D1123735

Life in the Victorian Age

JOURNEYS INTO THE PAST

LIFE IN THE VICTORIAN AGE

Published by
THE READER'S DIGEST ASSOCIATION LIMITED
LONDON NEW YORK SYDNEY MONTREAL CAPE TOWN

CARVING THE JOINT A British family and their pet present a cosy domestic scene in the 1850s.

THE DAILY ROUND The maidservants at an English country house stand ready for their day's work. Ironing (left) was one of the least popular household chores.

BROADWAY
New York office buildings loom high on either side of a traffic-jammed Broadway in the 1870s.

FREE PRESS
A French paper lampoons the politician Adolphe Thiers in 1870.

A FARMER'S LIFE A small-scale farmer from the North of England poses with his family and a dairy 'house cow'.

LIFE IN THE VICTORIAN AGE
Edited and designed by Toucan Books Limited
Sole author: Andrew Kerr-Jarrett

First edition copyright © 1993
The Reader's Digest Association Limited,
Berkeley Square House, Berkeley Square,
London W1X 6AB

Copyright © 1993
Reader's Digest Association Far East Limited
Philippines copyright © 1993
Reader's Digest Association Far East Limited
All rights reserved

Reprinted with amendments 1994

No part of this book may be reproduced, stored in a retrieval system, or transmitted in any form or by any means, electronic, electrostatic, magnetic tape, mechanical, photocopying, recording or otherwise, without permission in writing from the publishers.

® Reader's Digest, The Digest and the Pegasus logo are registered trademarks of The Reader's Digest Association, Inc, of Pleasantville, New York, USA

Printing and binding: Printer Industria Gráfica S.A., Barcelona

ISBN 0 276 42121 3

**Previous pages: (page 1) New York's Lower East Side; (pages 2-3) an American family.
Front cover: (centre) textile workers; (clockwise from top left) chimney sweep; advertisements for 'penny-farthing' and early vacuum cleaner; lawn tennis in a biscuit advertisement; 1888 flat disc player.
Back cover: (centre) US grocery store; (clockwise from top left) wedding portrait; 'hokey-pokey' stall; cookery books advertised; baked-potato seller.**

CONTENTS

A KISS IS STILL A KISS A couple in evening dress demonstrate the art of elegant kissing.

A MODERN COLOSSUS An American cartoon satirises the railroad magnate William Vanderbilt, with his associates Cyrus W. Field and Jay Gould.

A DAY AT THE SEA Late Victorian bathers enjoy the full fun of the seaside at the popular Belgian resort of Ostend.

OUTBACK LABOURERS An Australian blacksmith of the 1870s stands outside his forge, with his family and assistants.

OFFICE LIFE A German publication shows the changes in office life, such as the use of women typists.

Who Were the Victorians?

Never had the world changed so fast as for the Victorians. Industry and technology were transforming everyday life, and faith in the steady onward march of 'progress' seemed invincible. Life was often grim for the workers, but for the middle classes the opportunities seemed boundless.

FOR QUEEN VICTORIA it was 'one of the greatest and most glorious days' of her life. For thousands of her subjects, as well as many foreign visitors, May 1, 1851 (declared a public holiday in Britain that year) was a day they would certainly never forget.

Dawn broke clear, though a little chilly, and not long afterwards horse-drawn 'omnibuses' started plying through the streets of London carrying people towards the extraordinary cathedral-like structure of glass and steel which, since the previous September, had sprouted in the capital's Hyde Park. Aptly named the Crystal Palace, it covered 19 acres along the Park's southern edge and rose to 108 feet (enclosing several large elm trees). It had a steel frame of 3300 columns and 2300 girders and boasted nearly 300,000 panes of glass. A former gardener, Joseph Paxton, had designed it, and it was unlike anything anyone had ever seen before.

At 8.30am the gates opened and visitors started to pour in. By 10 there was standing room only inside the Crystal Palace, and by 11.30 the Park and surrounding streets were thronged. Then came the clatter of hooves and ringing cheers as, under briefly darkened skies and a few worrying spatters of rain, a procession of nine carriages rolled up Constitution Hill from Buckingham Palace and into the Park. Shortly afterwards, a fanfare of trumpets rang out through the glass halls, and Britain's 32-year-old Queen appeared, accompanied by her German-born husband Prince Albert and their two eldest children. Colourful ceremonies followed, interrupted at one point by a Chinese man in rich satin robes who suddenly prostrated himself at the Queen's feet – he owned a junk on the River Thames and the gesture was a publicity stunt to draw more visitors (which it did). Finally, amidst the dying echoes of a 100-gun salute, Queen Victoria declared officially open an event that was as novel and, in its way, as awesome as the building that housed it: the 'Great Exhibition of the Wares of Industry of All Nations'.

The generations that succeeded one another between 1837 when Victoria ascended the British throne and her death 64 years later in 1901 lived in a world which was changing faster than ever before. The Victorians transformed landscapes; industry,

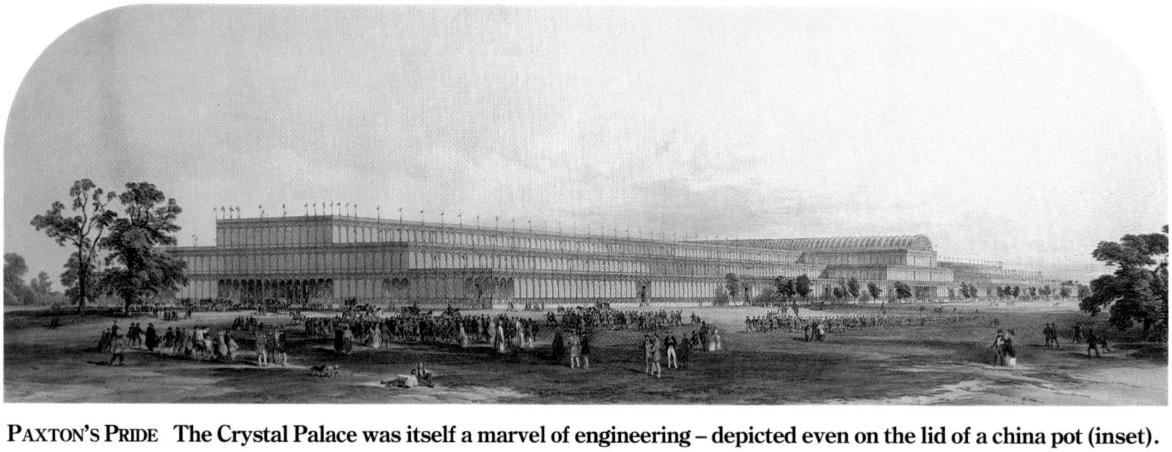

PAXTON'S PRIDE The Crystal Palace was itself a marvel of engineering – depicted even on the lid of a china pot (inset).

ROYAL VISIT Victoria and Albert open the Great Exhibition. The first Ferris wheel featured at the World's Columbian Exposition at Chicago in 1893.

pioneered in Britain in the 18th century, spread out and took root in continental Europe and North America. Factories sucked workers from the countryside and overseas; filthy, desolate slums often provided the workers' only housing. The middle classes – businessmen, factory owners and professionals – gathered wealth and influence, asserting what would eventually be seen as the characteristic Victorian values: thrift, hard work, piety and moral earnestness (with the inevitable counterpart, hypocrisy) and a love of home with all its domestic duties and comforts.

At the same time, there was an astonishing faith in the age's technological achievements, and optimism for a future in which these would yield more and more benefits for mankind. As the Frenchman M.A. Javary wrote in 1850: 'If there is any idea that belongs properly to our century ... it is the idea of Progress conceived as the general law of history and the future of humanity.'

There were few more splendid temples to that faith in progress than the Great Exhibition – and the many similar exhibitions that followed it: in Paris (several times), London again (in 1862), Vienna (1873), Philadelphia (1876) and Chicago (1893).

TEMPLE OF PROGRESS

Like its successors, the London Exhibition – masterminded by Prince Albert – was a dazzling treasure house of all that was best in an age supremely confident in itself and in the prospect of its steady forward march. Half devoted to Britain and its huge empire and half to the rest of the world, its exhibits ranged from brand-new devices such as Colt revolvers and McCormick reaping machines (a particular draw

BIG GUN A giant gun by the German firm Krupp was shown at the Paris Exposition of 1867; it would be used against Paris during the Prussian invasion of 1870. The Eiffel Tower was built for Paris's 1889 Exposition.

for intrigued farmers) in the large American section to more traditional wares such as carpets from Tunisia and Sèvres china from France (after Britain, the biggest contributor). Nothing was too ambitious or large – the Americans had a scale model of the Niagara Falls, the British a huge astronomical telescope. Nor was anything too small – a particular favourite with Queen Victoria (who, like many people, revisited the Exhibition several times) was an engaging group of stuffed frogs sent by the German state of Württemberg, one frog carrying a tiny umbrella, another equipped as a barber and preparing to shave its companion.

The Exhibition inspired awe in many people – the English clergyman and writer Charles Kingsley was 'moved to tears', and felt as if he was 'going into a sacred place'. Indeed, it seemed like living proof of everything that he and many Victorians most fervently believed in. They were under no illusions about the obvious horrors of their age – rising crime, the miseries of the slums, the prevalence of disease – but in the first flush of an intoxicating technological

'Industry of the Tyne' A painting by William Bell Scott expresses a fervent belief in the benefits of industry.

EYEWITNESS

An American Feat of Suspension

New York's Brooklyn Bridge spanning the East River took 14 years to complete and was responsible for more than its share of casualties. The bridge's designer John Augustus Roebling was killed in one accident during construction, and his son Washington, who succeeded him in charge of the project, was crippled as a result of another.

Even so, when opened in 1883, no one was in any doubt that the Brooklyn Bridge was among the greatest wonders of Victorian engineering – as a French visitor, Paul Bourget, testified:

MULFORD, CARY & CONKLIN,
Leather and Findings,
NEW YORK.

CROSSING THE EAST RIVER An advertisement of 1887 reveals something of the sheer majestic scale of the Brooklyn Bridge.

❛ You see great ships passing beneath it and this indisputable evidence of its height confuses the mind. But walk over it, feel the quivering on the monstrous trellis of iron and steel interwoven for a length of 1600 feet at a height of 135 feet above the water; see the trains that pass over it in both directions, and the steam-boats passing beneath your very body, while carriages come and go, and foot passengers hasten along, an eager crowd, and you will feel that the engineer is the great artist of our epoch, and you will own that these people [the Americans] have a right to plume themselves on their audacity, on the go-ahead which has never flinched. ❜

revolution they felt there was nothing that progress (and the correct application of engineering, in particular) could not put right.

In the words of the British historian Lord Macaulay at the very start of Victoria's reign, progress 'has lengthened life; it has mitigated pain; it has extinguished diseases; it has increased the fertility of the soil; it has given new securities to the mariner; ... it has spanned great rivers and estuaries with bridges of form unknown to our fathers; ... it has enabled man to descend to the depths of the sea, to soar into the air [in balloons], to penetrate securely into the noxious recesses of the earth, to traverse the land in [railway] cars which whirl along without horses, and the ocean in [steam] ships which run ten knots an hour against the wind.'

Across the Atlantic, the American writer Ralph Waldo Emerson was no less confident 30 years later in 1867, and in a United States that had recently emerged from civil war he gave his faith a patriotic slant: 'Was ever such coincidence of advantages in time and place as in America to-day? – the fusion of races and religions; the hungry cry for men which goes up from the wide continent; the answering facility of immigration, permitting every wanderer to choose his climate and government. Men come hither by nations. Science surpasses the old miracles of mythology, to fly with them over the sea [in steamships], and to send their messages under it [by telegraph cable] ... Who would live in the stone age, or the bronze, or the iron, or the lacustrine? Who does not prefer the age of steel, of gold, of coal, petroleum, cotton, steam, electricity, and the spectroscope?'

Certainly, history seemed to be marching at a remarkable pace. 'I am very young, and perhaps in many, though not in all things, inexperienced,' Victoria had written in her journal after the June dawn when messengers brought news that her uncle King William IV had died, 'but I am sure, that very few have more real good will and more real desire to do what is fit and right than I have.' The dutiful 18-year-old – typical in this, as in so much else, of the age that would bear her name – found herself Queen in a world where railways were in their

AMERICAN PERRY A Japanese artist left this portrait of the American Matthew Perry.

infancy and stage coaches still hooted across the countryside. On the other side of the English Channel, her maternal relative Louis-Philippe, the 'Bourgeois Monarch', ruled in France; Germany was a motley collection of independent states large and small, from Prussia (ruling important parts of the Rhineland, as well as its heartland in the east) to the tiny fragmented realm of Saxe-Coburg.

In the United States – undergoing something of a financial crisis that year, due in part to the failure of a number of British firms with large investments there – Martin Van Buren had moved into the White House as 8th President in March. Buffalo and the Indians still roamed the plains of the West largely undisturbed, while in the South, American settlers in Texas had defeated Mexican troops at San Jacinto in April. They thus secured the independence of their recently proclaimed Republic of Texas – integrated into the Union only in 1845. Africa, meanwhile, was still almost entirely unexplored by Europeans, except around its fringes. In the Pacific, Japan kept itself firmly closed to the outside world.

A World of Change

Events of the next 60 years would change much of that. In 1848 an explosion of revolutions across much of continental Europe – though not Britain – saw crowned heads tumble and societies reformed (temporarily, at least) along more liberal, even socialist, lines. One victim was Louis-Philippe in France who fled hastily to England. Within a few months his place had been taken by Napoleon's nephew, first as elected President, then (from 1852) as Emperor Napoleon III. Thus was born the French Second Empire during which Napoleon with his beautiful Spanish-born wife, the Empress Eugénie, would do much to set the tone for fashionable life across the mid-Victorian world.

April 1853 saw the American Commodore Matthew Perry break Japan's centuries-old isolation when he sailed with two armed steam frigates and two sailing ships into Uraga harbour. It was an event that captured the world's imagination and started a growing fashion for Japanese-style ornament in both America and Europe. October that year also brought grimmer news, however, in the outbreak of the Crimean War, pitting Britain and France against Russia. This was where the Englishwoman Florence Nightingale first practised her new nursing methods. It also saw the birth of on-the-spot war reporting in the despatches of the London *Times* correspondent, W.H. Russell.

Peace returned to Europe in 1856, but five years later in 1861 cruel, civil war broke out between South and North in the United States. The Southern states were determined to retain the institution of slavery; the North, under President Abraham Lincoln, was determined to end it and to preserve the Union. By the time of the North's victory in 1865, over 600,000 lives had been lost. The subsequent pain of reconstruction in the South was immense, but for the North, at least, as well as the West renewed peace unloosed the unmatchable prosperity and industrial vigour of America's 'Gilded Age'. Elsewhere in the world, France suffered Prussian invasion in 1870 and the downfall of the Second Empire (succeeded by a republican regime). This humiliation was compounded the next year when the 'Iron Chancellor' Otto von Bismarck chose the mirrored halls of the former royal palace of Versailles outside Paris to proclaim a new, unified German Empire, with King Wilhelm of Prussia as its Emperor.

These events left few people's lives untouched, and at the same time, everyday life was being transformed

Smile, Please **Portrait photography required sitters to keep still for a long time – hence this joke device suggested by the French cartoonist, Honoré Daumier.**

LIFE IN PARIS Paris's vibrant street life made it 'fun capital' of the Victorian world. The foreign policy of Napoleon III – unmistakable with waxed moustaches and pointed beard – is satirised in a cartoon showing his flirtations with the Italians, Hungarians and Poles.

in countless ways too. Travel, for example, became steadily easier as railways spread out across the globe in an ever-growing network, and as faster and more comfortable steamers plied back and forth across the Atlantic or between Europe and the East. In 1875 the New York firm E. Remington and Son (hitherto gunsmiths) manufactured the first typewriters. The next year the Scots-born Alexander Graham Bell demonstrated the first primitive telephone in America, and by the end of the decade the first telephone exchanges had appeared. At the same time, Thomas Edison in America and Joseph Swan in Britain were perfecting the incandescent light bulb. In transport,

FORTUNES OF WAR Technology could be used for war as well as peace. Here, Parisians flee the German invasion of 1870 (above) and American homesteaders (left) find themselves driven from their homes during the Civil War.

the German Carl Benz revealed a spindly, three-wheeled ancestor of the modern motor car in 1885.

Various forms of photography, meanwhile, especially the processes named after the Frenchman Louis Daguerre, had been around since the early Victorian years, but in 1888 the American George Eastman introduced a new dimension when he brought out the first hand-held Kodak box camera. Around the same time, the growing craze for bicycles was offering thousands of young people a freedom they had never dreamt of before.

Queen Victoria saw the new century in by just over a year. She died at 6.30pm on January 22, 1901, at Osborne House on the Isle of Wight off Britain's south coast, surrounded by a crowd of children and grandchildren – including her devoted grandson, the young Emperor Wilhelm II of Germany, who insisted on supporting her on his right arm (the other was withered) throughout her last hours. To a large extent the Victorian age had been the age of Britain and its Empire, dominating the globe with its commerce, its navy and its armies. But the world Victoria left behind was still changing fast. The British Empire remained mighty, but Britain itself was no longer the world's foremost industrial giant, having lost its lead to both the United States and Germany. Everyday life had been transformed in a way that few visionary enthusiasts at the time of the Great Exhibition of 1851 could have dreamt of.

But progress was not necessarily a reliable idol. Prince Albert and the other organisers of the Great Exhibition had talked of uniting the world in peace through the products of its industry and technology. In fact, within 15 years of the Queen's death, industry and technology would be the instruments of horrific bloodshed in World War I.

LIFE IN THE VICTORIAN FAMILY

For the Victorians, family life offered a haven of security in a rapidly changing world. Presided over by the benign presence of the mother – the 'Angel in the House', in the words of the British poet Coventry Patmore – the family acquired enormous sentimental importance. At the same time, children were treated less as miniature adults and more as children, with their own books and toys. In grim contrast, meanwhile, was the plight of the orphans and waifs who wandered the streets of the growing cities.

Courtship, Love and Marriage

Despite their strait-laced reputation, the Victorians loved romance and passion. On the other hand, they also liked romance to be tempered with judicious concern for social respectability and such all-important matters as financial means.

WHEN IT CAME TO LOVE and marriage, the Victorians were a curious mix of romance and realism. In 1846, for instance, William Smith, a cobbler from Shropshire in England, was introduced to the young woman who would later become his wife. Many decades later he left a touching, and definitely romantic, record of their first meeting. 'She was dressed in black, having just lost and buried her brothers. She was very dark with long black hair and dark eyes which she modestly fixed to the ground. And she gave me such a shake of the hand that I have felt it hundreds of times since then and I sometimes feel it now. I was smitten at once. It was love at first sight.'

Romance and realism, sentiment and hard common sense – the Victorians' view of the family was a balance of all these forces. Certainly, they raised the family as never before to heights of almost religious importance, and right across the Victorian world from Chicago to St Petersburg, from Glasgow to Naples, popular painters, preachers, writers and politicians were almost unanimous in choosing it as one of their favourite themes: the family united in prayer; the family gathered in domestic bliss around the fire or, at Christmas time, around the dining-room table; the family also in times of distress – when mothers have to part with sons or, worse, when a family member falls into disgrace. But these were never purely sentimental visions. For, in the prevailing Victorian view, the family also had a clear social purpose. It was the family, after all, that 'civilised' the individual human being, that – on a

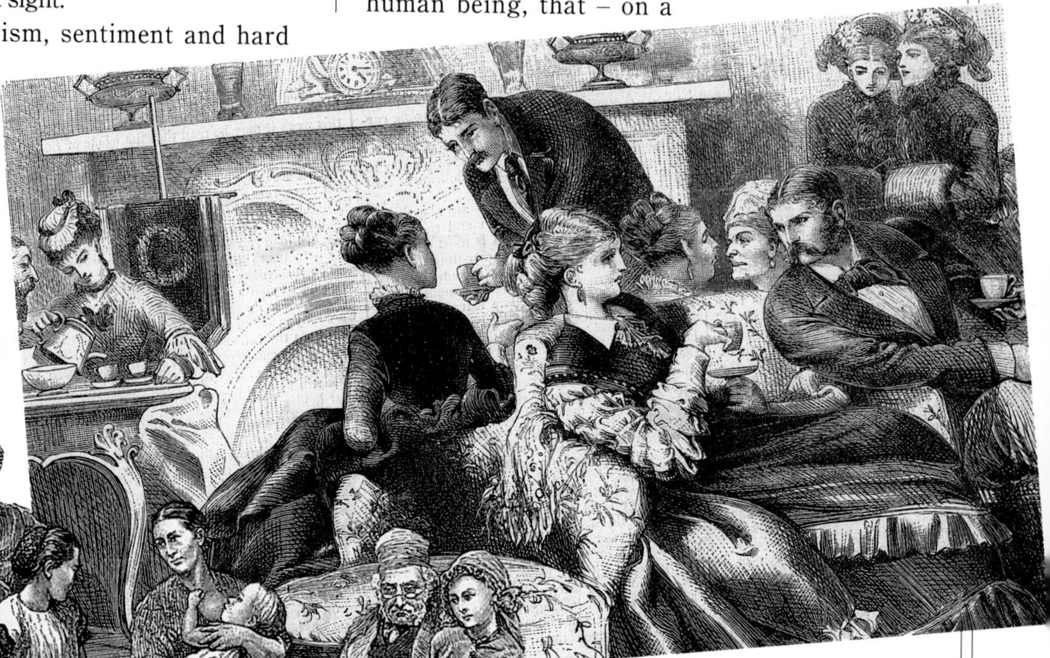

SOCIAL CONTRASTS
The well-padded luxury of a wealthy home contrasts with the scene in a farmer's kitchen. But whatever the setting, family was still all in all.

HOME WELCOMES
A new baby is centre of attention for the American Hatch family. A father's welcome home from work inspires a painting of the 1890s.

very practical level – made him or her a worthier, more useful member of the larger family of society.

It was, of course, an intensely patriarchal view of the family, in which the father was the revered head, earning his family's living and directing its relations with the outside world. The woman's role, meanwhile, was definitely subordinate. But restricted though the woman's role was, her place within the home was all-important, especially in her influence on the man. As the popular American monthly *Godey's Lady's Book and Magazine* put it: 'The perfection of womanhood ... is the wife and mother, the center of the family, the magnet that draws man to the domestic altar that makes him a civilized being, a social Christian. The wife is truly the light of the home.'

The actual practice and reality of family life was undergoing important changes during the Victorian period. As industry struck deeper roots, and the cities grew, so the extended family of grandparents, uncles, aunts and cousins gave way in some measure to the nuclear family of parents and children. Inevitably, this involved a loss of old ties and systems of mutual support – and there was no shortage of commentators to bemoan the passing of the old ways and to prophesy the collapse of family values.

In fact, however, the picture was more complicated than that. The extended family did survive in a number of places, notably among the various peasant communities of countries such as Italy, Spain, France and Germany, but also to some extent in the industrial cities of North America and Britain. And then the nuclear family – particularly among the growing middle classes – had its compensations, too. In the 1860s, the British philosopher John Stuart Mill commented, for example, on a greater tenderness and affection in many family

TENDER MOMENTS Victorian love takes a passionate turn on the sands of the popular British seaside resort Great Yarmouth. For another young couple things are a good deal more domesticated, while for a third pair ball gowns and formal evening dress set the tone for an elegant upper middle-class courtship.

relationships, especially among men. Earlier in the century, the strongly domesticated German Biedermeier style of living, painting and furnishing – named after the typically middle-class character 'Papa Biedermeier', somewhat akin to the American Uncle Sam or British John Bull – had emphasised the same family values.

At the same time, the French official Christophe de Villeneuve had noted similar trends among the bourgeoisie of Marseilles: 'The family father, obliged to occupy himself with difficult business problems during the day, can relax only when he goes home. Everyone crowds around him. He beams at the children's games; he prides himself on knowing them well and their accomplishments delight him. Family evenings together are for him a time of the purest and most complete happiness.'

FOR LOVE OR MONEY

The basis of family life was marriage, and on the subject of marriage the Victorians and the books they read had plenty to say. The cynical side of the case was neatly summed up by the French Academician Joseph Droz in a popular book entitled *Essai sur l'art d'être heureux* (*Essay on the Art of Being Happy*).

'Marriage', he wrote 'is in general a means of increasing one's credit and one's fortune and of ensuring one's success in the world.' And no doubt it was true that some Victorian men and women saw marriage in these terms, as a way of advancing themselves socially and financially, and that they – or their ambitious parents – made their arrangements accordingly.

On the other hand, it was probably equally true that middle-class Victorians as a whole laid more emphasis on love in marriage than any of their forebears. What resulted was a typically Victorian compromise. It was generally reckoned that for a marriage to be balanced and successful there should be love, but also that the couple's material circumstances should be taken into account.

ARM IN ARM The Victorians were no strangers to the cosy intimacies of love.

Ideally, there should be a rough parity between the fortunes and ages of both – or if not, then the perhaps new wealth of one should be offset, say, by the better-established social standing of the other.

Love, then, within limits, was important, but that did not mean you waited starry-eyed for its arrival. For most girls, in particular, the chief business of life was to win the right husband – and for men, too, being married was always a sure badge of respectability.

In the middle and upper classes this procedure was extremely well lubricated, with the paraphernalia of balls, dances, weekends in the country and, later, tennis parties to bring young unmarried men and women together. In these settings the Victorians could be surprisingly liberal – flirtation, for instance, was positively encouraged: 'Flirting is to marriage what free trade is to commerce,' remarked *Godey's Lady's Book*. 'By it the value of a woman is exhibited, tested, her capacities known, her temper displayed, and the opportunity offered of judging what sort of wife she may probably become.'

The Europeans (including the British) laid great emphasis on chaperones – mothers, aunts or elder married sisters – to make sure that no girl was exposed to undue temptation in the company of a young man. The Americans, on the other hand, were a good deal more relaxed in such matters. Later in the Victorian age, the various crazes for roller and ice skating and for bicycling had an important liberating effect on young people everywhere, in allowing them to go off together unsupervised.

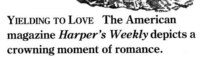

YIELDING TO LOVE The American magazine *Harper's Weekly* depicts a crowning moment of romance.

For working people, the business of meeting suitable members of the opposite sex could be more difficult, especially in the industrial cities. Middle-class Victorians tended to look on the factories and mills, where women and men worked side by side, or at least in adjacent areas, as dens of the most shocking sexual immorality. As so often, they probably exaggerated, and in any case (in accordance with the prevailing double standards of the age) working men would not necessarily want to marry girls they had enjoyed a 'fling' with in the mill.

For those with a religious bent, such as William Smith and his wife, chapel or church was one good place for men and women to meet and assess each other. In some French towns there were special marriage bureaus, acting rather like early versions of the modern dating agency. For the rest, it was a

EYEWITNESS

A SUITOR IN MOSCOW

ANGUISH IN LOVE had a romantic appeal for the Victorians. And few lovers were more anguished than the Russian writer Count Leo Tolstoy while courting the 18-year-old Sofya Behrs in 1862, as his diary testifies:

' *12 September* Wandered around the whole day, and went to gymnastics. Had dinner at the club. I'm in love in a way that I would never have believed possible. I'm crazy, I'll shoot myself if things go on like this. Spent the evening at their [the Behrs family] house. She's delightful in every way ... I'm made beautiful by my love. Yes, I'll go to their house tomorrow morning. There have been moments, but I didn't take advantage of them. I was afraid; I should just have spoken out quite simply. I yearn to go right back there now and make my declaration in front of everyone. Lord, help me. '

Five days later Tolstoy at last screwed up the courage to propose. He was accepted.

RUSSIANS WITH LOVE Courtship was fraught with crises for Tolstoy.

question of young people making the best of family contacts, pubs and bars, and the various fairs and festivals that lasted into the industrial age.

For country people, things were simpler, since a number of time-honoured rural courting practices had survived. Among the Italian and French peasantry, arranged marriages were still very much the norm, with parents employing the services of expert go-betweens (often travelling drapers) to bring to their notice suitable young men or women from neighbouring villages. In both North America and much of Europe, the old ritual of 'bundling' remained common. In its simplest form, this consisted of a young couple sleeping together, with their parents' consent, but without undressing or, alternatively, with a separating blanket between them.

The Silliness of Rice and Old Shoes

Wedding rituals varied as much as courting ones, and similarly depended a good deal on class and region. In many country areas, people went on celebrating marriages much as they had done for centuries. Entire communities would turn out for the festivities, which might well last a day if not longer. At night there would often be the traditional cat-and-mouse pursuit of the bride and groom: the young couple doing their best to find privacy together, the boisterous youths of the village doing their best to interrupt them.

Among the middle classes, things were a lot more sedate and, at the beginning of the Victorian period at least, a lot more simple. Most early 19th-century American couples, for instance, preferred to get married at home, with a minister presiding and just a few close family and friends around them. Only gradually did the proceedings become more elaborate, with most of the trappings of a modern wedding falling into place.

A Peep Through the Wedding Ring
A Valentine card reveals a suitably domestic prospect.

By 1887, the American bride Julia Finch was sounding an authentically modern note of bridal exasperation when she complained to her fiancé Cass Gilbert: 'I doubt if we shall have anything to do with the managing of our wedding, there are so many others to do it for us. If we are on hand to say "I will" at the right time, that will be all that will be necessary.'

Blanche, fiancée of the young Bostonian botanist Oakes Ames, complained in similar vein (and in idiosyncratic spelling) of all they had to endure, in particular 'the silliness of rice and old shoes and the assenine temprement [sic] of people who indulge in such things at weddings'. The wedding itself generally took place on a Sunday or a weekday, but rarely on a Saturday. A popular rhyme in America and Britain went:

Monday for wealth,
Tuesday for health,
Wednesday the best day of all;
Thursday for losses,
Friday for crosses,
And Saturday no luck at all.

For small weddings, invitations were usually given by word of mouth. For grander affairs they would be printed, though even these would often be sent out only a week or so in advance.

Brides generally – though not always – wore white, and the veil (a comparatively recent innovation, symbolising the purity of the bride) became increasingly popular. Queen

Art and Love
Illustrators thrived on depicting episodes from love's progress: the governess tilting her charges' hats when with her suitor; a couple hiding behind a fan.

Signing the Register A bride wears blossom in her hair, in contrast to the rustic simplicity of her father's smock, in a work by the British artist James Charles.

Wedded Bliss
A certificate depicts scenes of married life.

THE ROTHSCHILDS

The most glittering of the Victorian business dynasties suffered all the usual stresses and tragedies of family living.

A MOTHER'S DEATH in childbirth was a tragedy suffered by many Victorian families, and one that not even the fabulous wealth of the Rothschilds could spare them. In late 1866, Evelina de Rothschild (a Rothschild by both birth and marriage) was injured in a railway accident and a few weeks afterwards died at her London home while giving birth to a stillborn son.

She had been one of the liveliest and most engaging members of the family, and was sorely missed. 'O shocking, sad day!' her cousin Constance wrote in her diary. 'It seems almost impossible to write about it. And yet it took place. We were happy, merry, even joking, without the slightest thought of such a terrible event.'

The bereaved husband Ferdinand had been on a trip to Vienna when Evelina died and was devastated.

ZEBRA POWER Walter was a noted (and eccentric) naturalist.

'She opened her life with wisdom and in her speech was the law of kindness. My darling wife,' he had inscribed on her tomb.

The Rothschilds were a remark-

WHERE IT ALL BEGAN A high desk and metal-bound chest were the sparse furnishings of Mayer Amschel's counting house in Frankfurt.

FOUNDING FATHER Mayer Amschel founded the family fortune through trade and banking during the Napoleonic Wars.

GRAND MATRIARCH Gutle, Mayer Amschel's wife, bore 19 children in all, of whom 10 survived.

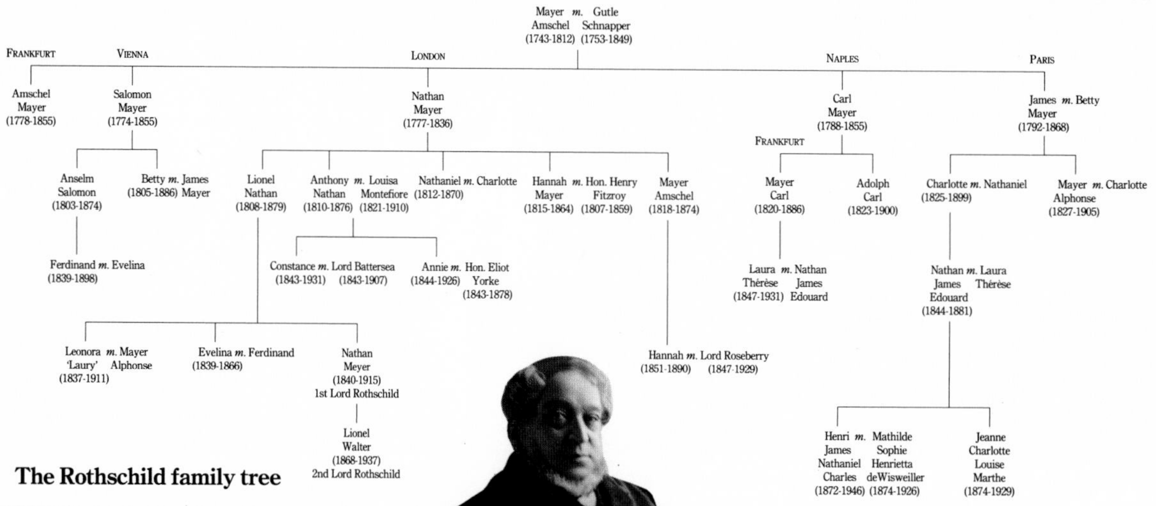

The Rothschild family tree

JEWISH FIRST Lionel was the first practising Jew to become a British MP.

PARIS WEDS LONDON Alphonse from the French branch married Leonora from the English branch in 1857. Alphonse was one of the family's wiliest business heads.

able family, in their private as well as their professional lives. Nearly half a century before Evelina's death, her great-grandfather, Mayer Amschel Rothschild, had sent his five sons out from their home in the old Jewish quarter of Frankfurt to establish themselves in the major European capitals.

Since then the sons and their offspring had rarely failed to make their mark. They became easily the most powerful of Victorian banking dynasties, the friends of royalty and prime ministers. Baron James de Rothschild, the longest-surviving of Mayer Amschel's sons and head of the Paris house, also found time to build a large art collection. In England, one of Mayer Amschel's grandsons, Lionel de Rothschild, became the first practising Jew to enter Parliament.

Rothschilds owned vineyards, were notable sportsmen and sportswomen, produced outstanding naturalists and had homes – such as Mentmore, Waddesdon and Tring in the Vale of Aylesbury in England – that were among the most fabulous of Victorian palaces.

And underpinning it all was the basic solidarity of the family, in all its various branches. This was maintained by a deliberate policy of intermarriage. From an early age cousins were marked down for cousins (Ferdinand and Evelina, for example, had long been destined for each other), with Baron James in Paris going so far as to marry his niece Betty.

Not surprisingly, this practice produced a mixed bag of results. Ferdinand and Evelina's brief marriage was blissfully happy; so was the much longer-lasting union between another English Rothschild, Sir Anthony, and his cousin Louisa Montefiore. Others, however, were less fortunate, as were the children they produced.

In an age when Paris was notorious for its libertinism, the puritanical Laura Thérèse, for example, was determined that her children Henri and Jeanne should escape any contagion. To try to ensure this, she brought them up in almost complete isolation from young people of their own age – with the result that Jeanne fell in love with the coachman and Henri was seduced by their German governess.

Later, one of his uncles secretly helped Henri to acquire a mistress and later again, but still aged only 23, Henri decided to get married. The girl in question was of impeccable Jewish upbringing, but his mother was none the less outraged when he told her: 'The unexpected news had stunned her,' he remembered later. 'She was furious that I had become engaged without her knowledge, humiliated that I had taken this decision without at least asking her advice, without enabling her to gather information about the young woman ...'

THE BUILDER Ferdinand built the sumptuous Waddesdon Manor.

SOLID AS A BANK Sir Anthony was a pillar of the British house.

Victoria, for her wedding in 1840, wore a white satin dress trimmed with orange blossom, and on her head a small veil of Honiton lace with more orange blossom tucked into her hair. The attendant bridesmaids and groomsman or best man also became standard features in Victorian weddings.

After the ceremony came the reception or wedding breakfast (another increasingly popular event), at which all the presents were carefully displayed and labelled. In earlier times, couples had normally made their way, after their marriage and any celebrations that followed, to their new home. This gave way in many places to the custom of making a 'bridal tour', to visit various friends and relatives.

Finally, the idea of the honeymoon, with the couple going off alone together, took root: middle or upper-class British people might make a tour of the Continent, or if that was not possible spend a week or two at Brighton, say, or on the Isle of Wight; Americans might head for Florida.

Of course, wedding nights followed wedding days, and here Victorian myth and reality can be hard to extricate. In the Frenchman Gustave Droz's popular *Papa, Mamma and Baby* – commended by no less an authority than the novelist Emile Zola as depicting 'characters which certainly live as excellent studies of the society of the period' – he gave fictionalised accounts of a wedding night from the point of view of both the groom and bride. His narrative, distinctly overwrought to modern eyes, none the less reflects the kind of thoughts and feelings that Victorians would have considered appropriate to such an occasion. First, the groom alludes to his bride's ignorance of what is to come. As the last guests are leaving the reception, her 'mother whispers something in her daughter's ear, about a sacrifice, the future, necessity, obedience, a holocaust ... The poor child does not understand anything about it, except it be that something unheard of is about to take place, the very anticipation of which makes her quiver with impatience and alarm.'

At last all the guests have left. The bride retires to her room; the young husband waits impatiently to join her. Finally, he knocks and enters: 'I bent over the bed, and in the softest notes, the sweetest tones my voice could compass, I murmured, "Well, darling?" ' After a few more such exchanges, he tries to slip under the bedclothes, only to be greeted by 'a cry of terror'.

Confounded, the young man whispers: 'I love you, my dear child, I love you, little wifey; don't you think that I do?' She replies 'in a voice broken by emotion and so soft, so low, so tender that it

MARRIAGE STYLES
Guests loll elegantly at a fashionable New York wedding. A couple from Indiana are rather stiffer as they pose for a wedding portrait.

penetrated to the marrow of my bones: "I love you too. But let me sleep, it would be so kind of you to let me sleep." ' The unfortunate husband can only comment: 'A smack in the face would not have humiliated me more. Yes, I was a coarse swashbuckler, and I felt myself blushing to the tips of my ears.'

But patience is to be rewarded. After his rebuff, the husband retires to an armchair by the fire. But he cannot stay away for long, and soon he is back at the bedside of a now much more yielding wife.

What Women Should Know

The Victorians' naivety and repression in sexual matters is legendary. And many women (not to mention some men) undoubtedly entered marriage with an astonishing ignorance of what consummation involved – especially in the Anglo-Saxon world where the puritanical Evangelical revival of the early 19th century had left deep marks.

What little information was vouchsafed to well brought-up, middle-class girls tended to be extremely negative, with sex very often portrayed as no more than a duty and a burden. A comment by the American Eliza Duffey in her book *What Women Should Know: A Woman's Book About Women* was fairly typical: 'the consummation of marriage is frequently attended with inconvenience, and even physical prostration.' Sex was there for reproduction, certainly not for pleasure; on that both Protestant and Catholic writers and preachers were unanimous.

Even the highly secular French army doctor Auguste Debay, whose *Hygiène et physiologie du mariage* (*Hygiene and Physiology of Marriage*) was certainly one of the most explicit manuals of the period – and never translated into English – felt bound to say: 'The wise man does not see in [sexual] union the frivolous objective of pleasure; he considers another, more serious one, that of producing offspring. It is on this objective that a man should fix his attention if he wants to look forward to a future of happiness in the number, strength and beauty of his children.'

Encapsulating in disastrous form many of these attitudes and values was the marriage of John Ruskin, the British art critic and prophet of social reform, to the pretty but (for him) uncongenial Effie Grey. In 1854, six years after they were married, Effie Grey appealed for help to her parents: 'I do not think I am John Ruskin's Wife at all – and I entreat you to assist me to get released from the unnatural position in which I stand to Him.' Apparently,

Bridal Touches A bride of the 1890s prepares for her fate.

Hard Truth Honeymoon pictures contrast with mail-order bridalwear.

EYEWITNESS

A Wife in the American West

American women who went West had to make their homes in lonely places. Here, Virginia Wilcox Ivins describes a day in the 1850s, in the two-roomed home her husband built for them in California:

❛ One lovely day in the latter part of summer Mr Ivins went to Tomales for a load of vegetables. It being fifteen miles out he started very early, taking the ox team which served for all occasions, sometimes as a carriage. After he left the hours dragged slowly, and it seemed as if the day were a week long, that night never would come. Drunken Indians rode past making the air hideous with their whoops and howls, but no other human being came in sight. After what seemed a day almost interminable the night closed down. I put my little ones to bed and waited. Outside the cloth and paper house the coyotes barked, and there were all sorts of alarming sounds. I felt as if I should almost die of fright. I could not leave or carry my children, and the nearest neighbour was almost a mile away. It was midnight when I heard a shout on the hill back of the house, and shortly after my husband came, driving the big ox wagon straight down a steep hill a half mile high, without any signs of a road ... All the vegetables in the state would not have tempted me to live over again that dreadful day. I knew of the grizzly bears that had been killed so near the place, and although my husband assured me that dead grizzlies would not hurt me, I was afraid there might be live ones left. ❜

Simple Living A frontier family pose outside their home.

the marriage had never been consummated, with Ruskin putting forward at various times a number of excuses for not doing so: 'Hatred of children, religious motives, a desire to preserve my beauty, and finally this last year [he] told me the true reason (and this to me is as villainous as all the rest), that he had imagined women were quite different to what he saw I was, and that the reason he did not make me his Wife was because he was disgusted with my person.'

Ruskin's experience was probably more the exception than the rule. In practice, other Victorians – whatever lip service they may have paid to prudery in public – could be a lot more positive in their approach to sex ... even the most 'respectable' of them. Sometimes, this actually involved experimentation before marriage. In the 1860s the American Lester Ward, later to become a distinguished and pioneering sociologist, kept a diary (in French) recording his courtship of Lizzie Vought – *la fille*, 'the girl', as he invariably refers to her – who was to become his first wife. Its entries reveal a sometimes tortured process of exploration mingled with occasional misgivings. Even so eminent a Victorian as the reforming British clergyman and writer Charles Kingsley, at one time chaplain to the Queen herself, was happy to confess that he and his future wife, Fanny Grenfell, 'did all we could, before we were one!'

Innocence and Experience

There was also the question of double standards. In theory, the laws of Victorian sexual morality were as binding on men as on women. In reality, however, while middle-class women were expected to remain strictly chaste, a little discreet sowing of wild oats by young men was usually tolerated and even sometimes expected.

Prostitution was rife in every major Victorian city: 'That libertinism of the most demoralising character flourishes in London, in Paris, and in New York, cannot be a secret,'

Modesty A lady's ankle sufficed to excite men.

Tempting to Ruin **Paris prostitutes take a rest in a painting by Henri de Toulouse-Lautrec. An American drawing warns of the danger of girls being lured into prostitution.**

remarked the British commentator Francis Newman; 'nor that it is confined to no grade of society. But alas, the chief cities do but impress the imagination more, by the scale of the evil.' Figures for the numbers of prostitutes vary widely and were no doubt often exaggerated by well-meaning social reformers, but the British medical journal the *Lancet* may have been fairly close to the mark when it reckoned in 1857 that there were about 80,000 prostitutes in London – that is, one in every 16 women in the capital earned her living on the streets. Paris, with about half London's population, was thought to have about twice as many prostitutes.

Indeed, the French – despite the fact that they, too, participated in the Victorian cult of the family – had a particular reputation for sexual activity: 'It is rare to find in the present state of our morals boys who are virgins after 17 or 18,' observed one commentator, Dr Louis Fiaux, in 1880. A boy's first visit to a brothel was almost as standard a rite of passage as his first communion. Many older French men, meanwhile, vied with each other at their different social levels for the favours of courtesans and mistresses.

Rebels with a Cause

Where adultery and extra-marital sex were concerned, the Victorian world was again definitely a man's world. Some women could and did get away with a vigorous succession of affairs, but they usually belonged to the bohemian world of artists and writers, which had different codes of behaviour. Perhaps the most famous example of a free-living woman was the French novelist George Sand, who scandalised respectable opinion by her habit of wearing men's trousers and enjoyed a string of lovers, including the poet Alfred de Musset and the composer Frédéric Chopin.

George Sand and the English novelist George Eliot, who also chose to write under a man's name and lived with her lover, were able to brazen it out. Others were less fortunate. The art and literature of the Victorian period is scattered with portrayals of so-called 'fallen women': the Frenchman Gustave Flaubert's *Madame Bovary*, for example, and the Russian Leo Tolstoy's *Anna Karenina*.

Among the working classes, attitudes were generally a lot more relaxed. Yet even here women could fall foul of the prevailing code, especially among the better-off, more 'respectable' workers. The British clergyman Francis Kilvert, with a parish on the Welsh borders, noted such a case in his diary in 1871. 'This morning Edward Morgan of Cwmpelved Green brought his concubine to Church and married her. She was a girl of 19 rather nice looking and seemed quiet and modest.' A few weeks later he visited the Morgans' cottage and commented on its neatness: 'A vase of bright fresh flowers stood upon each table and

I could have eaten dinner off every stone of the floor ... The oven door was screened from view by a little curtain and everything was made the most and best of. I don't wonder Edward Morgan married the girl. It was not her fault that they were not married before. She begged and prayed her lover to marry her before he seduced her and afterwards. She was very staunch and faithful to him when she was his mistress and I believe she will make him a good wife.' In spite of all which, the 'girl said no one ever came near the house to see it, and she kept it as clean and neat and pretty as she could for her own satisfaction'.

Such treatment and attitudes did not go totally unchallenged. Throughout the Victorian period there was a small but often insistent chorus of campaigners in favour of freer attitudes towards marriage and love: figures such as the Englishman G.R. Drysdale, who argued in 1854 that 'if a man and woman conceive a passion for each other, they should be morally entitled to indulge it, without binding themselves together for life.' Americans such as the formidably energetic women's rights campaigner Elizabeth Cady Stanton believed firmly in marriage – 'The right idea of marriage is at the foundation of all reforms,' she stated – but she wanted it to be more equal and more truly based on love: 'I hold that it is a sin, an outrage to our holiest feelings, to pretend that anything but deep, fervent love and sympathy constitute marriage.'

THE AWAKENING CONSCIENCE 'Fallen women' were a favourite theme – as in this painting by the Pre-Raphaelite William Holman Hunt.

HIM WHOM YOU LOVE

Certainly, sex and seductiveness in marriage did seem to be regarded as less and less of a crime as the age wore on, even among the preachers and moralists. In France, Gustave Droz was urging wives to reclaim their husbands from the arms of their mistresses: 'For mercy's sake, ladies, tear from the clutches of the hussies, whose toilettes you do very wrong in imitating, your husbands' hearts. Are you not more refined, more delicate, than they? Do for him whom you love, that which they do for all the world; do not content yourselves with being virtuous, be seductive ...' At the same time, birth control methods – earlier regarded with horror by many people, as a crime against nature and God's law – were becoming more sophisticated and widely used, allowing the pleasures of marriage to be enjoyed without the succeeding burden of childbirth (or, in the worst case, abortion).

And it was not merely from the male point of view that sex was enjoyed. In *Hygiène et physiologie du mariage*, Debay put forward an argument frequently used by the Victorians to excuse, or at least explain, much of male infidelity: 'If one encounters some women who are too amorous, there are many more who sin by the contrary excess, and show an indifference, a frigidity in accomplishing their conjugal duty, that freezes a husband, who is sometimes secretly scandalised by it.' But while certain attitudes were relaxing, others remained fairly rigid.

Divorce was one knotty area. In France it had been banned altogether when the Bourbon dynasty returned to power after the defeat of Napoleon in 1815, and remained illegal through successive regimes until 1884. A few smaller countries such as Sweden and Scotland had relatively liberal divorce laws which treated husband and wife more or less as equals. But the attitudes revealed by the English Matrimonial Causes Act of 1857 – itself an improvement on what went before – were all too typical. The husband could sue for divorce on the grounds that his wife had committed adultery; the wife, by contrast, had to prove not only her husband's adultery, but also that he had been guilty of some further offence, such as rape or cruelty.

Since in most countries a wife's property automatically became her husband's on marriage (in France, women were officially treated as minors in business affairs), a divorce could leave her penniless. Only by considerable ingenuity or persistence could such restrictions be got around. One who succeeded was the German socialist leader Ferdinand Lassalle, on behalf of his friend Countess Sophie von Hatzfeldt. Between 1846 and 1854 he brought no fewer than 35 different lawsuits against the Countess's estranged husband, and eventually so wore him down that she obtained her divorce and a reasonably fair share of her property.

In the United States, Elizabeth Cady Stanton – as daughter of a judge of the New York Supreme Court – was in a particularly good position to understand the laws discriminating against women. It was largely thanks to her efforts that the state of New York, at least, gave property rights to married women.

In England, meanwhile, a bizarre form of popular divorce survived long enough to feature in Thomas Hardy's novel *The Mayor of Casterbridge*, published in 1886. Wife-selling (also known as a 'Smithfield bargain', after the London meat market) involved bringing a wife of whom her husband had grown tired to a market place or pub, usually with a halter around her neck. There she would be displayed – sometimes with her disenchanted husband – while bidding commenced in what was often a well-organised auction. In earlier ages, respectable artisans and shopkeepers occasionally acquired wives in this way; by Victorian times, however, it was growing much rarer.

In general, the Victorians – in common with earlier generations – viewed homosexuality with outrage. 'With all its disgusting and ignominious horrors, how can it exist in an advanced civilisation like ours?' was the comment of the liberal French *Encyclopédie Larousse* in the 1860s. Homosexuality was a criminal offence in most countries, in spite of which male prostitution thrived in cities such as Paris and London – Queen Victoria's own grandson, the Duke of Clarence, was reputed to be a client of male brothels.

Blackmail associated with homosexual activity was also common, although less so in the late Victorian age when there seems to have been a greater official tolerance of homosexuality. At that point a number of prominent literary and artistic figures, such as the American poet Walt Whitman, the French novelist Marcel Proust and his friend Comte Robert de Montesquiou, were able to practise and write about it with relative freedom. The most famous victim of the laws against it was the Irish playwright and wit Oscar Wilde, who unwisely provoked the anger of his lover's father, the Marquess of Queensberry, and ended up sentenced to two years' hard labour.

REBEL WOMEN George Sand, George Eliot and the actress Sarah Bernhardt all defied moral conventions.

CHILDHOOD AND UPBRINGING

Childbirth was a dangerous time for both mothers and babies, and childhood ailments were often fatal. For all that, and despite appalling conditions for many poor children, growing up was happier for many Victorian youngsters than for most of their ancestors.

THE VICTORIANS may have idolised the family, but Queen Victoria for one was under no illusions about the business of childbirth. 'What you say of the pride of giving birth to an immortal soul is very fine, dear,' she wrote in 1858 to her daughter, 'but I own that I cannot enter into that; I think much more of being like a cow or a dog at such moments; when our poor nature becomes so very animal and unecstatic.'

Childbirth generally meant appalling pain and the all-too-possible prospect of the death of either the child or the mother – or both. Infant mortality was consistently high throughout the period, with over 150 babies in every 1000 born alive in Britain, for example, failing to reach their first birthday.

The story of Isabella Beeton, author of the famous *Book of Household Management*, illustrates the kind of fate that awaited many women: her first child died when only three months old, the second at three years old; Mrs Beeton herself died, aged just 28, of a fever

GROWING FAMILIES One American family, complete with baby carriages, is photographed outside its home. A print shows the beginnings of another.

THE PERILS OF GIVING BIRTH

QUEEN VICTORIA – a mother of nine – helped to popularise the use of chloroform in labour. Here, she describes the labour of a niece in a letter to one of her daughters:

❛ Oh! dear child, thank God! darling Marie is safe with her magnificent baby but it was an awful labour! And at last at two in the morning of Friday ... after she had three hot hip baths in all her agony, borne without a murmur or more than a little, gentle, piteous moan ... Dr Farre said she must not be allowed to go on or she would be exhausted and the child would die and so instruments must be used!! Poor Ernest [Marie's husband] was in despair and crying – and so I sat by her and they put her completely under chloroform and she was like as if she slept, I stroking her face all the time and while Dr Farre most skilfully ... delivered her without her knowing or feeling anything, and only woke when she heard the child cry and immediately said she wished to have a prayer read to her for she was so thankful, and wishing only she could give her life for me and restore beloved Papa [Prince Albert] to me!! ❜

BABE IN ARMS Queen Victoria holds her youngest-born, Princess Beatrice.

contracted during the birth of her fourth child in 1865.

And yet several advances were made in childbirth practices during the Victorian age. In most European countries, professional midwives were trained and qualified; chloroform became increasingly popular; and obstetricians and midwives started using a variety of instruments to help with difficult births: forceps, dilators and so on. Correctly used, these saved some lives. Unfortunately, medical attendants were sometimes too keen to use them and inflicted permanent damage or death as a result. Another difficulty was the modesty of some women. It meant that male obstetricians had somehow to carry out their job while groping around under an elaborate screen of sheets.

Once safely delivered, the child embarked on the stately process of a Victorian upbringing. In this, the authority of parents and other adults tended to loom large: 'The first duty which devolves upon the mother in the training of her child is the establishment of her authority over him – that is, the forming in him the habit of immediate, implicit, and unquestioning obedience to all her commands,' stated the American Jacob Abbott in his best-selling *Gentle Measures in the Management and Training of the Young*.

SEEN AND OFTEN HEARD

Many Victorians undoubtedly suffered appalling childhoods. The Englishman Augustus Hare was brought up by a wealthy aunt, who would have tasty-looking cakes made, offer them to the boy and then

Bringing up Baby: Victorian Childcare

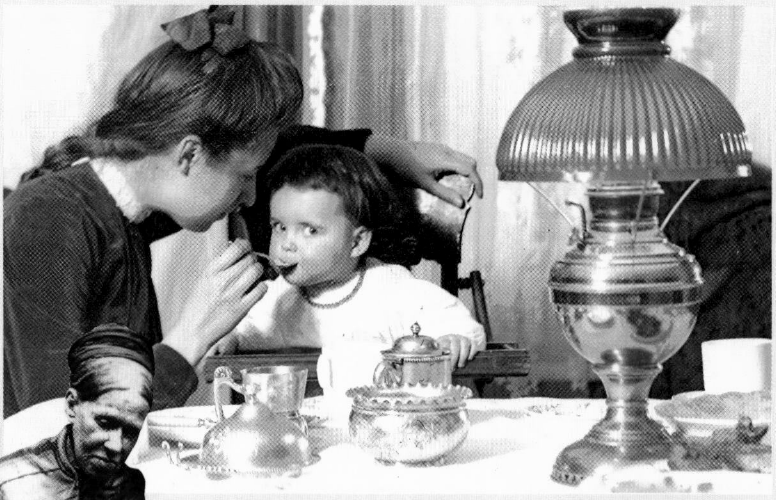

Rich and Poor Childhood meant very different things amidst the comforts of a rich American home and on the streets of London's slums.

VICTORIAN WRITERS were surprisingly modern in some ways. They turned against the fashions of Georgian times and advised mothers to breast-feed. In 1860, for example, the American doctor J. Stainback Wilson urged the readers of *Godey's Lady's Book* to shun both wet-nursing and 'hand-raising' (artificial feeding) 'if they can possibly perform their maternal duties themselves'.

And such recommendations were widely echoed, together with lists enumerating all the various benefits of breast-feeding: 'This operation, independent of the pleasant sensations it communicates, kindles [the mother's] best affections,' wrote the British doctor John Conquest. In further support of his case, he affirmed as 'a matter of universal observation ... that at no period is the countenance of the female more attractive' than when breast-feeding.

For all such confident assertions, however, the process of feeding and bringing up a young child was an anxious one for Victorian mothers. Throughout the period the rates of infant and child mortality – regardless of families' wealth and class – remained astonishingly high. In New York City, for instance, 220 out of every 1000 babies born live in 1860 died before they reached the age of one; by 1870 the figure had risen to 240.

In all this, ignorance, on the one hand, and over-anxiety, on the other hand, unquestionably played a part. One common cause of death was diarrhoea – very often this resulted from an anxious mother feeding her baby excessively until it became constipated, then purging it with over-generous doses of laxative.

And yet the period was not without its advances, either. Breast-feeding may have been best, but for those who did not choose it methods of artificial feeding improved considerably. Feeding bottles had been available since the start of the century, and rubber nipples since the 1830s; by the 1880s well over a million bottles were being sold each year in the United States alone. The invention of pasteurisation was another important development, meaning that it was now safe to use animals' milk.

In other areas too there were significant changes. In many countries, the old practice of swaddling babies into rigidly bound bundles largely disappeared. At the same time, a more tender relationship was widely encouraged between mother and child. In previous centuries, crying had been considered good for a baby; now it was seen as a symptom that something might be wrong.

Mothers were encouraged to cuddle their babies (almost impossible in the days of swaddling), and their role in nurturing more than just the child's physical health was increasingly recognised. As one British writer put it, 'no adverse circumstance in after life [can] altogether destroy the advantages which result from the early bias given in the mind by the judicious attention of a really good mother.'

CLASSROOM ORDER Pupils standing to attention reveal the stern face of Victorian schooling. Welcoming a newcomer presents a gentler face.

suddenly whip them off with instructions that they were to be given to the poor. Parents may have aimed at instilling 'unquestioning obedience' into their children, but generally speaking they preferred to work through love rather than fear, using the 'gentle measures' recommended by writers such as Jacob Abbott – who disapproved, for example, of corporal punishment.

The Victorians, despite the way they dressed their offspring, were among the first people to treat children as children, rather than miniature adults. They wrote special books for them – including many of the greatest children's classics: Hans Christian Andersen's *Fairy Tales* (1835-42), Lewis Carroll's *Alice's Adventures in Wonderland* (1865), Anna Sewell's *Black Beauty* (1877), R.L. Stevenson's *Treasure Island* (1883). They also devised splendid games and toys, and widely insisted that childhood should be a time of special magic and appeal.

There were also, of course, noticeable variations among different countries and cultures. Middle-class British people were unusual in having a structure of nannies and nurseries. The Germans had a reputation for beating their children; on the other hand, they produced some of the most popular children's literature of the period – most famously the fairy tales collected by the scholarly Brothers Grimm. In the late Victorian period, they also produced the best toys: wonderful lead soldiers, dolls, dolls' houses and perfectly functioning miniature steam locomotives and sewing machines.

Foreign visitors to Britain often commented on the lack of physical intimacy between middle-class children and their parents, partly a result of the habit of secluding the children in the nursery and the growing – and to many foreign eyes, barbaric – custom of sending them away to boarding 'public' schools. On the other hand, this encouraged

EAST SIDE STORY A mother tends her family in a New York tenement.

Victorian Scandals

An increasingly powerful press exposed the lives of the great to public scrutiny and helped to influence popular opinion.

SCANDAL, AIDED BY an increasingly powerful popular press, touched the lives of some of the greatest men and women of the Victorian Age, sometimes in ways that altered the course of history.

The numerous liaisons of the Prince of Wales never seriously jeopardised his prospects as the heir to the throne, but on occasions he caused considerable anxiety to his mother, Queen Victoria. In 1891, for example, he appeared in court as a witness in the 'Baccarat Case'. He had been playing baccarat with some friends at a country house, Tranby Croft, when one of the guests, Sir William Cumming, was caught cheating. The other guests, including the Prince, promised to keep the matter secret, in return for Sir William's undertaking that he would never again play cards for money. The story none the less leaked into the newspapers, Cumming brought a court action, and the Prince was obliged to appear as a witness. Some churchmen condemned the Prince for having anything to do with gambling, and a German cartoonist suggested a new motto for him, '*Ich* Deal' (a parody of *Ich Dien*, 'I Serve').

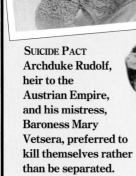

SUICIDE PACT Archduke Rudolf, heir to the Austrian Empire, and his mistress, Baroness Mary Vetsera, preferred to kill themselves rather than be separated.

The Prince survived this affair and succeeded to the throne in 1901 as a popular monarch. In 1889, another prince, the Archduke Rudolf, son of the Emperor Franz-Josef of Austria, killed himself in what must have been a suicide pact with his mistress, the 17-year-old Baroness Mary Vetsera, in the imperial hunting lodge at Mayerling. The imperial government succeeded in covering up the matter, but this personal tragedy affected history, for the succession then passed to Archduke Franz-Ferdinand, whose assassination at Sarajevo in June 1914 triggered World War I.

In the same year as the 'Mayerling affair', another sex scandal brought down a member of the British House of Commons. Charles Stewart Parnell was an Irish nationalist, a leader of the struggle for Irish Home Rule, and one of his colleagues in the cause was the MP Captain William O'Shea. But O'Shea's wife, Kitty, was Parnell's mistress and had been since 1880. Finally, in December 1889, O'Shea filed a petition for divorce, citing Parnell as the co-respondent – this may have been a political manoeuvre, with O'Shea acting as a pawn for Parnell's enemies. Parnell, who never attempted to defend the suit, was a broken man. He married Kitty O'Shea in June 1891 and died just four months later at Brighton.

ROYAL AFFAIR The liaison between Lily Langtry, a married woman, and the Prince of Wales was accepted by society.

Scandal marred the career of one of the United States's greatest men, Ulysses S. Grant, who led the Union to victory in the Civil War and became the 18th President in 1868. While he was campaigning for a second term in 1872, newspapers

PRESS POWER Politicians Charles Stewart Parnell and Ulysses S. Grant suffered from the attentions of the press. Left: Society felt betrayed by Oscar Wilde.

discovered that some of his political associates were linked with a shady corporation, the Credit Mobilier of America, which was illegally siphoning profits from a railroad company.

Following this, some of Grant's officials, including his private secretary, were shown to have been involved in an illegal whisky ring that was defrauding the government of tax revenues. Though Grant was himself quite innocent, his reputation was clouded by this evidence of corruption among his associates.

At the end of the era two tragic scandals revealed deep fissures under the apparently stable surface of Victorian society. In 1894 an obscure French Army captain, Alfred Dreyfus, serving at the War Ministry, was convicted by a court-martial of selling military secrets to the German military attaché and sentenced to life imprisonment on Devil's Island. Dreyfus was a Jew, and the 'Dreyfus affair' revealed an unsavoury streak of anti-Semitism in French life. In 1898, new evidence brought a further court-martial, but Dreyfus was again found guilty. The verdict was so blatantly unjust that the French president offered Dreyfus a pardon. Even so, it was not until 1906 that he was finally cleared of all charges.

In 1891, Oscar Wilde, shortly to win fame as a successful playwright, met the young Lord Alfred Douglas, son of the Marquess of Queensberry, and the two formed a close friendship. Although Wilde was a married man, his manner and his writings hinted at a decadence that infuriated Douglas's father, who left a note at Wilde's club accusing him of 'posing as a sodomite'. Urged on by Douglas, Wilde brought an action for criminal libel, which, when it came to court, went some way to exposing him as a probable homosexual. Wilde dropped the action. His friends urged him to flee the country, but he refused and was arrested and brought to trial. In May 1895 he was found guilty and sentenced to two years' hard labour.

PREJUDICE Alfred Dreyfus, whose case had divided France, returned to Paris after his release and 'rehabilitation'.

greater solidarity among the children and allowed them greater freedom to enjoy their games together. The Americans were closer to the continental Europeans in this respect: their children lived in much closer intimacy with their parents and were more used to speaking out, for example, in adult company.

BOYS IN SKIRTS

The Victorians believed in wrapping their children up warmly, and to that end young boys as well as girls were often dressed in layers of thick skirts. It was a great day for a boy, usually around his seventh birthday, when he was finally released from the constricting skirts and given his first pair of breeches.

Life on the Edge

If a middle-class Victorian childhood could be exceptionally happy and secure, there never lacked reminders of those who were less fortunate. In his book *The Children of the Poor* (1892), the Danish-born journalist and investigator of the conditions of the New York poor, Jacob Riis, described Tony, one of the more engaging of the many street 'ragamuffins' he came across in his researches:

'A ragged coat three times at least too large for the boy ... trousers that boasted a seat once, but probably not while Tony has worn them; two left boots tied on with packing twine, bare legs in them the colour of the leather, heel and toe showing through; a shock of sunburnt hair struggling though the rent in the old straw hat; two frank, laughing eyes under its broken brim – that is Tony.'

Clearly, life for children such as this was quite different from that of their wealthier counterparts. Not that all children were as threadbare as Tony, but life was frequently precarious for working-class families: the fear of destitution or the death of a parent was constantly at hand for even the steadiest and most respectable of families.

In such circumstances, a child's ability to contribute to the family's earnings was extremely important. As a result, the various laws passed in most countries during the Victorian age to limit the number of hours that children (and women) could work were not always welcomed by the workers themselves.

Children had to help in other ways, too. With mothers obliged to go out to work, older children had

Schooldays
Tom Brown slugs it out in the English novel *Tom Brown's Schooldays.* An English village school (above) and American classroom (right) offer more ordered scenes.

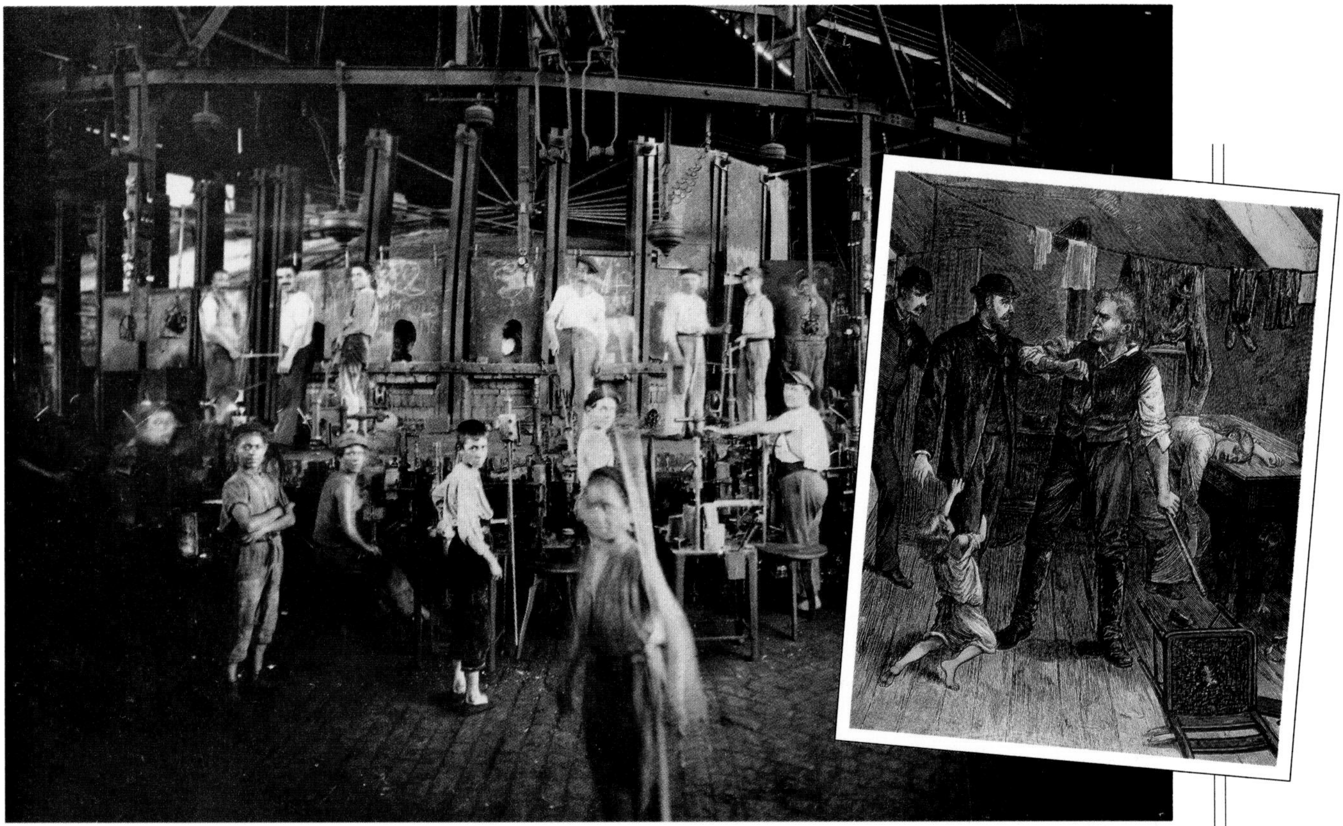

BOY WORKERS Despite laws against it, child labour was still common in many places, as in this French glassworks photographed at the end of the 19th century. In a scene from New York, officials intervene to prevent the illegal use of child workers.

to look after younger ones as well as taking their fair share of the household tasks: for the boys, cleaning the boots and fetching and carrying the coal and water; for the girls, helping with the cooking, sewing and darning. All this left many children with little time for lessons or school, let alone play.

At least such children had parents, however. In 1875, some 93,000 of the children born in France were abandoned by their parents. That same year, one French child in 14 was illegitimate. By the end of the century, for every 15 French families with both mother and father living, there were six lacking one or both parents.

Similar pictures could be drawn for most countries across the Victorian world. Orphans and abandoned children were among its most obvious and heart-wrenching social problems, providing many of the child chimney sweeps, street-crossing sweepers and other waifs who have survived as lasting images of the time's evils, thanks in part to the novels of Charles Dickens, Victor Hugo and others.

A LONDON SWEEP The sooty faces of boy chimney sweeps were all too familiar on Victorian streets.

The descent from relative prosperity to the destitution of the streets could be appallingly abrupt. The English investigative journalist Henry Mayhew, with a similar approach to Riis's, interviewed one bare-footed crossing sweeper he encountered in the late 1840s huddled in a doorway just off the Strand in London: 'a good-looking lad, with a pair of large mild eyes, which he took good care to turn up with an expression of supplication as he moaned for his halfpenny.' The boy's father had died some five years before, followed by his mother; and then his older sister, with whom he had been living, threw him out and told him to fend for himself.

Such stories were not unique to London. Similar unfortunates could have been found in New York, Melbourne, Paris, Berlin, Madrid and most other Victorian cities. To try to cope with them, most continental European countries had state-run orphanages. The United States had poorhouses and Britain workhouses – but conditions in them were in the majority of cases hardly less grim than on the streets, with spartan buildings and ferociously authoritarian regimes

TAKE YOUR PARTNERS ... Training for social graces often started early, as in this English children's ball.

(they were deliberately designed in this way to deter people from entering them except in the most extreme need). Usually it was left to the initiative of charitable organisations such as the remarkable Foundling Asylum of the Sisters of Charity in New York and in Britain Dr Thomas Barnardo's National Incorporated Association for the Reclamation of Destitute Waif Children to provide more humane help.

Similar organisations also set out to reform the practice of baby-farming, whereby parents would farm out babies to people who undertook to look after them for a fee. This was open to the cruellest abuses. As Jacob Riis put it: 'An infinitely more fiendish, if to surface appearances less deliberate, plan of child-murder than desertion has flourished in New York for years under the title of baby-farming. The name, put into plain English, means starving babies to death.'

What frequently happened was that the babies were kept seriously underfed and quietened with doses of the opium-based drug laudanum. In 1870 a particularly notorious case, of two sisters, Margaret Waters and Sarah Ellis, was brought to trial at the Old Bailey in London. During the course of the trial one witness told of his grandson, the illegitimate offspring of a 17-year-old daughter. The baby had been perfectly healthy when entrusted to the sisters; a few months later it was unrecognisably gaunt, filthy, wet and drugged – it died shortly afterwards. Sarah Ellis got away with 18 months' imprisonment; her 36-year-old sister, however, was found guilty of murder and hanged.

LOVE AND PASSION

Posterity has given the Victorians a bad name for repression, hypocrisy and the social horrors of the growing industrial cities. Such abuses undoubtedly existed, and yet it is also true that the Victorian family could be a centre of extraordinary warmth. 'I anticipate unspeakable delight in your embrace,' the highly respectable, Harvard-trained American lawyer and journalist Joseph Lyman wrote in a letter to his wife Laura in 1865, after seven years of marriage.

'Oh how I love you,' she wrote back. 'How I long to see you – how I long to "be all night in the hollow of my husband's shoulder" ... How I long to feel the contact of my mind against yours.'

And such love was no monopoly of the middle classes. The British miner and early trades union activist Edward Rymer recalled the death of his wife: 'She lingered and suffered until Jan. 22nd, then sank to rest in my presence, while my very soul seemed to lose its hope somehow, and set me adrift on a dark and trackless future – lonely and desolate without her. We had braved the storm and ruthless tempest in all its fury for 40 years.' Evidently, the qualities of love and passion were at least as common in Victorian family life as repression and hypocrisy.

LIFE IN THE VICTORIAN HOME

No effort was spared on the Victorian home. Factories were turning out ever-more affordable furnishings, and for the first time many decorative objects such as china and wallpaper came within the reach of ordinary people – not just the rich. For people of all classes, meanwhile, a stream of inventions, from the sewing machine to electric lighting, tinned meat to gas cookers, were transforming the everyday routines of housework.

UPSTAIRS, DOWNSTAIRS

Mrs Beeton, the English-speaking world's best-known writer on domestic affairs, compared the housewife to 'the Commander of an Army'. Certainly, the Victorian housewife was an all-important figure with an impressive range of duties.

Mid pleasures and palaces though we may roam,
Be it ever so humble, there's no place like home;
A charm from the skies seems to hallow us there,
Which, seek through the world, is ne'er met with elsewhere,
Home, home, sweet, sweet home!
There's no place like home! there's no place like home!
J.H. PAYNE, 'CLARI, the Maid of Milan'

SETTING UP HOME was as exciting, though sometimes as exasperating, a business for young Victorian couples as for all others. In Vienna, in 1882, the imagination of one newly engaged, 26-year-old doctor, Sigmund Freud, was especially fired at the prospect. Their home, he wrote to his fiancée Martha Bernays, would be a 'little world of happiness'. It would not be large, with just 'two or three small rooms', but it would be amply furnished with 'tables and chairs, beds, mirrors, a clock ... [and] an armchair for an hour's pleasant day-dreaming'.

They would have 'carpets to help the housewife [in other words, Martha] keep the floors clean, linen tied with pretty ribbons in the cupboard ... glasses for everyday [use] and others for wine and festive occasions, plates and dishes'. To complete the domestic scene, there would be 'an enormous bunch of keys – which must make a rattling noise', and then 'the books and the sewing table and the cosy lamp'.

Were they right to set their hearts 'on such small things'? Most certainly they were, opined the future father of psycho-analysis, 'and without hesitation'.

In that statement, at least, the young Freud showed himself to be a true Victorian. For if the Victorians worshipped the family, they also worshipped the family home – in all its smallest details. In an industrialising world that was changing so rapidly – and often so distastefully – around them, home was a treasured haven of peace and security. As a result, no amount of care, love and imagination was considered too much to be lavished upon it. 'I don't think there is a wiser way of spending money than in making the home beautiful,' the architect Andrew Wells told an audience of Australian colleagues in 1892.

Moral considerations were as important as aesthetic ones. A well-ordered home life initiated men, in particular, into the 'public virtues'. A slovenly home, by contrast, left them open to the all too real lures of drink and other dissipations. On this subject, the American domestic writer Mrs M.H. Cornelius was especially clear: 'Many a day-laborer, on his return at evening from his hard toil, is repelled by the sight of a disordered home and comfortless supper ... and he makes his escape to the grog-shop or the underground gambling room.'

Clearly, there were huge and glaring contrasts in what different Victorians could call 'home', from the 100-room mansions of European aristocrats and American millionaires, to the detached middle-class villas of the burgeoning suburbs, to the dripping, one-room cellar dwellings of the slums. But whatever people's social level, it was felt that they should at least make an effort to decorate their homes as attractively as they could. The New

DAILY FARE Managing the servants was one of the wealthy housewife's chief tasks. Here, a cook is given her day's instructions.

Mrs Leoni at Home **A cluttered abundance of furnishings was one of the hallmarks of wealth – as in this well-draped New York interior of the 1890s. English children (right) enjoy the festivities of a Victorian Christmas.**

York journalist Jacob Riis noted with approval the capacity of the city's black population to make pleasant homes, even in the direst circumstances: 'The poorest [black] housekeeper's room in New York is bright with gaily-colored prints of his beloved "Abe Linkum" [Abraham Lincoln], General Grant, President Garfield, Mrs Cleveland, and other national celebrities, and cheery with flowers and singing birds ... '

For more comfortable, middle-class Victorians, meanwhile, the choice of the kind of home they could look forward to was growing. The choice between apartments and houses tended to follow national lines. In England and America, those who could afford it increasingly chose houses in the suburbs. The Scots and continental Europeans, on the other hand, had long been in the habit of living in apartment-like tenement buildings. Following Baron Haussmann's trend-setting remodelling of Paris in the 1860s, living centrally in Parisian-style apartment blocks became the norm for many of the Continent's urban middle classes.

If the home, whether house or apartment, was 'a sacred place, a vestal temple, a temple of the hearth watched over by Household Gods' – in the somewhat high-blown words of the British art critic John Ruskin – its priestess was the housewife. Mrs Isabella Beeton, the most famous of the Victorian age's domestic writers, chose more military images when she wanted to convey something of the housewife's importance: 'As with the Commander of an Army, or the leader of an enterprise, so is it with the mistress of a house,' begins her best-selling *Book of Household Management*, first published in 1861.

The Victorian age certainly made high demands of housewives. Never before had they been so well provided with numerous different manuals, full of highly practical advice on all their various duties: the works, for example, of Mrs Beeton and Eliza Haweis in Britain, Mrs Cornelius and the redoubtable Julia McNair Wright in America, Frau Davidis in Germany,

THE VICTORIANS AT TABLE

For the better off, meal times provided an opportunity to enjoy and broadcast their wealth and social status.

WELL-TO-DO VICTORIANS ate on a scale not seen since the days of Imperial Rome. Eating a substantial meal in the evening rather than in the afternoon was a recent habit – the young Victoria led the fashion by dining at eight – and the dinner party became an opportunity for the display of wealth, not only in the food itself but in the use of fine silver and glass and the attendance of butlers and footmen.

Among country squires and prosperous farmers at the beginning of the period there was a lingering suspicion of 'fancy French dishes', but in fashionable circles everywhere French cuisine was predominant. The French themselves plunged into the joys of food and its preparation with an enthusiasm unrivalled elsewhere.

By the middle of the 19th century many of the great houses of Europe and North America boasted French chefs. Among the greatest of these was Alexis Soyer, who left France during the Revolution of 1830 and became chef to the Reform Club in London. A remarkable man, he went at his own expense to establish soup kitchens in Ireland in the famine year of 1847 and later to organise the victualling of hospitals in the Crimea. His published books had an enormous influence on the cookery of English houses. In one of them he imagined a housewife, 'Mrs B', whose husband started out as a small shopkeeper and later became a prosperous merchant.

In the early years of Mrs B's marriage, a typical week's menus included roast beef, potatoes, greens and Yorkshire pudding; boiled beef and bones, vegetables and spotted dick pudding; and boiled pork, pease pudding and greens. After a few years, Mr B had greatly prospered, and the couple were giving dinner parties in the French manner, with as many as 20 dishes served simultaneously in two great courses.

QUIET REVOLUTIONARY Mrs Beeton's advice on menus and managing a household revolutionised many women's lives.

The dinners of the rich would be more like the one served to Queen Victoria that included four soups, four fish, four hors d'oeuvres, four *relèves,* 16 entrées, with three joints on the sideboard including a haunch of venison, and a second service of six roasts, six *relèves,* two *flancs,* four *contreflancs,* 16 *entremets* – 70 dishes in all. (The Queen preferred plain food, but is reputed to have had curry

REFORMING SPIRIT The Reform Club's kitchens were rebuilt to the plans of Alexis Soyer, and were a model of efficiency. Right: Soyer's sauce was a great boon to hard-pressed cooks.

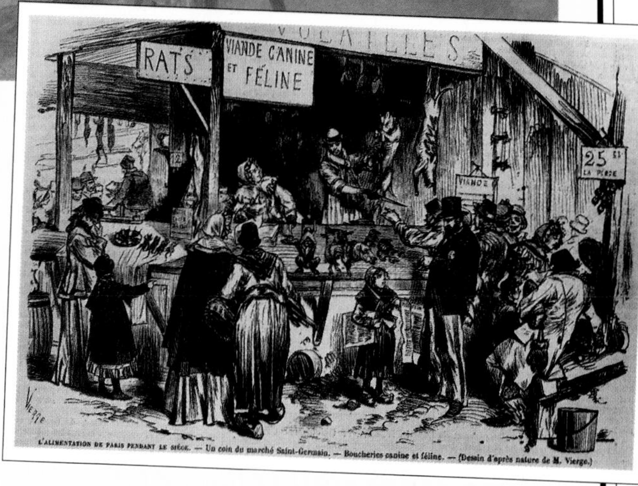

EATING OUT Fashionable men and women dine out together. Right: During the siege of Paris the inhabitants survived on cats, dogs, rats and anything else that was edible.

prepared in the palace kitchens every day in case a visiting Indian prince should ask for it.)

Of course, these enormous dinners were partly for display. Guests would decline some dishes, or take only token helpings from them. What was left over would go to the servants or, in country districts, to the poor. But even so, there was enormous waste, at a time when a large proportion of the population were subsisting on potatoes or beans or bread and tea, eked out irregularly with bacon, cheese and sausage.

In the 1860s, Mrs Beeton was still proposing menus in the French manner, but in the last decades of the century fashionable society began to dine *à la russe*, the dishes being placed on the sideboard and then served in sequence by the footmen. Roughly two-thirds of the way through, the guests would pause to refresh their stomachs by eating sorbets before turning to roast game or poultry, followed by a variety of puddings, ices and savouries, followed again by dessert, coffee and liqueurs.

In these decades, too, it became fashionable for men and women to eat out in hotels and restaurants; formerly only men had eaten out, in clubs and chop houses.

In contrast, during the siege of Paris by the Prussian army (1870-71) the city's inhabitants were reduced to eating domestic pets and the more edible animals from the zoos. The Jockey Club's menus included *salmi de rat* and 'rat pie', and one resident claimed that he had eaten 'camel, antelope, dog, donkey, mule and elephant, which I approve in the order in which I have written.'

The Etiquette Book in Action

In an age with a growing middle class, whose members were often uncertain of themselves socially, the etiquette book flourished as never before. Figures such as Florence M. Hall and the editors of *Godey's Lady's Book and Magazine* in the United States, Madame Emmeline Raymond and Baroness Staffe in France, and numerous, mostly anonymous British writers (sometimes designating themselves 'one of the Aristocracy', 'an Officer's Widow', or the like) – all at various times published their advice and opinions on a wide variety of social issues. These topics ranged from the correct ways for ladies and gentlemen to dress on different occasions to the genteel accomplishments of singing, dancing and playing cards (and even, for gentlemen, duelling); from how to entertain and be entertained to the proper way to propose marriage.

One of the most instructive of these books was the anonymous *Habits of Good Society* (first published in 1859), whose unnamed author claimed to be a worldly-wise London clubman – 'an old bachelor' who had 'passed a varied life'. He had no qualms about giving his advice on every aspect of social life, including many feminine ones, such as the use of rouge and other cosmetics (of which he disapproved) and the custom of wearing flowers in the hair at balls (of which he approved).

He also gave some very detailed advice on different kinds of entertainment. Take the dinner party, for example. Here, his first recommendations were obvious enough: excellence in the food and wine ('A dinner, like a pun, should never be made public unless it be very good') and careful consideration of the size and composition of the guest list – he preferred smaller dinners of six to ten people 'at which all the guests can join in a common conversation'.

'A dinner party breaks up at about eleven,' stated the author, with like-minded, bachelors evidently in mind. 'At eleven you go home, and having had a walk, put on your white necktie for the next event of the evening.' This would generally have been a grand ball.

Street Etiquette **Most writers disapproved of couples who were too demonstrative in public.**

Madame Pariset in France, Pellegrino Artusi in Italy, and many others.

Equally, however, the standards expected of the housewife had never been so high or so refined. In previous ages, middle-class women had often helped their husbands in the hurly-burly of their workshops or places of business. Now, the world was increasingly divided into the public, masculine domain of work and business and the private, feminine sanctuary of the home.

A Woman's Work

In this the woman was expected to be a true prodigy: hard-working yet always cheerful, frugal yet able to put on a good show, charitable, resourceful and beyond moral reproach. Even women who were comparatively well-off found their lives all too frequently dominated by the sheer, hard slog of the home. The Huntington family of Rochester, New York, owned a prosperous seed and nursery business, and their daughter Alcesta did not suffer either from inexperience or lack of means, but she still found herself a near-slave to the housework: 'I have been very busy in the kitchen most of the day,' she wrote in a letter in 1868. 'The state the kitchen is in most of the time would drive you frantic. And the more you try to put things in order the greater the confusion.'

For less well-off families, without the benefit of domestic help, the pressure was even greater: the wife frequently rose before the rest of the family to make breakfast and went to bed after them to give her time to clear up and prepare for the next morning.

The list of these women's duties was impressive, with most days assigned their particular chores –

CHORES RELIEVED Monday was usually washing day – the most dreaded day of the week. Sewing machines and, to a lesser extent, 'home washers' helped to revolutionise housework from the 1860s.

aside from the daily routines of cooking and cleaning. Monday, for instance, was laundry day in most homes. This, if you could possibly afford it, you gave out to a washerwoman. For those who could not, it meant a hard day's work, making Monday many women's least favourite day of the week.

First, they had to sort the clothes (separating out the whites and delicate fabrics, the calicos and ginghams, and so on). Then they had to fill a large washtub with hot, soapy water. The whites and delicate fabrics went in first, the whites scrubbed vigorously on a board, the delicates rubbed more gently. Next, the washed clothes were spread out in a second, empty tub. Boiling water from the kitchen heater or from a cauldron bubbling on the stove was poured over them. More soap was added; the tub was covered, and the clothes were left to stew for half-an-hour or so.

Finally, they were tipped out, drained, rinsed in clean water (usually with a special bluing agent added), wrung out (by hand or with a mechanical wringer), and hung up to dry, before the whole process was repeated with the next batch of clothes.

With the clothes clean and dry, Tuesday was ironing day. This task was still less popular than washing, involving the use of heavy cast-metal irons, heated up on the stove. Even families who could not afford to put out their washing sometimes managed to find someone to do their ironing for them. Tuesdays – or sometimes Thursdays – were also baking days in many American and British households. For Anglo-Saxon housewives, baking their own bread was often something of a point of pride, even if they had a cook to do everything else in the kitchen. In France, by contrast, buying baker's bread was increasingly the norm, even among working-class families.

Saturday was another baking day in America and Britain, and it had the added burden that the housewife was supposed to get as much preparation as possible done on Saturday, in order to keep the Sabbath free of work – 'busy fixing for Sabbath as usual on Saturday,' was a rather sour little note in the diary of Almira MacDonald, the well-to-do wife of an American lawyer.

As well as all these weekly chores, there was also, of course, an annual round of tasks. Some of these were relatively pleasant (such as the seasonal business of bottling fruit and making jams, pickles and the like), but others were less so – such as the upheavals of spring and autumn cleaning.

These twice-yearly cleanings involved a wholesale turning-out of the house and its furnishings, and might take a week or longer. Carpets were pulled up and beaten, windows and curtains washed, mattresses aired, storerooms emptied and rearranged, winter or summer clothes checked and packed away.

Not tied to any particular season, but equally important, was sewing. Here, the invention of the cotton-machine worker Elias Howe, from Spencer, Massachusetts, probably had as much impact on the workaday lives of Victorian women as any of the age's other technological advances. For five years Howe spent every moment of his spare time devising a workable sewing machine, finally obtaining a patent for one in 1846.

Although Howe himself scarcely profited from his invention until just under a decade later, it was the basis of the modern sewing machine as refined by Isaac Merrit Singer.

Once the design was well established, it soon caught on – the 'Queen of Inventions' is how the popular American monthly *Godey's Lady's Book and Magazine* described it – and by 1860 over 110,000 machines were being produced and sold each year in the United States alone.

Paradoxically, the sewing machine did not always reduce the busy housewife's workload. Now that sewing was so much easier and faster, the pressure was on women to do still more of it: 'With the help of this useful invention,' wrote Mrs Beeton,

A LANGUAGE IN CARDS

Paying calls and receiving them played an important part in the weekly round of many Victorian ladies. So did the ritual of leaving visiting cards. This was a language in itself. If a lady folded down the top right-hand corner of her card, it meant that she had come in person – rather than sending a servant. If she folded it in the top left-hand corner, she was conveying congratulations – for the engagement of a daughter, say. If she folded down the bottom left-hand corner she was offering condolences.

'a lady can, with perfect comfort, make and mend every article used by herself and children, and do a great deal towards repairing and making her husband's clothes.'

Individual women may or may not have heeded such advice, but observers noted that many became much more fashion conscious – to the irritation of the more puritanical – since it was now so much easier for them to run up new outfits or adapt old ones. This in turn helped to iron out some of the old class differences in dress, as poorer women were better able to emulate the styles and fashions of the wealthy.

Mistress and Servants

The other side of the middle-class housewife's job was managing the servants. Households varied hugely in size, of course, from vast aristocratic establishments which might employ 40 or 50 indoor servants alone – including house steward, butler, housekeeper, valet and lady's maid, footmen, nursemaids, scullery maids, housemaids and many others – to the far more numerous middle-class homes, which might have just one overburdened maid-of-all-work. Roughly two-thirds of all female domestics throughout the Victorian world were maids-of-all-work employed on their own.

Mrs Beeton, as usual, had a great deal of very precise advice to give on the subject, including a scale showing how many servants people should think of employing at various levels of income. She reckoned in 1861 that those with about £1000 a year could reasonably expect to have a staff of five: a cook, an upper and an under housemaid, a nursemaid and a man servant. At around £150 a year, they were lucky to have a maid-of-all-work, as well perhaps as a 'girl' who came in from time to time to help.

Generally speaking, middle-class families were prepared to make fairly substantial sacrifices in order to employ at least one servant – if only as a badge of their middle-class status: 'I must not do our household work, or carry my baby out: or I should lose caste,' was the rather astonishing complaint of an

Servants and Masters
Servants far outnumber family at the English country house Ketteringham. Tasks varied hugely from those of the footman polishing silver to the humbler skivvying of a maid-of-all-work.

A Footboy in the Seventies

THE ENGLISH farmer's son William Lanceley ended his working life in royal service, as steward to the Duke of Connaught. But his beginnings were more humble. In the 1870s, aged 16, he was footboy in the household of the local squire:

'My duties, which started at six o'clock A.M., were as follows: first light the servants' hall fire, clean the young ladies' boots, the butler's, housekeeper's, cook's, and ladies'-maids', often twenty pairs altogether ... then lay up the hall breakfast, get it in, and clear up afterwards. Tea was provided at breakfast for the women servants and beer for the men. I was not rated as a man, but was allowed tea with the women servants, and was duly railed at by the other men ... The food generally consisted of a large dish of stew served on a flat pewter dish; a big joint of cold beef with bread and cheese completed the menu ... My day's work followed on with cleaning knives, housekeeper's room, silver, windows, and mirrors; lay up the servants' hall dinner; get it in and out and wash up the things, except dishes and plates; help to carry up luncheon; wash up in the pantry; carry up the dinner to the dining room and, when extra people dined, wait at table; lay up the servants' hall supper; clear it out and wash up. This brought bedtime after a day's work of sixteen hours.'

BOY LABOUR 'Service' started early for many, such as this London bellboy in the 1880s.

English assistant surgeon's wife in 1859. 'We must keep a servant.' The whole relationship between masters and servants was changing. In the old days, servants on farms or even in merchants' houses had been more like members of the family. Family and servants had usually eaten together; in Germany masters had addressed their servants using the familiar *Du*; in parts of Brittany servants had addressed their master and mistress as *oncle* (uncle) and *tante* (aunt).

In a few country areas such habits survived the Victorian era, but in most places the old family-like relationship gave way to a much more formal one. A contributor to *The British Mothers' Family Magazine* in 1864 was quite stern: 'Friends in servants, indeed!' she snorted. 'Expect servants to be our friends! I have tried, but it cannot be; it is not in their nature to soften or yield to kindness.'

Happily, relations could be a lot less tart than that. One of Alcesta Huntington's married sisters, Susan, spoke highly of a new maid of hers: 'Maggie and I get along splendidly. She takes care of all the back part of

SYMBOLS OF OFFICE Servants hold symbols of their duties in a British household of the 1880s.
A British cartoon pokes fun at the unwieldy size of many households.

A World of Choice Large new stores – such as New York's Hill Brothers – catered for every need.

the house, upstairs and down, cleans the lamps … and takes the baby whenever I want her to do so.' Another Huntington sister spoke appreciatively of her 'girl [who] is taking hold nicely and doesn't need to be told anything twice … I have finished up the little cleaning that wasn't done, and have realized more fully all that I have escaped.'

Varieties of Service

From the servants' point of view, experience was equally varied. Those in large aristocratic households had a general reputation for being extremely pampered. At the same time, they were often highly snobbish, with 'upper' servants (the steward, butler and housekeeper) lording it over 'lower' servants (the ordinary footmen and maids).

There was little pampering for maids-of-all-work in less grand households, by contrast. They would usually work between 80 and 100 hours a week, with one afternoon off, perhaps, and part of Sunday. And they had much more to contend with. One not uncommon hazard was the attention of people such as the master of the house, or one of his sons, or simply one of the menservants. A significant proportion of all unmarried mothers in Victorian times had been domestic servants when they got pregnant. Few were lucky enough to keep their jobs in such circumstances, and many ended up in prostitution.

Yet a maid's life was not always bleak. Some mistresses were undoubtedly harsh and inconsiderate, and it was not for nothing that most of the household manuals found it necessary to remind their readers that 'servants are human beings … with rights no amount of service money can buy', as the American Josiah Gilbert Holland put it. But there were always others who were kind and just. Work might be hard and living conditions spartan, but the faithful servant did often come to feel like a member of the family, and would frequently be looked after as such, in both sickness and health.

As the Victorian age wore on, more and more women opted for the better pay and working conditions of shops, food-processing factories and offices. Even so, at the turn of the 20th century the majority of working women across the world were still employed as domestic servants. And service still had much to attract young girls, most of them coming from the country in Europe, or from among the immigrant communities in the United States.

CRIME AND DETECTION

Victorian society was rocked by a series of violent crimes, but the science of detection developed to meet the challenge.

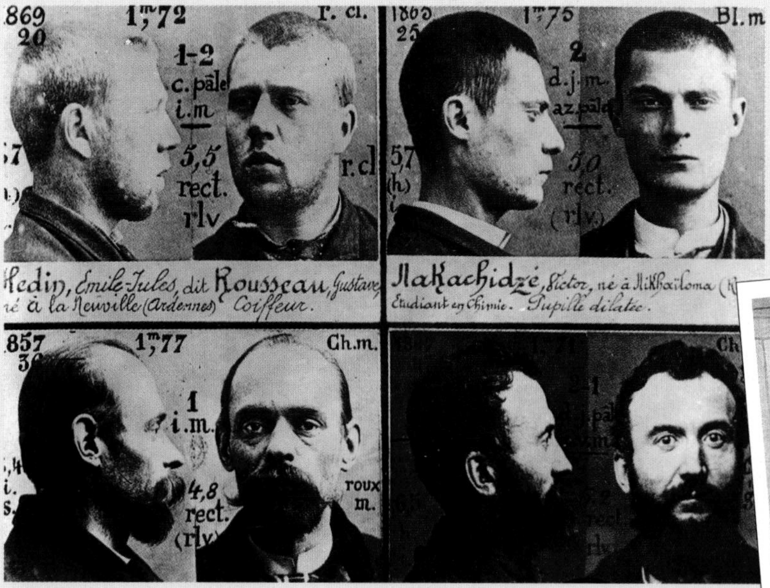

ROGUES GALLERY The Bertillon method included full-face and profile photographs together with several measurements, such as height, circumference of head, length of ears, length of feet, and a description of facial features and bodily characteristics.

BY THE VICTORIAN PERIOD, most Western countries had regular police forces and were beginning to develop scientific methods for the investigation of crime. One of the most widespread of these was the system of identification developed by Alphonse Bertillon for the French Sûreté, where he had started work as a records clerk. This was based on the theory that no two human beings have the same combination of body measurements, so a typical Bertillon record would include photographs, a systematic description of physical characteristics, and measurements.

The Bertillon method was most useful for tracing criminals from witnesses' descriptions of them and for identifying habitual criminals, who might otherwise try to pass themselves off as first-time offenders under assumed names. What it could not do with any degree of certainty was to link a criminal to a particular crime. Bertillonage therefore rapidly fell out of use at the end of the 19th century when the technique of fingerprinting was developed.

In 1892 the British scientist Sir Francis Galton published his book *Fingerprints*, in which he set out the basic features – arches, loops and whorls – by which fingerprints could be classified. His book was read by Sir Edward Henry, Inspector General of Police in Bengal, who expanded the system. Within a few years, the Galton-Henry system was being used by police forces around the world.

In Argentina, a police officer, Juan Vucetich, had read Galton's book and set up his own system of fingerprint identification. Vucetich probably deserves the credit for convicting the first murderer – a woman who had killed her own children and tried to put the blame on a neighbour – with the aid of fingerprints.

It was the evidence of doctors rather than Bertillon records that featured in many of the great murder trials of the 19th century, particularly in the poisoning cases that were such a feature of the age, although doubt lingers about some of them to this day. In May 1889, the American Florence Maybrick was convicted of the murder of her husband, but although traces of poison were found in his body there is considerable evidence that James Maybrick,

INCRIMINATING PRINTS Fingerprinting enabled police to link a person to a particular crime.

FORENSIC FIRST **Professor Webster murders Dr Parkman. Despite Webster's attempts to dispose of the body, the victim was identified by his dentures.**

POISONOUS INTENT **Dr Thomas Cream earned the nickname 'the Lambeth Poisoner'.**

a hypochondriac who regularly used arsenic as an aphrodisiac, may have taken it himself.

There is very little doubt about the cases of Dr William Palmer and Dr Thomas Cream. Dr Palmer was hanged for murder in 1856 after poisoning as many, possibly, as 14 people for financial gain. Cream, born in Glasgow, graduated as a doctor from McGill University in Canada and practised in Chicago, where in 1881 he was given a life sentence for the murder by poisoning of a man called Stott, the husband of Cream's mistress. Released in 1891, he moved to London, where he murdered at least four prostitutes with strychnine. He was hanged in November 1892.

Forensic dentistry also played a part in 19th-century criminology. In 1849 Dr John Webster, a Harvard professor, killed one of his associates, Dr George Parkman, in a quarrel over money. He then dismembered Parkman's body and destroyed most of it by burning it in a furnace. In a subsequent investigation, however, a dentist, Dr Nathan Keep, identified the charred remains of the dentures he had constructed for Dr Parkman, and Professor Webster was found guilty of murder and hanged.

At the end of the Victorian age there appeared the first and greatest of fictional detectives, Sherlock Holmes, created by Sir Arthur Conan Doyle. At about the same time came the most notorious of unsolved murders, those of 'Jack the Ripper'. The Ripper, who killed and horribly mutilated at least five women in London's East End in the 1880s and taunted the police with boastful letters, has variously been identified as a prince, several prominent doctors, a midwife and a Jewish ritual slaughterman. It is most probable, however, that he was a psychopath who died in obscurity and whose identity will never be known.

'Jack the Ripper' shares his celebrity with an American contemporary, Lizzie Borden. In August 1892 her father and stepmother were found dead with their heads smashed in at their home; a freshly cleaned axe blade was found nearby. Lizzie Borden was duly charged with their murder, but found not guilty.

TRAPPED BY SCIENCE **Sherlock Holmes conducts a chemical experiment. He used analytic methods of investigation that were beyond the capacities of the police of his day.**

HOME COMFORTS

Plushly upholstered sofas, drawing-room pianos or organs, running water and, later, water closets – all came to be essential features of middle-class homes. Many families who were less well-off also aspired to a piano and a neat front parlour.

PURITANICAL though the Victorians were in many of their attitudes, few had any qualms about comfort and ornament in the home. Quite the contrary: 'If the care we take over our person and clothes is a mark of deference towards other people, it is an obligation to ourselves to ornament our homes in such a way as to make them pleasant and to inspire in us the taste for staying there.' So wrote the French authority Charles Blanc in the opening sentence of his *Grammaire des arts décoratifs* (*Grammar of the Decorative Arts*). The American writer on family life Henry C. Wright, was equally emphatic: 'Man needs a home for the body as well as the soul. It is natural and right that a man and a woman, living in the conjugal relation, should seek to surround themselves with material beauty and elegance, as well as comfort.'

LOVE SEAT The cosy vis-à-vis was a Victorian favourite.

Certainly, a well-developed taste for comfort was an outstanding Victorian characteristic. No age has produced such a luxurious array of different kinds of sofa and easy chair, for instance: the plumply upholstered and buttoned ottoman, the conveniently S-shaped vis-à-vis (allowing couples full intimacy in their conversations), the 'cosy corner', the American-style rocking chair, the smoker's chair (with handy spittoon hidden in a drawer beneath) and the cushion-like pouffe – to name but a few.

At the same time, the Victorians' love of ornament was beyond dispute. Typical interiors were lush, and to many modern eyes overwhelming; displays of strong colours and patterns, with heavily draped furnishings, often in a multitude of styles, covered large amounts of floor space, while pictures and photographs were massed along the walls from the ceiling almost to the floor.

In part at least, all this was a response to the new social and industrial conditions of the age. For it was, supremely, an age of possessions. Political stability, relative prosperity and the new industrial processes of production meant that for the first time large numbers of people other than wealthy aristocrats could afford to buy and accumulate objects. Not everybody's possessions were of the highest quality, of course – one reason for the Victorian habit of covering tables and chests with heavy cloths was to hide the inferior quality of the factory-made furniture beneath.

Another factor was the widening horizons of the Victorian world. As new parts of the globe were explored on the one hand, and as popular historians opened up new understandings of the past on the other, so the habit grew of raiding and mixing the styles of different eras and cultures. Such 'eclecticism', with its abundant jumbling of effects (mock-Gothic, Japanese, rococo and so on), seemed a natural response to newly discovered riches and few Victorians would have felt any embarrassment about it. Equally, their world's widening technological horizons played a role.

One of the English-speaking world's most influential books on interior design was Charles Locke Eastlake's *Hints on Household Taste*, published in 1868. In it, he railed against the 'commonplace taste' of the mid-Victorian age which compelled people 'to rest on chairs

MASS PRODUCTION Ordinary people could afford decorative china.

and sit at tables which were designed in accordance with the worst principles of construction and invested with shapes confessedly unpicturesque', which 'bade us ... furnish our houses after the same fashion as we dress ourselves, and that is with no more sense of real beauty than if art were a dead letter'.

In Britain, many of Eastlake's views were echoed by the Arts and Crafts movement – led by the visionary William Morris and calling for a return to traditional crafts skills – and he also had an indirect influence on the Art Nouveau movement which emerged in many countries in the 1890s. In the United States, his influence was, if anything, greater still, generating an 'Eastlake style' which emphasised simple, relatively unornamented surfaces and remained popular for the rest of the century.

A Proliferation of Rooms

On the subject of how to decorate the home's different rooms, Eastlake and most of the Victorian domestic writers had a good deal to say, and often in some detail. One characteristic of the middle-class Victorian home was its sheer proliferation of rooms, each with its own special function: drawing room, dining room, breakfast room, smoking room, library, billiard room, nursery, dressing room, bathroom, conservatory and so on – depending on the wealth and pretensions of the family. And even in the smallest home, each room was supposed to have its own distinctive character. In the drawing room, for instance, the sensitive, feminine touch was supposed to be most evident. According to the American Mary Gay Humphreys, it 'should convey a sense of elegance, good taste, recognition of the polite arts, and of graceful, social

Age of Ornament **An American lady, Ina Leland, reclines in richly ornamented rooms. Even the less wealthy, meanwhile, could hope for a fine brass bedstead or for goods offered by the Chicago mail-order firm, Sears, Roebuck.**

Design for Living **A rich profusion of furnishings, as in the American interior above, reflected a delight in colour and ornament. Manuals on interior design illustrated effects that could be achieved (right).**

amenities'. Rather like the Victorian home as a whole, the drawing room had a dual role: as bastion of family privacy, on the one hand, and on the other, as public statement, in a highly status-conscious age, of the family's wealth and taste.

In Australia, the *Illustrated Sydney News* best summed up these considerations: the drawing room, it wrote, 'is an important room, if for no other reason than that it is the link between the outside world and the inhabitants of the house – the neutral ground where callers can penetrate without further approach to intimacy, and from that standpoint gather their impressions of what lies beyond – of what are the tastes, intellectual pursuits and characteristics of the occupiers of the house'.

Here, during the late morning, the mistress of the house might sit, preferably engaged with a little light needlework ('none other is appropriate in the drawing-room,' wrote Mrs Beeton), while she received the calls of friends and neighbours. Here too, after dinner, the family would gather round the velvet-covered central table for one of the cosy evenings beloved of many Victorians. They might play cards or chess – taking advantage of what might be the one good source of light in the room, a paraffin lamp hanging over the table – or the father or elder son might read aloud from some popular, and suitably edifying, work of fact or fiction, while the wife and daughters sewed or embroidered.

Alternatively, one of the children might strike up on the piano or parlour organ – essential drawing-room accoutrements for any household with pretensions to gentility – while another sang. In German families it was not uncommon for different family members to play different instruments, so that they could perform small chamber pieces together. Under cover of the others' activities, a daughter of the family might retreat to a conveniently shadowy

Busts and Bustles: The Evolution of Fashion

Even in its heyday, the complex, often highly constricting apparatus of Victorian dress – especially for women – had its critics. In the early 1850s, for example, the American women's rights' campaigner Mrs Amelia Jenks Bloomer was vehement in her castigation of the impractical fashions adopted by so many of her contemporaries. In her eagerness to counteract such trends, she even tried to devise a more sensible form of female garb with baggy, Turkish-style trousers as one of its most distinctive features.

It was all to very little apparent effect. Mrs Bloomer was laughed to scorn in the Press and elsewhere – though the trouser-like garments named after her would make a comeback some 40 years later. And most women with any pretensions to stylishness continued to array themselves in corsets, stays, layers of petticoats and skirts.

Then, in the mid-1850s, the cage crinoline made its appearance, much encouraged by the example of the Empress Eugénie, the beautiful Spanish-born wife of Napoleon III of France. At first this represented something of a release for women. Constructed from light steel hoops sewn into a special petticoat, the crinoline meant an end to all the heavy layers of extra petticoats needed to puff skirts out. But it had its drawbacks too, such as a tendency to fly up in the wind.

Then came the bustle, a hallmark in fashion for much of the 1870s and 80s, as the crinoline had been for the years of Napoleon III's Second Empire. This consisted of a horsehair pad or small steel cage attached to the waistband at the back, which helped to create what was then the desired look of full bust and ample behind.

Divided knickerbocker dresses or bloomers at last came into their own as garments for cycling, and the efforts of the dress reformers – the Rational Dress movement of the 1880s in Britain, for example – began to pay off after long years of ridicule. Corsets were abandoned, or at least untightened, with the looser, more flowing style exemplified by the American 'Gibson girl' look coming to dominate.

March of Fashion **Ladies had to be rich to wear crinolines (right), since they needed at least one maid to help them put it all on. By the 1880s, fashions (above) had become a little simpler.**

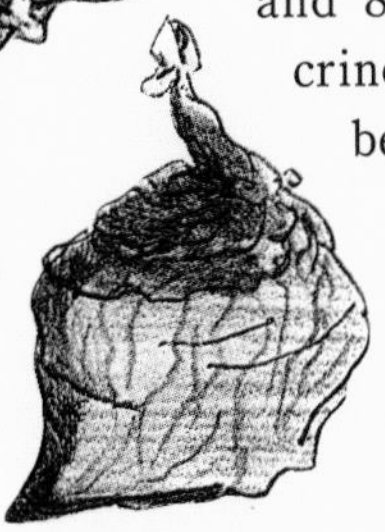

'Oop La! Wind-blown crinolines could be revealing.

The Victorian Kitchen

The pace of change in the kitchen matched that in the home as a whole. At the start of the Victorian age, for example, the standard means of cooking in most middle-class homes, and in some poorer ones as well, was the 'open' range: a cast-iron monster with an open, coal- or wood-fired grate and ovens to the side. Then came the more sophisticated 'closed' range, with an iron hotplate over the grate and a more efficient system of flues to direct the heat around the ovens. In the 1850s the first gas cookers were manufactured. Finally, in the 1890s, a few early electric cookers made their appearance.

Among all these different cookers, or 'kitcheners', however, the range (which also often had a water heater attached) unquestionably reigned supreme – though many poor families went on cooking over small open grates. As late as 1886, for instance, the American Susan Huntington Hooker was rejoicing in her 'hot and cold water and new magic range [which] make the work so much easier that when we are settled it seems as though we had saved one-half of our work'. Not that ranges, even the most advanced closed ones, were by any means labour-free. Early each morning they had to be raked out and, in thrifty households, the cinders sifted through to separate out those that could be burnt again. A coat of black-lead (a mix of iron and carbon) was applied like shoe polish to the surface, and once a week the build-up of soot had to be removed from the flues.

Elsewhere in the kitchen, the Victorians managed to accumulate an impressive range of useful gadgetry. Table-mounted apple parers, devices for stoning cherries, coffee and meat grinders, and large-scale equipment such as the space-saving 'Hoosier' cabinet (with built-in flour and sugar dispensers and a fold-down work surface) – all made their appearance, especially in America where obtaining servants was generally more difficult than in Europe. New materials also began to emerge, such as the popular and near-unbreakable 'granite ware': utensils made from steel with a light porcelain-like coating. At the same time, more luxurious items such as primitive refrigerators or 'ice-chests' were becoming more common, triggering a late Victorian craze for ice-creams and sorbets.

Kitchen Treasures **Baking powder, egg beaters and lemon squeezers – all transformed kitchen labours.**

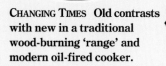

Changing Times **Old contrasts with new in a traditional wood-burning 'range' and modern oil-fired cooker.**

HOME ENTERTAINING Shawls decorate a 'Gilded Age' American interior. Elegant ladies exchange confidences, and a young American strums his banjo.

window corner with a visiting friend or suitor.

Even in small working-class homes, families would try to set aside the front room as a kind of special sanctum with all their best possessions: studio photographs of stiffly posed family members; prints of the president, monarch or national heroes; mementoes from seaside holidays; even perhaps a piano. Unlike the middle-class drawing room, the working-class front parlour was rarely in everyday use, however. People would sit there only on special occasions and when 'company' visited – though, like the drawing-room window nook of middle-class homes, it was a favourite retreat for courting couples.

HOME HYGIENE

Among the home's other rooms, the dining room was considered the next most important. According to Mary Gay Humphreys, 'it should be the most cheerful and most enjoyable room in the house', since the family met there at least three times a day. Further advice abounded: the walls should be painted rather than papered, as wallpaper was believed to soak up food smells; for similar reasons the seats of dining-room chairs should be leather-covered or wickerwork, rather than covered with velvet or tapestry. Bedrooms, meanwhile, were not for show, and therefore tended to be more spartan. Their chief items of furniture were usually a washstand, with washbowl and water pitcher, and a simple iron bedstead – it was the Victorians who by and large abandoned the old, curtained four-poster bed (a free flow of air as one slept was considered healthy).

As for bathrooms, it was also the Victorians who first got into the habit of having special rooms set aside for this purpose. Even so, the habit never became universal: as late as the 1880s five out of six town-dwellers in the United States had no bathroom in their home. Where a bathroom was not available, hip baths and various forms of mobile shower bath remained popular.

More and more homes had plumbed-in hot water, heated in a boiler attached to the kitchen range or

stove and then piped upstairs. But again it was still on the whole more common for people to use 'toilet cans' to carry their hot water upstairs with them from the kitchen.

If this was too laborious, there were various ingenious alternatives. The metal gas bath was filled with plumbed-in cold water and then heated by gas burners underneath – it was important to remember to turn off the burners before you got in – or there was the geyser, which heated the water inside a small boiler in the bathroom.

The modern flush toilet was another Victorian invention, claimed by the British firm of Bostel in Brighton. Once more, the alternatives were numerous, including the Revd Henry Moule's earth closet, invented in 1860. This managed to survive competition from the water closet, and as late as 1900 was being advertised in Britain as 'serviceable in bedrooms and nurseries' and 'invaluable' in 'sickrooms, in hospitals, and in infirmaries'.

At first, homes supplied with water closets had them secluded in the basement or back yard – most people went on using chamberpots at night. Only gradually did the water closet begin to make its appearance, first in a room adjoining the bathroom and then in the bathroom itself. Even then, authorities such as the British *Cassell's Book of the Household* regarded it as unhygienic and complained in 1890 about 'the objectionable practice of placing a w.c. in the bathroom ... common to suburban homes'.

Porridge, Potatoes and Pasta

The importance of good food, meanwhile, was as much appreciated as that of comfort and an attractive home. It was a Frenchman, the great Antoine Carême, cook to Tsar Alexander I of Russia and the millionaire banker Baron Jacques de Rothschild, who regarded most highly the value of fine cooking. It was, he stated, 'the most ancient of the arts and the art which has rendered the most important services to civil life'. Across the Atlantic, *Godey's Lady's Book* was hardly less emphatic, though rather more down-to-earth: 'If we are to be a vigorous and

Labour Saving **Carpet sweepers and bread cutters were among new household gadgets. Water closets, meanwhile, came shaped like Grecian urns or dolphins.**

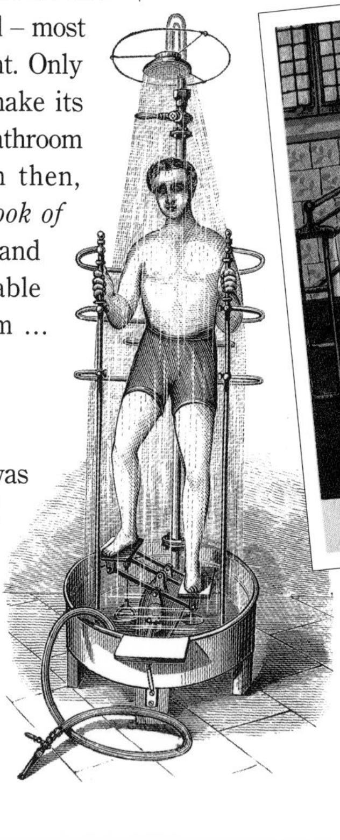

Cleanliness **Bathrooms and various showering devices were all novelties.**

Bedroom Hygiene Wooden washstands were still the norm in bedrooms, as in these English (above) and French (right) examples.

enduring race, we must have both well-selected food and good cookery,' it commented in 1870.

Of course, such apparent unanimity was to some extent superficial, and behind it lay huge variations in what different people in different countries and classes ate, and how they ate it. Karl Marx's collaborator Friedrich Engels, who spent many years managing the English end of his family's textile business, gave a detailed account of the diet and eating habits of the working classes in Manchester in his *Condition of the Working Class in England*, written in 1844.

These habits in themselves varied a great deal. In good times, the family of a well-paid worker could expect to eat reasonably well, with meat for the main midday meal every day, and a lighter evening meal of cheese and bacon. Lower down the economic scale, families would have meat just two or three times a week, and proportionately more potatoes or bread. At the bottom of the scale meat disappeared from the diet altogether, leaving 'only bread, cheese, porridge, and potatoes, until on the lowest rung of the ladder, among the Irish, potatoes form the sole food'.

All of this assumed that the family had at least one wage-earner. Among the unemployed, a family's entire diet might consist of no more than 'potato parings, vegetable refuse, and rotten vegetables ... eaten for want of other food'. The rural poor, living closer to the sources of food, fared marginally better than their urban counterparts, though their diet was rarely luxurious. The English writer Richard Jeffries noted that a typical Wiltshire farm labourer in the 1870s lived chiefly off 'bread and cheese, with bacon twice or thrice a week, varied with onions, and if he be a milker (on some farms) with a good "tuck-out" at his employer's expense on Sundays'.

The poorest French peasants had an equally monotonous diet, often consisting of vegetable soup bulked out with bread three times a day, varied with *bouillie* – a porridge made by boiling maize or rye in water or milk. In comparison, many Italians seem to have come off tolerably well. For them, pasta played a key role. Pasta factories sprang up in villages and towns, and the whole process of producing it became something of a ritual, rather like grape-picking.

Food's Great Tradition

But it was among the middle and upper classes that the enjoyment of good food really took root. Clearly, the pleasures of the table had always been important to those who could afford them, but it was during the

Victorian age that the habits of good eating came to be more widely disseminated.

In this the French, naturally enough, led the way – it was during the 19th century that France firmly established its supremacy as the home of fine food. Bourgeois French families would regularly spend two or more hours over one meal consisting of perhaps 10, or even 15, courses. At the same time, a crop of books by great chefs such as Antoine Carême laid down the law about how to produce the sumptuous dishes off which the rich fed.

In America and Britain, many middle-class people tended to take a certain pride in dismissing what they regarded as the fopperies of continental European cuisine – one observer noted the English habit of answering questions about food with no-nonsense assertions such as 'My living is plain, always roast and boiled.' For all that, they never stinted themselves in the quantity of what they ate, nor in the quality of the ingredients (thanks in part to more advanced agricultural methods in both Britain and America).

The simplest of middle-class breakfasts would consist of bacon, eggs, ham, broiled haddock, toast, coffee and perhaps some seasonal fruit in summer. In addition to this the Americans already had their own morning delicacies such as waffles. They also astonished foreign visitors by the huge amounts of iced water they drank throughout the day.

After that, middle- and upper-class people, unlike the working classes, usually had a light lunch around midday. This was followed a few hours later in Britain by another Victorian invention: afternoon tea (in the old days tea had been taken in the evening, after an early dinner eaten while it was still daylight). Then came dinner, the main meal. Here, a different set of class distinctions came into play: generally speaking, middle-class families had dinner at around 5 or 6pm (after the husband had returned from work); while the more leisured classes had it later, between 8 and 9pm.

The Victorian age did see changes in the way food was cooked and served. One was a slow move away from the almost impossible richness of the dishes favoured by many of Carême's successors. Urbain Dubois, among the best-known cooks of the latter half of the 19th century, criticised the 'extravagant superabundance' of much contemporary cooking – though his own food was scarcely simple. Others began to react against dishes in which the extraordinary assortment of flavours (particularly in the sauces) more often than not drowned the taste of the basic ingredients. The real revolution, however, led by Auguste Escoffier in favour of a simpler, more scientific cuisine, came only in the years immediately following Queen Victoria's death. An earlier revolution, meanwhile, had affected the way food was served. At the start of the Victorian age, the standard way of serving a meal was *à la française*. The meal had three main courses, as well as numerous slightly lighter, intermediate ones. For each of these the table was laden with a huge array of dishes – rather like a modern buffet

STAFF OF LIFE Bread remained the staple of poor people's diets, and in the cities shortages – as in Berlin in 1847 – could cause riots.

HOT POTATOES A London baked-potato seller of the 1870s poses for the pioneer photographer John Thompson.

SUNRISE STORES **The grocery store at Sunrise, Wyoming offers elegance and a plentiful array of goods. Mrs Beeton's *Book of Household Management* offers tips on cuts of meat, among other things.**

– from which you simply took your pick; hence the sheer size of some Victorian menus. The trouble with this was that by the time all the dishes had been arranged on the table and people had helped themselves, much of the food had grown cold.

As a result the later fashion for service *à la russe* (Russian-style service), which first started to appear in western Europe and America in the 1860s, caught on fairly swiftly. This was essentially the modern way of serving a meal, with fewer dishes, each brought on individually and then handed round by servants – the only problem with service *à la russe* was that it meant much more work for the servants.

A World of Change

By the time Queen Victoria died in 1901, a good deal more had changed in domestic life than the way in which meals were served. For, as in most other areas of life during her long reign, the home had seen some substantial technological advances.

When the young Queen ascended the throne in 1837, the tools and equipment available to the housewife or her servants had on the whole been fairly primitive. There were the usual brushes and brooms, while only a few useful gadgets had as yet made an appearance: the dirt-prone kitchen range to cook on, for instance, and the mangle for pressing

EATING UP THE DIRT A few early, electrically powered vacuum cleaners and 'aspirators' were being advertised by the turn of the century.

sheets and heavy linen (though that had been in existence since the 17th century at least).

Just 60 years later the position was quite different, with many areas of household work now supplied with handy gadgets to make life easier. Carpet sweeping, for instance, was widely hated: 'the hardest torture of the week', according to the American magazine *Household* – 'prosecuted', it went on graphically, 'until every nerve is throbbing in fierce rebellion at the undue pressure to which it is subjected'.

Help was at hand: as early as the 1870s some of the first carpet sweepers, almost identical in design to the modern carpet sweeper, were being manufactured at Grand Rapids, Michigan. At the very end of Queen Victoria's reign the first, rather unwieldy, hand-pumped vacuum cleaners were just beginning to appear. Also in the 1870s, some early washing machines were being made: 'Have you got running water in your house?' asked a surprisingly modern-sounding newspaper advertisement placed by one manufacturer from Binghamton, New York. 'Well, – if you have enough pressure on it I'll make it do all your washing without any work. You can just throw the clothes into the tub, turn a tap, and our new Self-Working Washer will do the rest.' In fact, these early washing contraptions were chiefly notable for leaving rust marks and tearing the clothes with their paddles, but refinements were not slow in following. And so it was with many of the household chores. In the kitchen, for example, water heaters were becoming more common, and by the 1880s the first gas cookers began to be sold on a commercial scale.

From the 1860s tinned meat (mostly from the great meat-processing plants of Chicago and Cincinnati) had started to appear on shop shelves throughout the Victorian world. The stringy blobs of meat floating in congealed fat inside the tins were scarcely appetising, but at least it was cheap – half the price of butcher's meat –

TELEPHONE BELL

The telephone was a Victorian invention. Alexander Graham Bell demonstrated an early prototype at the American Centennial celebrations in Philadelphia in 1876, and within four years the United States had 138 local exchanges. In 1883 a successful long-distance link was made between New York and Boston, and just four years after that 150,000 American homes and businesses had telephones. By the same year Britain had some 26,000 telephone subscribers, Germany 22,000, and France 9000.

PHONE ORDERS A promotion for biscuits shows one of the early uses for telephones.

SIXTY YEARS OF PROGRESS
The magazine *Illustrated London News* celebrated Queen Victoria's Diamond Jubilee in 1897 with this memorial to the technological advances of her reign.

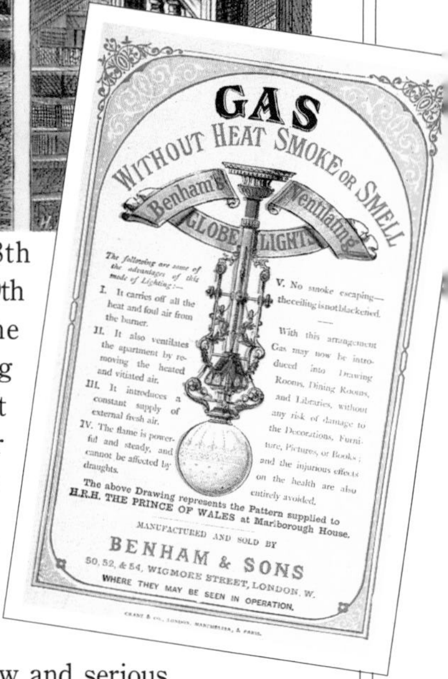

LIGHTING THE HOME Cragside, above, was the home of the armaments millionaire Sir William Armstrong and in 1880 became the first house to be lit by electricity derived from water power. A little later, the 'incandescent mantle' would transform gas lighting.

and helped to improve the diet of poorer working people. Then in the late 1870s corned beef began to appear, and in 1880 came another technological breakthrough: the SS *Strathleven*, with a newly devised refrigerated hold, brought the first cargo of frozen beef and mutton from Melbourne in Australia to London. Soon, tons of meat were being imported each year into Europe from Australia, New Zealand, North America and Argentina. At the same time, a combination of railways, steam trawlers and techniques of ice preservation led to fish becoming a regular part of the diet even in inland areas.

Equally dramatic were the developments in lighting. At the beginning of Queen Victoria's reign people lit a room by night with candles or one of various kinds of oil lamp – burning fish oil, whale oil or, in the case of the island of St Kilda off the west coast of Scotland or of coastal North America, an oil secreted by the fulmar, a seabird. Then came a series of important discoveries. In the 1840s, Abraham Gesner in America and James Young in Britain devised ways of distilling what Gesner called 'kerosene' and Young called 'paraffin'. Within a few decades cheap and reliable lamps using this fuel were widely available. Gas lighting had first appeared in the late 18th century and by the mid-19th century had become the standard way of lighting town and city streets. It did not become popular for domestic purposes until the Austrian Karl Auer invented the 'incandescent mantle' in 1884.

But gas also had a new and serious rival. In 1879, the inventor Thomas Edison first successfully demonstrated his carbon-filament lamp: essentially, the modern electric light bulb. It, too, spread rapidly. Reactions to this new form of lighting were mixed. The British writer Robert Louis Stevenson was not enthusiastic. He looked back nostalgically to the heyday of the gas lamplighter running through the streets at nightfall lighting the lamps one by one.

Stevenson's worries were a little premature, however. It would be well into the 1930s before electricity overtook gas as the standard form of domestic lighting in many Western countries. Even so, his comments, made in the very last years of Queen Victoria's reign, were characteristic of an age which had seen so many changes in everyday, domestic living and which, while in most ways it exulted in them, also mistrusted many of them.

LIFE IN THE VICTORIAN CITY

As industry took root across the Victorian world, so the cities grew, and so too the everyday lives of millions of people were transformed. City life included the miseries of the slums, bad sanitation, rising levels of crime and the blight of disease. But there were other, more positive developments too: leafy suburbs around American and British cities, the bold rebuilding of parts of cities such as Paris and Chicago, large new department stores and improved urban transport systems.

The Changing Environment

By mid-century, Britain had become the world's first predominantly urban nation, and there were dramatic changes elsewhere, too. Chicago grew from almost nothing in 1800 to become America's second-largest city by 1890. Berlin quadrupled in size in the second half of the century.

THE GROWTH of the towns and cities was among the most startling and inescapable facts of life in the Victorian world. As the American journalist Horace Greeley put it in the 1860s: 'We cannot all live in cities, yet nearly all seem determined to do so … "Hot and cold water", baker's bread, gas, the theatre, and the streetcar … indicate the tendency of modern taste.'

Not that many of the millions who made their way in crowded immigrant ships across the Atlantic to New York or Boston, or who poured into the burgeoning industrial towns of the German Ruhr valley or the North of England, or who converged on Europe's fast-growing capitals, had such luxuries as hot and cold water or the theatre immediately in mind. For them it was the pressure of survival that drove them, and the need to escape a countryside that was less able to support them.

The results of these migrations were clearly revealed in the statistics. In 1851 a census showed that Britain, in particular, had become the world's first predominantly urban society. But in other countries, too, city living became increasingly the norm for huge numbers of people. Paris's population doubled between 1850 and 1900, Berlin's quadrupled. In the United States, Chicago's growth at the hub of an expanding rail transport system was particularly spectacular: from just 100 inhabitants in 1830, to 306,000 in 1870, to 1.1 million in 1890.

A New Style of Living

Such trends were hard to miss. In the first place, there was the purely physical side of this new environment, and it was in most cases bad enough. Apart from the miseries of the slums, bad sanitation, disease, regular epidemics, polluted air and thick 'pea-souper' smogs, it also included the sheer uniform dreariness of so many of the industrial towns and cities.

'The environs of [the French city] Saint-Etienne are generally monotonous and without charm,' wrote one visitor there in 1846; 'the countryside is furrowed with railroads. One encounters factories of various kinds almost everywhere, especially coal mines with smoking obelisks, and forges of coke that give off a thick, black smoke which can be seen from afar; it paralyses all vegetation and gives everything a black tint. At night these furnaces offer a truly astonishing spectacle, infernal to all who see the city for the first time.'

And then there were the social consequences. Never before had so many human beings been packed in such concentrated numbers. As the Englishman

PAGEANT OF THE STREETS A flower girl and paper seller ply their wares outside St Martin-in-the-Fields in London in the 1880s. Forty years earlier the German artist George Scharf had sketched many of London's poor.

CITY MASSES A flock of sheep adds to the confusion in this view towards London's St Paul's Cathedral.

Windy City **Chicago spread far inland from Lake Michigan by the 1890s – the streets around its Water Tower presenting a more leisured scene in the 1850s (inset). Britain's Black Country, meanwhile, was already known for its sooty industrial landscape.**

William Cooke Taylor observed, one 'cannot contemplate these crowded lives without feelings of anxiety and apprehension ... The population is hourly increasing in breadth and strength. It is an aggregate of masses.' The resulting loss of an earlier sense of community was widely lamented by contemporary observers.

Newburyport in Massachusetts, for example, was a comparatively intimate place. Even so, the editor of the first Directory of its businesses and inhabitants in 1849 felt that it had changed significantly in recent years: 'Since the introduction of the railroad, the erection and operation of cotton mills ... Newburyport is not what it was ten, or even five years since. We have been gradually losing that social knowledge of each other's residences and occupations.'

Yet, for all their problems, Victorian cities were by no means lacking in redeeming features. For a start, the age which produced the squalor of New York's Lower East Side and London's 'rookery' slums also produced the beginnings of the Manhattan skyline,

ANATOMY OF A CITY

For all the grime of their slums and polluted air, Victorian cities were often a source of pride to their citizens.

VICTORIAN CITIES grew faster than ever before, but – except in a few cases such as the brand new cities of the American West or the newly built extensions to cities such as Barcelona – their growth was rarely planned. In many parts of Europe, they grew upwards first, perching precarious lofts on top of older buildings as they squeezed expanding populations within the confines of medieval city walls ... until finally the strain became too much and the walls had to go.

CIVIC PRIDE City fathers expressed their pride with imposing municipal buildings, such as the Town Hall at Leeds in the North of England.

Elsewhere, they simply sprawled out over the surrounding countryside, as speculative builders covered increasing areas of former farming or common land with terraces or tenements of workers' homes.

The results were not very often beautiful. Smoke from the factory chimneys shrouded both cities and the nearby country in a smoggy pall

and deposited layers of sooty grime on buildings and plants alike. Canals and railways crisscrossed in the suburbs; municipal gasworks created strange silhouettes amid the factories. And yet such cities also generated a strong civic spirit. Among the millowners and professionals who profited from the new industries, there was usually a huge pride in their achievement, reflected often in grand new civic buildings. Even in the bleakest slums, there was often a vibrant community spirit.

CITY TRANSPORT London built the first underground railway – the Metropolitan Line opened in 1862.

BROADWAY FOLLIES New Yorkers were already complaining about the congestion of their streets – as in this satirical engraving of Broadway in 1859.

the much-loved café life and tree-lined boulevards of Paris, and the early 'Modernista' glories of Barcelona – to name just three examples. If communities died as the towns and cities grew, so too new ones often emerged.

Alongside their undisputed misery, many cities also often had an infectious vitality. One example was Châtellerault in central France, admittedly a relatively small city, which specialised in the manufacture of arms and cutlery. In the 1840s one of its citizens had no qualms about comparing it favourably with the far more ancient, and picturesque, neighbouring city of Poitiers: 'The noise of [Châtellerault's] streets contrasts with the silence of those of Poitiers ... Châtellerault is still so young that it seems to grow from day to day, while Poitiers is like the corpse of a large city.'

Certainly, the pressures on Victorian cities were unprecedented; and, lively though many cities were, they could also be distinctly overwhelming for those, rich and poor alike, who had to live out their daily lives in them. As early as 1837, for example, the New Yorker Asa Greene was complaining – albeit good-humouredly – about the ever-increasing volume of traffic in his native city: to cross Broadway, he wrote, 'you must button your coat tight about you, see that your shoes are secure at the heels, settle your hat firmly on your head, look up street and down street, at the self-same moment, to see what carts and carriages are upon you, and then run for your life'.

At the start of the century Americans had generally prided themselves on the orderliness of cities such as New York and the comparative absence of many of the inequalities of wealth and domestic comfort that were so characteristic of their European counterparts. They soon had to change their tune. Already in the 1840s, people were objecting to the sheer filth of New York's still unpaved streets, where mud and household waste accumulated at the sides in festering piles for weeks on end – kept in check only by the scavenging pigs that, until the 1860s, roamed most American cities as a primitive sanitation measure.

The problem of dirt was addressed some 20 years later, in 1866, when the New York Metropolitan Board of Health was set up, but by then the city's difficulties were far more complex and acute. Above all, they

LURE OF HIGH WAGES In a cartoon of the 1850s, a morose-looking British lion watches workers being lured across the Atlantic. An engraving of squatters' shanties near New York's Central Park reveals the grim reality that awaited many of them.

Ellis Island: the Immigrant Experience

More immigrants arrived in New York than in any other American port during the Victorian age. For most of them their first experience of the new continent was in the immigrant centres either at Castle Garden on Manhattan or, after 1892, on Ellis Island – the 'Isle of Tears', as it was often known.

Arrival was rarely a pleasant experience for the tired and apprehensive newcomers. Landing at the end of long and crowded sea journeys, they were pushed through a series of bureaucratic and humiliating procedures. They also often had to run the gauntlet of preying conmen trying to trick them out of their meagre savings with misleading (or downright false) offers of work or lodgings.

Arrival! Italian immigrants gather their belongings on Ellis Island.

For most, the whole process began when quarantine officials came on board the arriving ship to inspect it for infectious diseases. The ship then docked and, at Ellis Island, the passengers disembarked in a railed-off section of the wharf. This funnelled them through a door of the original wooden reception centre, up a staircase to the first floor and into a narrow corridor with wire-mesh walls on either side. The arrivals then moved in single file along the corridor to be inspected by medical officers. The newcomers now entered a large hall with, at the far end, a series of gangways or channels, each presided over by a registration clerk. One by one the immigrants gave the details of their names, ages, places of birth, whether they could read or write, whether they had prison records, whether they had the necessary tickets or funds for their onward journeys, and so on.

Having survived that grilling they were now free – unless, that is, they had fallen under the suspicion of one of the plainclothes 'contract labour inspectors', on the lookout for workers who had been illegally recruited in Europe and who were trying to slip in as ordinary immigrants. The inspectors had powers to detain anyone they regarded as suspicious.

If the immigrants passed that test, they could then collect their luggage and start their onward journey – to New York or beyond.

Cleared for Entry Immigrants get ready to disembark on Ellis Island.

FILTH AND SEWERS New sewer pipes helped to clean up London in the 1840s. A boy stands under a water-pump in New York's slums.

arose from the sheer pressure of numbers as more and more people poured in each year, some from rural America but many more across the Atlantic from Europe.

More than 5 million immigrants arrived in the United States in the 1880s alone. Most of them piled up in the cities of the Eastern Seaboard, creating distinct national ghettoes in each – even at the start of the 1880s around 80 per cent

LOWER EAST SIDE Street traders do brisk business among New York's immigrant communities.

of New Yorkers were immigrants or the children of immigrants (compared with London at the same time, where 63 per cent of the population was native to the city and all but 2 per cent came from Britain or Ireland). Such invasions created inevitable problems of assimilation, compounded in New York by what was probably the worst overcrowding anywhere in the Victorian world. In the notorious Tenth Ward, in particular, the density of population was 432 people per acre in 1880.

New York's problems were severe, but few of them were unique. Grim housing for the poor, wholly inadequate water supplies, sewers that were virtually non-existent – all these and more were near-universal characteristics of cities across the Victorian world.

In many cities, for example, it was not uncommon for poor people to be obliged to go begging from door to door in the richer areas for water. In Philadelphia in the United States the poor drew most of their water from the Delaware River, which was also where the city's various industries flushed out their waste. Some of their counterparts in the northern English city of Salford went further and sent their children to wash in the hot outflows from factory boilers.

Rising levels of crime were another problem of the cities, and teenage street gangs – some of them relatively harmless, others definitely not – also began to make an appearance: in the North of England the gang members were known as 'scuttlers'; in America, different gangs chose colourful names such as New York's Plug-Uglies and Dead Rabbits.

How quickly and effectively city authorities dealt

with these problems varied. Many early Victorians tended to regard the poor as more or less deserving of their lot, and as late as 1879 the otherwise liberal American academic John L. Hart seemed to have, at best, a very qualified sympathy for them: 'About one half of our poor can neither read nor write, have never been in any school, and know little, or positively nothing, of the doctrines of the Christian religion, or of moral duties ...' he expostulated, 'while the rich and more intelligent classes are obliged to guard them with police and standing armies ...'

Fortunately, many of the 'rich and more intelligent classes' (including, to be fair, Hart himself) were increasingly ready to take action on behalf of the poor. In 1859, for example, Glasgow in Scotland completed the Loch Katrine system, the first of many such schemes to bring water into cities from a long distance. The Glasgow authorities were also pioneers in buying out local gas companies in 1869, and making gas more cheaply available to their citizens. They were among the first to set about clearing the worst of their slums; they also established a magnificent system of public baths and wash-houses and did much to encourage an efficient urban transport system in their city.

At the same time, other changes were taking place.

THE NEW PARIS Baron Haussmann's rebuilt Paris gave the French capital grand new boulevards, such as the Rue Royale leading to the Church of the Madeleine. But satirists still complained of the congestion.

Sheffield Plate **Smoke belches from the chimneys of the British steel city Sheffield, which was also famous for its electro-plating industry.**

Above all, the various parts of cities were becoming increasingly distinct. There were the residential quarters for the rich as well as the working-class districts, and then the central business and shopping areas. The latter were often dominated by new department stores such as London's Selfridges, Paris's La Samaritaine and Chicago's Marshall Field's.

Boulevards, Suburbs and Skyscrapers

Here again city authorities often played a leading role, particularly on the continent of Europe. During the 1850s and 60s the prefect of the French department of the Seine, Baron Haussmann, embarked on his ambitious rebuilding of Paris. He transformed the central Ile de la Cité into an administrative district, and ruthlessly drove a network of grand boulevards through the city's maze of older, narrower streets. This part of the project had an important political purpose: to make it harder for potential rioters or revolutionaries to raise barricades, and easier for government troops to be deployed against them.

Haussmann also built four new bridges across the Seine and rebuilt three old ones. He had two new parks laid out, notably the Bois de Boulogne, along with Les Halles, the capital's principal food market, and an imposing opera house. He also gave Paris a brand-new system of sewers.

In the Anglo-Saxon world, by contrast, events had taken a slightly different turn. The suburb, seeking to combine the best of both town and country living, had emerged as the most distinctive development.

As early as 1841, G. Calvert Holland, a visitor to the British steel city of Sheffield, had noted that most

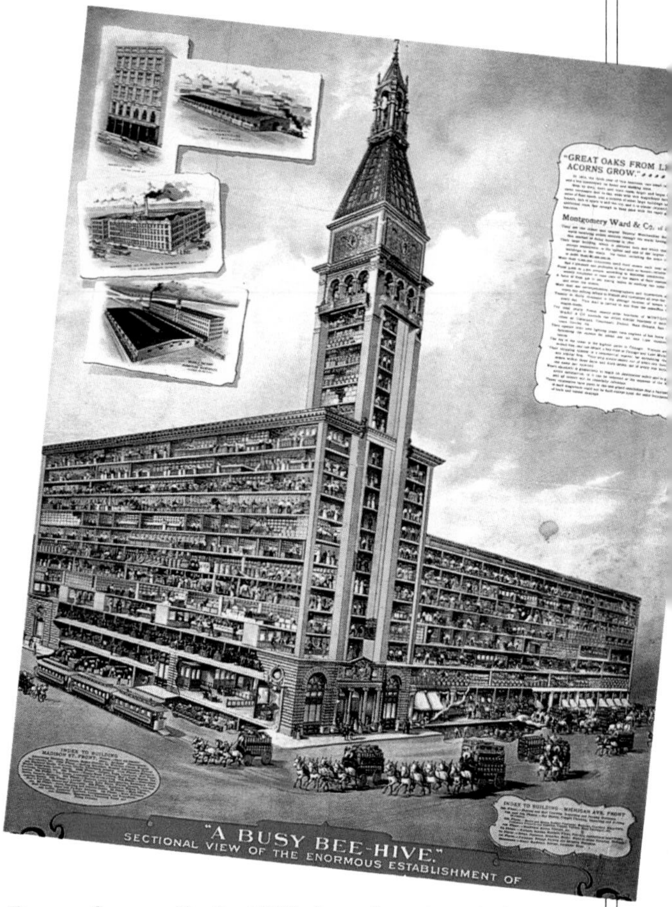

Beehive Stores **By the 1880s huge department stores – in America, often doubling as mail-order houses – had revolutionised the business of shopping.**

of those who could possibly afford to do so no longer wanted to live near their business premises in the centre, preferring instead to make their homes in outlying areas – hardly surprising in view of the pall of contaminated air that hung more or less permanently over the city. 'All classes, save the artisan and the needy shopkeeper', he wrote, 'are attracted by country comfort and retirement. The attorney, – the manufacturer, – the grocer, – the draper, – the shoemaker and the tailor, fix their commanding residences on some beautiful site, and adorn them with the cultivated taste of the artist.'

Subsequent improvements in transport greatly accelerated this process. In America it began, above all, with the arrival of the railways in the 1830s and 40s, which allowed wealthy merchants and businessmen to live in smaller, usually more attractive towns around the large cities and to commute daily to their city offices. The more specifically urban forms of transport – the horse-car, the tram and trolley bus, the underground and elevated railway – then led to the wholesale emergence of recognisably modern suburbs, the domain most notably of those with comparatively modest incomes.

HIGH-LEVEL STEAMING **Elevated railways (or 'L's'), such as this New York line, were one American answer to the problems of urban transport.**

ON THE RAILS **New Yorkers clamber on board a trolley bus around the turn of the century. Advertisements make a bright scene at a British railway station in the 1870s.**

THE TRANSPORT REVOLUTION

From stagecoaches to early motor cars, the Victorians saw astonishing changes in the means of getting around.

CALL OF THE WEST The railroads played a key role in opening up the American West.

QUEEN VICTORIA was a fairly early convert to rail travel. In June 1842 her technologically minded husband Prince Albert persuaded her – rather reluctantly at first – to take the train from Windsor to London. Her response to the experience was enthusiastic: 'We arrived here yesterday morning,' she wrote to her uncle, 'having come by the railroad from Windsor, in half an hour, free from dust and crowd and heat, and I am quite charmed with it.'

The sheer speed and volume of technological change in the Victorian age was remarkable. In few areas was it more impressive – or did it have greater impact on people's everyday lives – than in transport, and above all in the railways. When the world's first freight and passenger steam railways were opened in the North of England between Stockton and Darlington (1825) and Liverpool and Manchester (1830), they inaugurated a revolution. Over the next few decades it would shrink the globe and transform markets. In the New World in particular, it would result in the growth of entirely new cities and help to pull together these vast and developing countries.

Among the pioneering railway companies in the United States, was the Baltimore and Ohio Railroad Company, set up in 1830. Even more ambitious was the part played by the Union Pacific Railroad. In May 1869, at Promontory, Utah, it linked up with another line, the Central Pacific, heading east from California – thus creating North America's first transcontinental route.

In 1828, the first horse-drawn omnibuses, with room for between

WORK STATIONS Trains at London's Liverpool Street Station in 1884 contrast with the pioneering Stockton and Darlington line of 1825.

12 and 20 passengers, had appeared on the streets of Paris. Then came the horse-car – horse-drawn but running on rails – invented in 1832, though becoming popular only in the late 1840s. Some 40 years after that, in 1887, the first electrified tram or streetcar system was built in Richmond, Virginia, and soon these had become near-universal.

Meanwhile, in 1862, London had pioneered the underground railway which was soon copied in Budapest, Boston, Paris, Berlin and New York. New York also built the first elevated railway in 1867. Both underground and elevated railways were electrified in the 1890s.

Sea transport also changed radically. In 1843 the British engineer Isambard Kingdom Brunel's *Great Britain* became the first screw-propelled passenger ship – though it also used sails – to cross the Atlantic. Four years earlier, the Canadian-born Samuel Cunard had won a contract from the British government to carry mail across the Atlantic, and by mid-century his steamships were making regular crossings in just over 14 days. By the end of the century liners were making the crossing in seven days or less.

In 1885 and 1886 the Germans Carl Benz and Gottlieb Daimler had demonstrated their primitive forerunners of the modern motor car, and by the time Queen Victoria died in 1901 early motoring was well established.

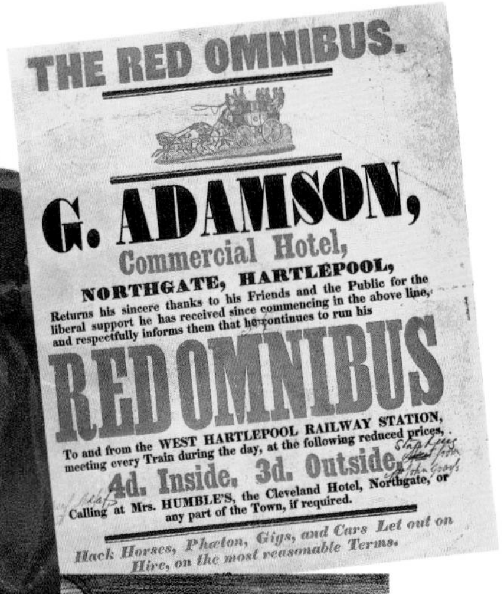

ON THE BUSES **Horse-drawn omnibuses appeared from 1828 onwards. Their well-filled interiors were depicted by the British artist William Maw Egley (above) and the French caricaturist Honoré Daumier (right). The operator of one North of England 'bus route drew respectful attention to his services.**

PUT OUT MORE FLAGS **Crowds cheered lustily for the launching of the SS *Great Britain* in 1843. By the turn of the century, motor cars, such as this early Daimler, were also appearing.**

The Coming of Technology

IT WAS NOT just in transport that the Victorian technological revolution was apparent. In 1837, the year Queen Victoria came to the throne, the first electric telegraphs revolutionised the speed at which news could be carried. They were demonstrated more or less simultaneously on both sides of the Atlantic, the American inventor being Samuel Morse who also devised the Morse code. By the 1860s telegraph cables had been laid, linking Britain to India and under the Atlantic to America.

Photography was also born. In 1839 the Frenchman Louis Daguerre revealed the so-called 'daguerreotype', refining an earlier process devised in the 1820s. During the same period, the Englishman W.H. Fox Talbot came up with his own photographic processes. By 1888 the American George Eastman was marketing hand-held box cameras under the made-up trade name Kodak.

And so it went on. The telephone, electricity for domestic purposes, the typewriter – all were Victorian inventions. 'As the nineteenth century draws to its close, there is no slackening in that onward march of scientific discovery and invention which has been its chief characteristic,' announced the British magazine *Popular Science Monthly* in 1898. 'At the beginning of the century the telegraph was as yet undreamed of, and the telephone and the dynamo [were] utterly unimaginable developments ... Today these things are considered commonplaces.'

More inventions would follow. In 1901, for example, Guglielmo Marconi transmitted the first radio communication across the Atlantic.

ENGLISH MECHANIC AND MIRROR OF SCIENCE

Engineering, Building, Inventions, Electricity, Photography, Chemistry, &c.

VOL. X.—No. 240. FRIDAY, OCTOBER 29, 1869. [PRICE TWOPENCE.

THE ELLERSHAUSEN PROCESS, PITTSBURGH, PA., U.S.—(Described on Page 145.)

MIRROR OF SCIENCE The engineer Isambard Kingdom Brunel (right) and radio-pioneer Guglielmo Marconi (below) look the picture of Victorian confidence. The magazine *Engish Mechanic*, meanwhile, is typical of many that fed wide popular interest in technology.

VISION BOX The hand-held Kodak box camera first went on sale in 1888.

LAKESIDE FLAMES Chicago's Great Fire of 1871 helped to give birth to the skyscraper. The city fathers encouraged tall new buildings to replace the old ones.

THE POLICEMAN ON HIS BEAT

The British 'bobby' was one response to rising levels of crime in the cities. In 1829 the British politician Sir Robert Peel – after whom the 'bobbies' were nicknamed – had set up the London Metropolitan Police, manned by salaried and uniformed officers, instead of the older, more haphazard system of part-time night watchmen and constables. During the Victorian age similar forces were established throughout Britain and its Empire; most American cities, starting with New York in 1844, followed suit. In 1842 the Metropolitan Police also set up a Criminal Investigation Division (CID), staffed by the first police detectives.

These new suburbs bore little resemblance to the elegant villas set in substantial grounds such as those described by Calvert Holland but, even so, many people considered them an important breakthrough in healthy city living. In 1851 a handbook for the American city of Cincinnati described one of its suburbs as 'unsurpassed for healthfulness, removed from the smoke and dust of the city, enjoying pure air and wholesome water'. A later advertisement for the west London suburb Bedford Park described it quite simply as the 'healthiest place in the world'.

The Americans, meanwhile, had made another contribution to urban living and working. In 1848 the watchmaker-turned-architect James Bogardus made history when he used cast iron to construct what then seemed an astonishingly high, five-storey factory building in New York. Over the next few decades he went on to build several such cast-iron 'cloud-scrapers'. During the same period, the engineer Elisha G. Otis perfected another key to the exploitation of tall buildings: a safety device for elevators, in case the cable broke. In 1857 he installed his first 'safe' elevator in a New York department store.

Then came the fire which in 1871 almost destroyed Chicago. The city's rebuilders favoured tall buildings to save space, and in 1885 the architect William Le Baron Jenney completed his 12-storey Home Insurance Company Building using a revolutionary cast and wrought-iron frame. With the work of Jenney and his Chicago colleague Louis H. Sullivan, the skyscraper had been born. It went on to make its home in New York as much as Chicago, with structures such as the classically inspired Graham Building which was completed in 1898.

SKY BUILDING Chicago's Home Insurance Building was one of the first skyscrapers. Louis H. Sullivan was a pioneer of building them.

A Soldier's Life

Harsh discipline, long periods of inactivity and campaigns fought in appalling conditions were the lot of the Victorian soldier.

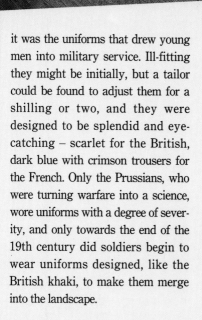

Staff sergeant J. MacMullen of the 13th Light Infantry (later the Somerset Light Infantry) published his memoirs of army life in 1846. In them he detailed the reasons why 128 of his fellow soldiers had enlisted. Two-thirds had been unemployed; eight were 'shady characters'; one was a convicted criminal; the rest had 'fallen on hard times' or gave other reasons. Except in countries such as Prussia, where military service was compulsory, these were the motives that drew men into the armies of Victorian times; however hard the discipline, and no matter that it combined long hours of boredom with short spells of extreme danger, army life was often preferable to life without employment in the industrial slums. For those with some education, or the capacity to learn a new trade, the armies of the 19th century, with their increasingly complex needs, even offered the possibility of a career. Encouraging many recruits was the prospect of promotion to the privileges, pay and material comforts of life as a non-commissioned officer.

Dressed to Kill The uniform of a French cadet, around 1850, was designed for show more than practicality.

Tending the Sick Florence Nightingale at the British hospital at Scutari, Turkey, where she worked in appalling conditions. The German army took the welfare of its men more seriously, even giving its officers medical examinations.

Whether volunteer or enlisted man, the army recruit, on arrival at the regimental depot, endured the same routine: he was issued with his uniform – in one of two sizes, 'too big' or 'too small' – bullied or cheated out of his pay by the veteran rankers, mercilessly drilled by sergeants practised in the art of humiliation, trained in musketry and the use of the bayonet, and set endlessly to the cleaning and polishing of his equipment. He would also learn the bugle calls that measured out the military day, from reveille in the morning to tattoo (or 'lights-out') that brought the day to a merciful close. This preliminary training was, then as now, a process carefully designed to break down the morale of slouching civilians and to re-create them as soldiers.

Apart from the alternative prospect of unemployment and hunger, it was the uniforms that drew young men into military service. Ill-fitting they might be initially, but a tailor could be found to adjust them for a shilling or two, and they were designed to be splendid and eye-catching – scarlet for the British, dark blue with crimson trousers for the French. Only the Prussians, who were turning warfare into a science, wore uniforms with a degree of severity, and only towards the end of the 19th century did soldiers begin to wear uniforms designed, like the British khaki, to make them merge into the landscape.

No Hope **In the American Civil War, the Confederate forces never had enough ambulances, trained medics or medicines to save their casualties from dying of their wounds. Below: A comrade tends a wounded Union soldier. Soldiers dreaded doctors, and many went to great lengths to avoid them.**

The American volunteers who flocked to join the different armies of the North and South at the beginning of the Civil War sported a confusing variety of uniforms, including imitations of the colourful Zouave costumes of the French colonial forces. Fatalities resulted, however, from this confusion in the first battles of the war, and uniforms were later standardised as blue for the Union troops and grey for those of the Confederacy. As the war went on, however, the South found it more and more difficult to provide uniforms for its men, who, increasingly, wore their own homespun and home-dyed clothing.

Infantrymen when on campaign marched 20 or 30 miles a day, and although officers might say that a soldier's best friend was his rifle, soldiers knew that their best friends were their boots. In the British Army until 1843, left and right boots were not differentiated and recruits were ordered to wear them on alternate feet on alternate days so as to shape them to fit both feet. Men who could afford to had their boots made to measure, and it was a rare soldier who hesitated to strip a fallen comrade of his boots if they were better than the ones he was wearing.

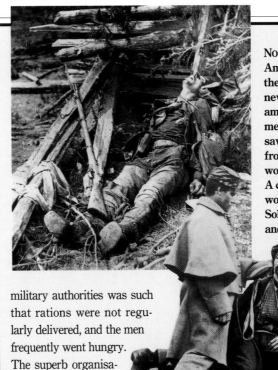

How well a 19th-century soldier ate on campaign depended on circumstances and on the competence of his superiors. Officially he was provided with basic rations for two meals a day. In the Crimean War, however, the incompetence of the British military authorities was such that rations were not regularly delivered, and the men frequently went hungry. The superb organisation of the Prussian General Staff, by contrast, meant that their men were usually well fed and well looked after.

To be left wounded on the battlefield is the greatest fear of all fighting men. Since the Napoleonic Wars, great advances had been made in ambulance services and field surgery, but the care of the sick and wounded in the wars of the 19th century still left much to be desired. The scandal of their treatment during the Crimean War led to the intervention of trained nurses under Florence Nightingale, and the creation, some 30 years later, of an Army Medical Staff. Volunteer nurses served in the US Civil War, which also saw the creation of a specially trained ambulance corps that became the model for European armies.

Field Kitchen **British Hussars in the Crimean War are served a meal. Before this time, troops had to cook for themselves.**

THE WORKING DAY

The work ethic ranked high with the middle classes, while for workers life was more a question of getting used to the strict routines of the factory. Many people, including some of the middle classes, lived with the constant fear of losing their hard-earned gains.

CITY LANDSCAPES were changing radically around them. Yet for most Victorian workers who were lucky enough to be in fairly regular employment, life was dominated by more mundane factors, such as the clock-work routine of the factory: 'obedience to the ding-dong of the bells', as one textile worker in the Massachusetts cotton city of Lowell put it.

Adjusting to new patterns of work was, in fact, one of the hardest of transitions for people used to the more flexible, though hardly less demanding, ways of the countryman or craftsman. Hours were often extremely long – a mid-century Austrian industrialist reckoned that 16 hours a day was about 'normal' for his workers – and although most countries introduced a variety of measures to limit working hours, these were all too frequently ignored. Workers also found it hard to get used to the strict weekly routine of the

PURSUIT OF EXCELLENCE Women workers strive dutifully to excel as they turn out crinolines in a 'model' New York factory in 1859. Young girls are kept hard at it in an American textile mill.

AN AMERICAN STEEL MAGNATE IN THE MAKING

THE Scottish-born steel 'king' Andrew Carnegie was a ferocious worker. He arrived in America as a young boy from Scotland, and by the 1860s, he was supervising the building of a new line for the Pennsylvania Railroad Company:

'... at one time for eight days, I was constantly upon the line, day and night, at one wreck or obstruction after another. I was probably the most inconsiderate superintendent that ever was entrusted with the management of a great property, for, never knowing fatigue myself, being kept up by a sense of responsibility probably, I overworked the men and was not careful enough in considering the limits of human endurance. I have always been able to sleep at any time. Snatches of half an hour at intervals during the night in a dirty freight car were sufficient.'

RAGS TO RICHES Andrew Carnegie was a classic case of an American who won wealth by drive and hard work.

factory. The old practice of what the British and many Americans called Saint Monday (taking Monday as a holiday) continued to flourish for a long time, in spite of the efforts of the millowners to eliminate it.

In Massachusetts, Lowell was regarded as something of a model city, known for its airy factories and exemplary workers' housing. Even so, the country girls drafted in to work there found it hard to cope with the noise and bustle. One described how in 'sweet June weather I would lean far out of the [factory] window, and try not to hear the unceasing clash of sound inside'. Another constant, nagging fact of life was the insecurity of employment. Employers could hire and fire more or less at will, so that the smallest dip in the trade cycle inevitably meant the loss of jobs and hard times to come.

In spite of all this, many labourers did take a surprising pride in their work when they had it. The workmen employed to build roads and railways, for example, were widely considered among the lowest beasts of burden of the working class. But they and their families also had their pride, as the child of one skilled British basketmaker discovered. A school-mate was a labourer's daughter, and she was in no doubt about her father's importance: '... she said that nobody could do his job. It was a high skilled job to keep that hammer going on top of that knob ... She said it was the most skilled job that was going. So they were proud of that job, see, and thought nobody was so good as them.'

Proud they may have been, but keeping a home together in such circumstances was hard. In Newburyport, Massachusetts, in the middle of the century an unskilled labourer might hope to earn \$300-350 a year – quite insufficient to raise a family on, thus obliging women and children to go out to work as well.

Systems of poor relief were rudimentary in most places, and in Britain and America for much of the Victorian age they were tied up with the grim prospect of the workhouse or poorhouse. Only in the 1880s did Germany's 'Iron' Chancellor Bismarck lead the way – chiefly as a political ploy to outwit his Social Democratic opponents – by introducing new

WAGE SLAVERY American industrialists outbid each other in the meanness of their wages.

SLUM LIFE

Grimy tenements, tightly packed 'back-to-backs' and dripping cellar dwellings were among the horrors of the slums.

THE HORRORS of existence in the slums of the growing industrial cities needed no exaggeration. In the 1880s investigators from the German newspaper *Das Volk* described one slum dwelling they had visited in Duisberg in the Ruhr valley, and their account was quite telling enough in its simplicity: 'we entered a narrow, low ceilinged room with two beds and a crib, lighted only by a small roof ventilation hole. A man with a severe lung illness sat on an old crate. He spoke only with great effort, labouring over every word.'

Conditions like these were far from exceptional. All across the Victorian world, in the tenements of New York, Glasgow and Berlin, the 'rookeries' of London, the 'back-to-backs' of the industrial North of England and the 'double-deckers' of Boston and Chicago, the poorest of the poor – first-generation immigrants from the countryside in many cases or, in North America, from Europe – eked out miserable lives that made a mockery of the age's idealised vision of the home. With entire families crammed into single rooms, drafty attics or even cellars, they suffered, in the first place, from appalling overcrowding. Then came overwhelming levels of filth, usually accompanied by a near-unbearable stench; running water and even the most rudimentary kind of refuse collection were for the most part unknown, so that all forms of waste simply accumulated in the streets and courtyards and oozed out as best they could.

MAKING DO A New York immigrant prepares a family meal.

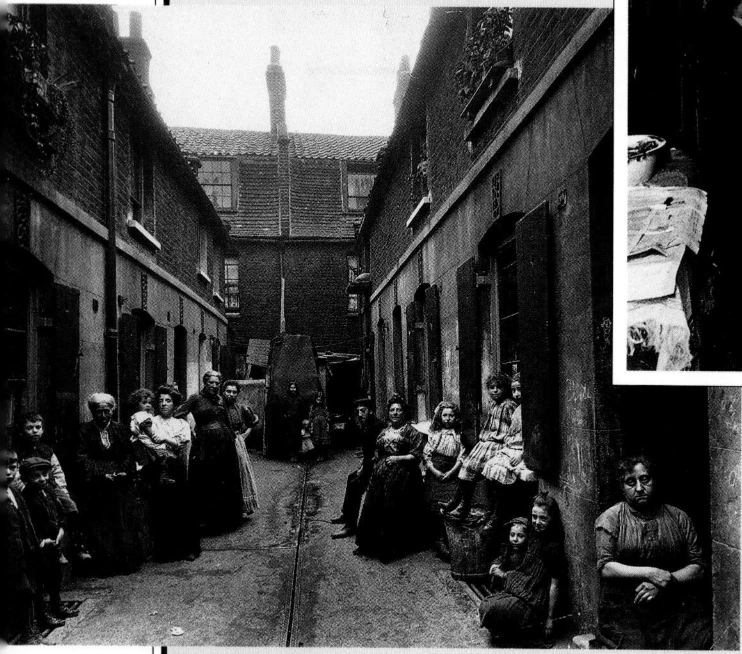

LIFE CARRIES ON British slum dwellers are pictured outside their homes. Neatness in spite of poverty marks a tenement home in New York's slums.

In such surroundings making any semblance of a home was difficult. The British Congregational minister Andrew Mearns listed some of the most startling cases of squalor and deprivation he and his colleagues had unearthed among the London slums: 'In one cellar a sanitary inspector reports finding a father, mother, three children, and four pigs! In another room a missionary found a man with smallpox, his wife just recovering from her eighth confinement, and the children running about half naked and covered with dirt.'

In the slums a family's entire stock of possessions was likely to amount to a few beds or mattresses, a cast-iron cooking pot, a rickety chair or two, a table and chipped crockery. Some families might also boast a primitive dresser and a few lithographs; the poorest would have just a board or two covered with rags to serve as makeshift beds – in cities such as Lille in northern France (which had some of that country's worst slums) their very cooking pot might be rented.

It was an existence with very few enjoyments. Landlords or their agents were often grasping, and evictions for non-payment of rent common. Filth and pollution encouraged pests such as fleas, lice and bedbugs, not to mention skin and respiratory diseases, and numerous epidemics of diseases such as typhus. Where conditions were so miserable and working hours frequently so long, home for many slum-dwellers was little more than a place in which to eat and sleep – providing little encouragement for a happy family life. Moreover, it was an existence from which it was supremely difficult to escape. Work, such as it was, and the bonds of a common culture and, often, a common dialect or language (especially among the various immigrant communities of North America) frequently kept people tied to the slums from which they must have longed to break free. And yet it was also an environment that produced several remarkably heroic spirits.

MEAN STREETS Little light manages to penetrate a slum alley in Glasgow.

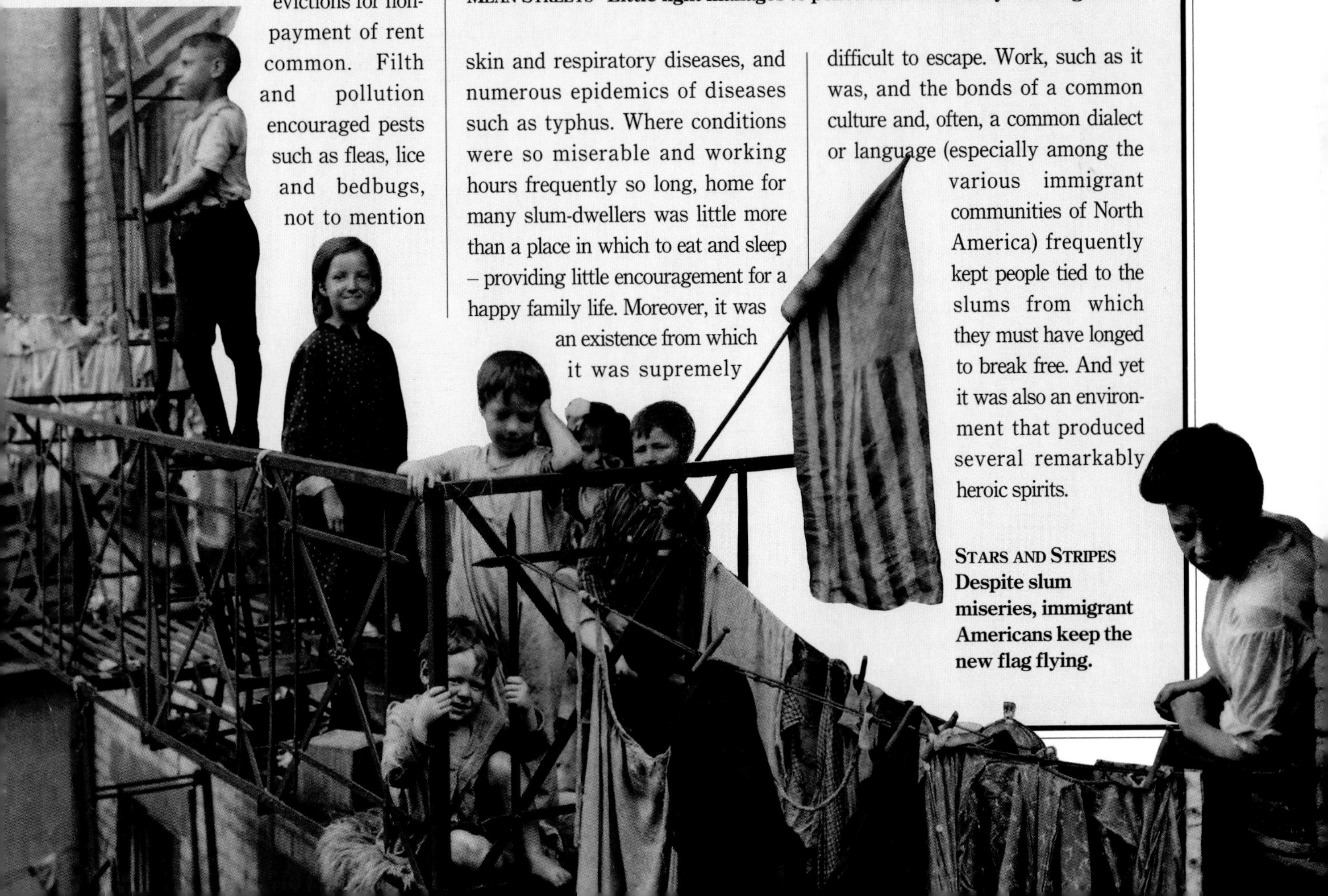

STARS AND STRIPES Despite slum miseries, immigrant Americans keep the new flag flying.

Family Sweatshop **Children and parents work as a team in the American tailoring trade. A Singer sewing machine holds pride of place by the window.**

state-financed social security measures, including provisions to insure workers against sickness, accident and old age.

In such conditions families tended to divide, along very Victorian lines, into those that were 'respectable' and those that were not. This did not necessarily have much to do with income. The daughter of a senior British railway worker (one of the grandest jobs a Victorian worker could have) remembered her parents as the very picture of respectability, going to church on Sunday, her father in 'his frock coat and silk hat, and mother with her silk cape'.

Equally, however, the children of a London navvy also had vivid memories of their parents' struggles to maintain 'respectable' standards. Both parents were illiterate and the family lived in grinding poverty. None the less, the children were taught to 'raise the hat to the ladies ... and we weren't allowed to talk over the table. ... You had to sit right and you had to hold your knife and fork right.'

In contrast were a family from Salford in the North of England, who were definitely not respectable. The children had no memories of going to church on Sunday, but very lively ones of petty shoplifting to help their hard-pressed mother.

The Discreet Rise of the Middle Classes

For the better-off, of course, life was in most ways quite different, with different preoccupations and priorities. One of the notable features of the Victorian age, along with the spread of industry and growth of the cities, was the rise in numbers and importance of the urban middle classes. They encompassed an

A DAY IN THE LIFE OF

A Dundee Factory Boy

Conditions in the flax and jute factories of the Scottish city of Dundee were notoriously harsh. Here are the memories of one survivor, published in 1850:

'When I went to a spinning mill I was about seven years of age. I had to get out of bed every morning at five o'clock, commence work at half-past five, drop at nine for breakfast, begin again at half-past nine, work until two, which was the dinner hour, start again at half-past two, and continue until half-past seven at night. Such were the nominal hours; but in reality there were no regular hours, masters and managers did with us as they liked. The clocks at the factories were often put forward in the morning and back at night, and instead of being instruments for the measurement of time, they were used as *cloaks* for cheatery and oppression. Though this was known amongst the hands, all were afraid to speak, and a workman then was afraid to carry a watch, as it was no uncommon event to dismiss anyone who presumed to know too much.'

Spinning Yarn **British textile workers pose outside their mill.**

TIME FOR A BREAK Women workers in the English mill town Wigan read letters and chat during their dinner hour. Workers at a British match factory strike for better pay in 1888.

increasing swathe of the population and, in Europe at least, gave rise to a host of subtle social nuances.

At the bottom end of the scale they included the families of lower middle-class clerks who were scarcely distinguishable from those of the skilled workers of the 'labour aristocracy'. At the top end, they included millionaire industrialists and financiers such as the German Krupps and Siemenses, the Catalan Güells, the American Vanderbilts and the various branches of the Rothschild clan, all of whom lived in much the same style (and increasingly in the same social circles) as the old landed aristocracy. Within their middle ranks, subtle distinctions prevailed such as those between business people and the members of the so-called 'liberal' professions (the law, medicine and so on), the latter often tending to give themselves a slight social edge over the former.

Not surprisingly, the gospels of hard work and orderliness generally ranked high with the middle classes, most of whom reckoned to have made their way in life through hard work and sober habits. But such a creed was not without its critics. As the early Communist writer Friedrich Engels put it in the 1840s when commenting on the German bourgeoisie: 'These people lead a frightful life and they are so content with it: the whole day long they bury themselves in figures in their offices, with a fury, with an interest that is scarcely credible; in the evenings at the appointed hour all go into company where they play cards, talk politics and smoke, and at the stroke of nine they all go home.'

At the other end of the Victorian age, the English brothers George and Weedon Grossmith were more gently satirical in *The Diary of a Nobody* (1892), their account of the life of the fictional Charles Pooter, a clerk in the City of London. He and his wife Carrie had a typically suburban address, 'The Laurels', Brickfield Terrace, Holloway, and their lives revolved around such weighty issues as an imagined slight Pooter received at the hands of a junior in his office.

Such people may have valued hard work, but definitions of what constituted hard work could vary considerably. The British novelist Anthony Trollope started his working life as a clerk in the London Post Office. He noted that the kind of 'man who came [into

HIGH SOCIETY

New industrial and business wealth injected an unsurpassed glitter into the life of the Victorian upper classes.

ELEGANT DIVERSIONS Wealthy New Yorkers take to their skates in a wintry Central Park of the 1870s. In London, fashionable ladies gather in the showrooms of the House of Worth, the pioneering couturier originally set up in Paris, in 1858, by the English-born Charles Frederick Worth.

BATH HOUSE, the London home of the hugely wealthy Lady Ashburton, was one of the grandest of the British capital's great aristocratic mansions; when the writer Thomas Carlyle and his wife Jane Welsh Carlyle received an invitation to a ball there in 1850, Jane Carlyle, at least, felt distinctly apprehensive. In the end, however, her husband persuaded her to go and (despite last-minute panics with her dress) she was grateful: 'I was glad *after* that I went,' she informed a cousin ' – all the Duchesses one ever heard tell of blazing in diamonds, all the young beauties of the Season, all the distinguished statesmen, etc. etc. were to be seen among the six or seven hundred people present – and the room hung with artificial roses looked like an Arabian Nights entertainment.'

Society (with a capital 'S') certainly exercised a special fascination in the Victorian age. In the three greatest cities of the time, London, New York and Paris, the elegance of older patrician ways combined with the influence of newly made wealth to create a social round of near-unprecedented glitter and opulence.

During the social Season each year (winter in New York; from Easter to August in London) life for those 'in Society' was an almost nightly succession of balls; huge, crushed receptions; smaller, more select dinner parties; nights at the opera; the exclusive *salon* entertainments of the great Parisian hostesses; and other such festivities. Days were often spent partly on horseback or in smart carriages, being seen to take the fashionable air of Central or Hyde Park or the newly laid-out Bois de Boulogne. When these amusements palled there were also the great sporting events of the social calendar – horse-racing at Ascot or Goodwood in England, for example, or at Auteuil in France.

After the Season New Yorkers usually retreated to resorts such as Newport, Rhode Island, with daily bathing or fishing parties for the

IMPERIAL SPLENDOURS **Officers' uniforms sparkle and ladies' dresses swirl elegantly at a court ball in the Austro-Hungarian capital, Vienna.**

young, as well as yachting excursions and, for more elderly ladies, sedate carriage rides along the coast. In Europe, meanwhile, the rich entertained each other at large country house parties. Alternatively, they withdrew to one of the continental spa resorts or, in winter, to the warmer climes of the South of France.

Although the domain of the leisured few, Society nevertheless managed to keep its members surprisingly busy. Every Season, for example, brought its new batch of debutantes, young girls – 18 was generally the favoured age – who were 'coming out' (that is, making their first official appearance) in Society. Mothers plotted anxiously to find suitable husbands for them and, in the European capitals, had them 'presented' at Court.

Society had still more to offer. Sooner or later most of the age's best-known artists, writers, scientists and the like were drawn into its bright circle, and many wealthy homes offered not only the most lavish entertainments but also the wittiest and cleverest company. The frisson of power was there too, especially in London, the world's most important capital, where Society was often the setting for the highest political dramas.

Small wonder, then, that it was so all-consuming for those involved in it. The American novelist Edith Wharton described a visit to one English country house on a 'Sunday at the end of a brilliant London season'. Her hosts were entertaining for the weekend 'the very flower and pinnacle of the London world', including numerous leading politicians as well as figures such as the American-born painter John Singer Sargent and the novelist Henry James. They may have formed a shining company but they were also, she noted, 'one and all so exhausted by the social labours of the last weeks ... that beyond benevolent smiles they had little to give.'

PARISIAN NIGHTS **Patterns of white, black and pastel pinks and blues dominate among guests at the salon of a grand Parisian hostess.**

THE PENNY POST

The world's first postage stamp was the Penny Black, bearing a portrait of Queen Victoria and issued in Britain in 1840 as part of a comprehensive scheme to reform the postal system. Until then, the person who received a letter generally paid for it, according to a hierarchy of charges which depended on how far the letter had come. It was the Englishman Rowland Hill's idea to make the sender pay a cheaper flat rate, depending only on the weight of the letter. Other countries were quick to follow suit, starting with Brazil and Switzerland in 1843. By 1878 the Universal Postal Union had been formed, including most countries in Europe and America.

the office] at ten, and who was always still at his desk at half-past four' – a comparatively modest feat that still often eluded the young Trollope – was usually considered an exemplary worker by his superiors.

On the other hand, many Victorians were prodigiously hard-working. When Trollope settled down to his writing career, which he pursued for a long time in tandem with his career at the Post Office, he set a formidable example. He would spend three hours between 5.30 and 8.30 each morning on his current novel, then put in a full day at the office, and after that enjoy an active social life in the evenings.

Hard work was also praised in one of the most colossal of all Victorian bestsellers, the Englishman Samuel Smiles's *Self-Help* (first published in 1859 and translated into many foreign languages, including Arabic, Turkish and Japanese). It made little of wealth or 'worldly success' as ends in themselves. Instead, Smiles's aim was to 're-inculcate those old-fashioned but wholesome lessons … that youth must work in order to enjoy – that nothing creditable can be accomplished without application and diligence.'

The Americans, meanwhile, were less abashed about the importance of success, as well as hard work. They were proud that, in their more democratic country, belonging to the right social class counted for less in the struggle for success than in Europe. In the words of a patent medicine advertisement in 1877: 'The first object in life with the American people is to get rich; the second, how to retain good health. The first can be obtained by energy, honesty, and saving; the second, by using Green's August Flower.'

NEW WEALTH The sober elegance of the Italian Guidini family reflects the new prestige of the upper middle classes. Businessmen – painted by Edgar Degas – gather in the Paris Cotton Exchange.

MIDDLE-CLASS PRIDE A British poulterer and his family present the very picture of lower middle-class 'respectability'.

THE VICTORIAN COUNTRYSIDE

Country people were not spared the changes of the Victorian age. Railways linked their villages and farms more closely to the cities – and their profitable markets – while newly invented agricultural machinery gradually wrought its own revolution. Mechanical threshers were early on the scene, to be followed by reaping machines, horse-driven combine-harvesters (first devised by Australian wheat farmers) and eventually the steam plough.

The Farming Year

Boom and bust was the pattern for many Victorian farmers. Hungry years in the 1840s were followed by the highly prosperous 1850s, 60s and early 70s. Then came bust, starting with a series of wet European summers in the late 1870s.

THE 1890s were a bad time for farmers on the Great Plains of North America – as they were, indeed, for their fellows in much of the rest of the world. 'At the age of 52, after a long life of toil, economy, and self-denial, I find myself and family virtually paupers,' was how one farmer from Kansas summed up his position at the start of the decade.

The rise and then sharp decline of Victorian agriculture – the mainstay, of course, of rural prosperity – was certainly dramatic. After the hungry years of the 1840s, which were dogged by bad harvests and the sufferings inflicted by potato blight (most notably in Ireland's Great Famine of 1845 onwards), came an era of very different fortunes. During the mid-Victorian decades farming seemed blessed with an unstoppable prosperity in many parts of the world. The growing cities provided rich and expanding markets for the farms' produce; and railways and steamships made it ever easier to reach them. Improved plant strains yielded increasingly abundant harvests, while more and more advanced machinery was available for exploiting them. With crops fetching steady high prices, land values rose to dizzy peaks, especially in the early 1870s. Agriculture and its related industries seemed one of the safest forms of investment – French sugar-beet refineries in the 1860s, for example, quite often rewarded their investors with dividends of 50 or even 60 per cent.

Then came the fall. In Europe, first, a series of wet summers in the late 1870s resulted in bad harvests and, in many areas, outbreaks of disease among the livestock. This coincided with tumbling crop prices, especially in wheat, where increased production on the plains of eastern Europe and Russia

MARKET DAY Stallholders wait expectantly by their stands in the cobbled square of an English market town. In contrast is a scene from the plateau of Oregon in the American Northwest (background). Early horse-driven combine harvesters – originally invented in Australia – were already beginning to appear there by the late 1880s.

was starting to add its weight to existing competition from North America. Farmers who had borrowed too freely in the good years in order to buy better equipment or stock found themselves suddenly overstretched. Many (whose families may have farmed the same land for generations) went out of business altogether; for the rest it was a question of fighting grimly on.

'This dismal, wet, dark, never-to-be-forgotten year is now at an end,' commented the English West Country farmer S.G. Kendall in his diary on New Year's Eve 1879. European agriculture was to remain depressed for most of the rest of the century.

For the Americans, meanwhile, especially those farming the Plains of the West, the turning point came later, in 1886. That summer scorching hot winds whistled across the prairies, drying out and blighting most of the crops before they had even been harvested. This was followed by a bitter winter. Massive blizzards in January 1887 dealt a death blow to the Plains' other farming mainstay: the melting snows later that spring revealed the rotting corpses of thousands of cattle.

As in Europe, increased competition from abroad and falling prices combined with widespread indebtedness and continued bad weather (a succession of bone-dry summers, in the case of the Plains) to create a major crisis. The same banks whose 'loan agents' had pressurised numerous farmers into borrowing more than they could properly afford foreclosed on many of their debtors, who in some cases were reduced to being tenants on what had previously been their own land.

While most farmers struggled on, a number simply quit. In western Kansas, in particular, between 1888 and 1892 more than half the families who had settled in the region only a few decades earlier left their farms and headed back East. 'In God we trusted, in Kansas we busted' was the angry slogan some were reputed to have daubed on the sides of their waggons as they departed.

New Meets Old

The years of comparatively easy prosperity may have been over by the end of the 1880s, but they had none the less transformed large parts of the countryside, and these changes were mostly there to stay.

Most obviously, the newly constructed railways left their mark: literally, in the embankments, cuttings, viaducts and tunnels that now crisscrossed the landscape; but also by helping to introduce new products and new customs to the countryside, and by breaking through centuries-old traditions of isolation and self-sufficiency.

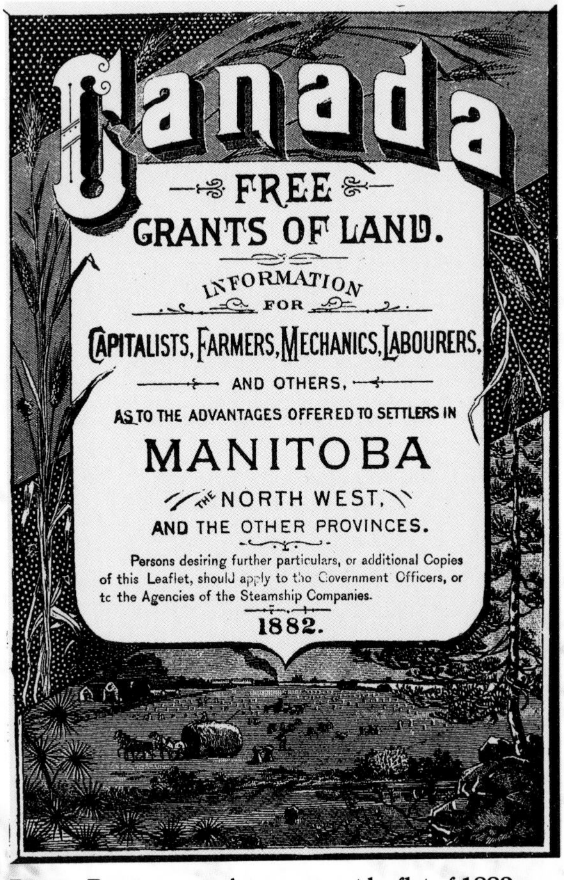

Prairie Pilgrimages A government leaflet of 1882 offers advice to hopeful Canadian settlers.

The village of Morette, for example, sheltering in the remote foothills of the Alps in Dauphiné in south-eastern France, was still almost entirely self-sufficient as late as the start of the 1850s. The various villagers made their own wooden farming implements, wove their own cloth and made a special nut oil for lighting their homes at night.

Things soon began to change, however. Around 1860 coffee made its first appearance in Morette, drunk initially on special occasions only, such as New Year's Day, but later replacing bread dunked in a local form of brandy as the standard breakfast fare. Other imported goods such as sugar, rice and macaroni followed later and by the 1890s Morette was thoroughly integrated with, and dependent on, the outside world.

Country ways elsewhere in the Victorian world, meanwhile, had experienced even more thorough-

HARD HARVESTS The French landscape presents a bleak scene, as peasant women gather in the potato crop – a staple of their diet – in a painting by Ernest Masson.

going change. Again the railways and improved transport were a key factor, as were inventions such as refrigeration. These meant that food could be safely transported over long distances and that cities, in particular, were no longer so dependent on their neighbouring areas to feed them. Different regions could thus specialise in a few crops or products which they then exported to the other side of the world, if necessary.

In Europe, this allowed places such as Denmark and Ireland to concentrate on high-quality bacon and dairy products. On the larger, worldwide scale it resulted in huge swathes of New World territory being colonised and given over to single forms of agriculture: sheep and dairy farming in different parts of New Zealand; beef, sheep and wheat in Australia; beef in Argentina; and beef and wheat on the Plains of North America.

This was farming on an industrial scale, and it was organised accordingly. During the boom years of the 1870s and early 80s, for example, European aristocrats and East Coast capitalists alike invested heavily in large cattle-raising syndicates in the American West. These giants included the XIT Ranch which controlled 3 million acres in the Panhandle region of northern Texas. While smaller farmers retained an important place among the Plains' wheat producers, they too found themselves more and

JOINT VENTURES Prosperous-looking Danish dairy farmers are proof of the benefits of the farming co-operatives pioneered in their country. Broom-makers, meanwhile, ply their craft in northern England.

FAMINE AND EMIGRATION: THE BLIGHTS OF THE LAND

THE VICTORIAN age's hungriest years – in Europe at least – were the 1840s. In that decade the effects of a string of bad harvests, rising food prices and the horrors of the potato blight (attacking the staple diet of many of Europe's poorest communities), all came together to bring catastrophe to a number of country areas, notably in Ireland and parts of Germany.

Of these, the blight, a fungal disease originating in America, was particularly swift to take hold and appalling in its consequences: 'On the 27th of last month I passed from Cork to Dublin,' wrote the Irish priest Father Theobald Mathew in August 1846, 'and this doomed plant [the potato] bloomed in all the luxuriance of an abundant harvest. Returning on the 3rd instant, I beheld with sorrow one wide waste of putrefying vegetation.'

POTATO BLIGHT Millions died in Ireland's Great Famine of the late 1840s.

In all, around a million people out of a total Irish population of 8 million died of starvation or disease as a result of the Great Famine, and another 1.6 million emigrated, mostly to North America. And they were not the only ones: during the same years 50,000 people died, for example, in the German region of Upper Silesia.

Better transport and more efficient agriculture meant that few parts of the Victorian world saw starvation on that scale again. But the countryside was never entirely free from misery, even in the mostly prosperous mid-Victorian years. In many parts of Europe peasants were driven off the land as larger farmers and landowners took over and enclosed what had for centuries been villages' common lands. Then came the aphid-like pest phylloxera (another American import) which in the 1870s ravaged most of Europe's wine-producing regions.

All of this was reflected in the emigration figures. Nearly 150,000 people left Sweden, for example, during bad years in the 1860s. In Germany, the figure rose to nearly a million in the 1850s and stayed high for the rest of the century. For all the hazards and uncertainties it entailed, the call of the New World clearly exercised a strong appeal for many people in the old continent's more battered rural communities.

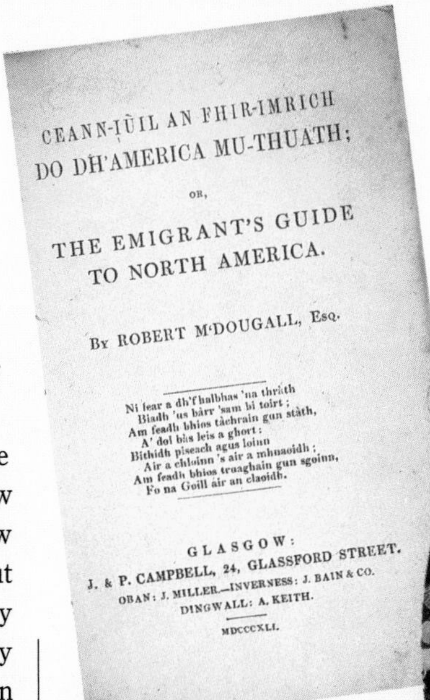

CEANN-IÙIL AN FHIR-IMRICH
DO DH'AMERICA MU-THUATH;

OR,

THE EMIGRANT'S GUIDE
TO NORTH AMERICA.

BY ROBERT M'DOUGALL, ESQ.

Ni fear a dh'fhalbhas 'na thràth
Biadh 'us bàrr 'sam bi toirt;
Am feadh bhios tàchrain gun stàth,
A' dol bàs leis a ghort:
Bithidh piseach agus loinn
Air a chloinn 's air a mhnaoidh;
Am feadh bhios truaghain gun sgoinn,
Fo na Goill air an claoidh.

GLASGOW:
J. & P. CAMPBELL, 24, GLASSFORD STREET.
OBAN: J. MILLER.—INVERNESS: J. BAIN & CO.
DINGWALL: A. KEITH.

MDCCCXLI.

LAST OF ENGLAND Emigrants watch the homeland disappear in a painting by Ford Madox Brown. A guide in Gaelic offers advice to Scottish emigrants.

THE COWBOY'S HOME American cattlemen round up their herds amidst the desolate grandeur of Montana.

THE MERITS OF SPIKED WIRE

Cattle-raising on the North American Plains yielded at least one widely used invention: barbed wire. Timber for fencing was scarce on the Plains and so ranchers used smooth iron wire stretched between a few wooden posts to make their fences. The trouble was that cattle rubbed against the wire and were constantly breaking it. Barbed wire – first manufactured on a large scale by Joseph F. Glidden of Illinois in the mid-1870s – put an end to this and was soon common throughout the Victorian world, despite the protests of a few humanitarians who regarded it as cruel.

more dependent on large capitalist organisations, such as the grain brokers of Chicago.

This new, more commercial approach to farming was seen in other ways too. From the 18th century Britain's aristocratic large landowners had been enthusiastic pioneers of new methods for improving their land, crops and livestock. Through organisations such as the British Royal Agricultural Society (set up in 1838), the US Department of Agriculture (1862) and the efforts of improvement-minded landowners

A DAY IN THE LIFE OF

SHEEP-SHEARERS DOWN UNDER

SKILLED SHEEP-SHEARERS could expect hard work but good pay during the annual shearings on New Zealand sheep stations. In December 1865 the Englishwoman Lady Barker saw one group in operation on a large South Island station:

'There were about twenty-five shearers at work, and everything seemed to be very systematically and well arranged. Each shearer has a trap-door close to him, out of which he pushes his sheep as soon as the fleece is off, and there are little pens outside, so that the manager can notice whether the poor animal has been too much cut with the shears, or badly shorn in any other respect, and can tell exactly which shearer is to blame ... A good shearer can take off 120 fleeces in a day, but the average is about 80 to each man. They get £1 per hundred, and are found [provided for] in everything, having as much tea and sugar, bread and mutton, as they can consume, and a cook entirely to themselves; they work at least fourteen hours out of the twenty-four, and with such a large flock as this – about 50,000 – must make a good deal.'

TROPHIES OF THE SHEARER'S ART Expert shearers, such as these Australian ones, could get through more than 100 fleeces a day.

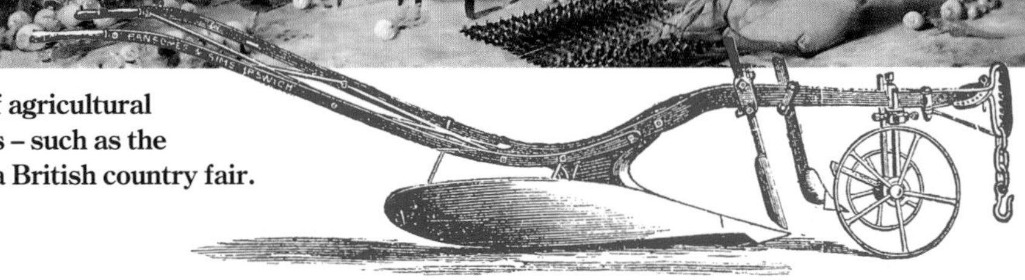

FOLLOW THE PLOUGH Makers of agricultural equipment show off their wares – such as the 'Newcastle' plough (right) – at a British country fair.

elsewhere – notably the Junker nobility of eastern Germany – this process continued in the Victorian age. Fertilisers (guano from Peru, nitrates from Chile) were increasingly used to enrich the soil, while experiments yielded more productive or disease-resistant crop strains and livestock breeds. Above all, the use of ever-more sophisticated machinery became a key part of agriculture.

This process had started well before Queen Victoria came to the throne, with the introduction of threshing machines – sufficiently common by the 1830s for bands of British labourers to go round smashing them as a threat to their winter livelihoods – and it continued right through the 19th century. Also in the 1830s, for example, the Scotsman Patrick Bell and the American Cyrus Hall McCormick had devised the first horse-drawn mechanised reapers, and these rapidly became popular after they were demonstrated at London's Great Exhibition in 1851. The Illinois blacksmith John Deere developed the first all-steel plough, while by the 1850s the wheat farmers of southern Australia started using a primitive form of horse-driven combine harvester.

By 1867 the American Albert D. Richardson was commenting on the impact of mechanisation on the Plains of the West: 'Machinery is increasing fourfold the efficiency of labor. This riding around the country on the spring seat of a mower or a planter is little like the old farming of New England! The great unsupplied need is the steam plow, but that will surely come' – as indeed it did. The first attempts at steam-ploughing had, in fact, been made as early as the 1830s in Scotland, but it was in the 1860s that more practical steam ploughs appeared.

SQUIRES, SERFS AND LABOURERS

While pioneer 'homesteaders' settled the Plains of the American West, many European aristocrats lived much as their ancestors had done for generations. The end of serfdom in eastern Europe and slavery in the American South forced people there to adjust to new ways.

THE VICTORIAN AGE saw enormous changes in rural life and rural ways. Yet, of course, it also saw continuity as well. In Britain, for instance, the role of the aristocracy and landed gentry in rural affairs, though to some extent diluted by 1900, remained crucial. The British aristocracy were still an essentially country-based group and it was in their large country houses that they tended to feel most at home and where they most freely displayed their considerable wealth and power.

As the French traveller and writer Hippolyte Taine noted in the early 1870s: 'they are rooted in their country seats; that is their true homeland, the loved domestic circle, the family centre, the place where they ... receive long visits from guests ... where they find at each step the memorial of their good deeds or of the good deeds of their ancestors ...' Their love of the rural sports of hunting, shooting and fishing was another tie that kept them bound to their estates.

The British were indeed unusual in this respect. Most other countries had long-established landed

THE SQUIRE AND HIS FAMILY The Englishman Edward Hussey sits with his wife Henrietta, six children and a friend in the grounds of his home Scotney Castle in Kent. A painting by John Frederick Herring gives a romanticised view of 'An English Homestead'.

WATER GATHERERS **An English countryman uses a yoke and pails to fetch water from the village pump. Another, older countryman wears the traditional smock, while a gamekeeper clutches a trophy of rabbits.**

aristocracies living substantially from the revenues of their country estates. But few, with the possible exception of the Prussian Junkers, bothered to live on their properties to the extent that the British did. They were notable in another respect too: for their grip on so much of Britain's best land. This was revealed by a survey in the mid-1870s which showed that some 80 per cent of Britain belonged to just 7000 families and that 55 per cent of it was owned in estates of 1000 acres or more. Other nations had giant landowners, such as the Russian Sheremetev family with 2 million acres or the American Livingstons with 300,000 prime acres in the Hudson Valley.

But thanks largely to the British system of primogeniture (which passed estates intact to the eldest son in each generation) only Britain had such a clutch of large landowners: ranging from magnates such as the Dukes of Sutherland and Bedford – with, respectively, 1.4 million acres and a more modest, but fertile 80,000 – to humbler squires with just 1000 acres or so. Not that many such landowners directly farmed their own land. Although many took a keen interest in agriculture, most left the day-to-day work to tenant farmers, many of whom were themselves extremely prosperous.

In 1880 the writer Richard Jefferies described two representative squires from the English West Country: the young and dynamic Squire Marthorne, popular alike with his social equals among the neighbouring gentry and with his tenants and labourers; and the older, stiffer, somewhat pedantic Squire Filbard, less well liked but still obsequiously curtsied-to and bowed-to by the local cottagers. In fact, neither was especially wealthy by the standards of their class – though both lived in fine mansions set in extensive parkland and the wives of both felt it necessary to try to keep up the appearance of high fashion. For all that, both men were figures of considerable influence in local 'county' affairs, not least through their roles as magistrates or Justices of the Peace. Both too were closely involved in all the minutest doings of their estates and neighbourhoods. In Squire Filbard's case this had a distinctly gossipy aspect and was fed by the daily reports of his trusted steward: 'One morning perhaps [the steward] would come in to talk with the squire about the ash wood they were going to cut in the ensuing winter, or about the oak bark which had not been paid for. Or it might be the Alderney cow or the poultry at the Home Farm, or a few fresh tiles on the roof of the pig-sty, which was decaying ... One of the tenants wanted a new shed put up, but it did not seem necessary; the old one would do very well if people were not so fidgety.'

A HOME IN THE WEST

The lives of American homesteaders who settled the Great Plains in the post-Civil War decades were very different. In 1885 – just before the crash in American agriculture – the aristocratic German-born entrepreneur Baron Walter von Richthofen wrote an enthusiastic description of these and the surrounding regions of the West and of the opportunities they offered to people with a pioneering spirit: 'Those who have traveled through the West from the Missouri River to the Rocky Mountains, or still farther, are full

THE COUNTRY HOUSE

THE MELLOW evenings of late summer saw the English country house at its most attractive. The London social 'Season' over, landed families returned to their estates to enjoy the pursuits of country life – hunting, shooting and entertaining their friends.

These mansions were often worlds almost of their own. Whether the hubs of huge ducal estates or the more modest establishments of squires, they employed large staffs of indoor and outdoor servants, far outnumbering the family they served.

The hierarchy among the servants was complex. At the top, in the grandest households, was the house steward, responsible for the overall running of his employer's homes. Then came the butler and the employer's personal valet – roughly equal in status – and the housekeeper, the most senior female servant. Under them was a pyramid-like structure of lesser servants, from cook, coachman and lady's maid, down through the footmen and gardeners, to the most junior kitchen and scullery maids and stable boys.

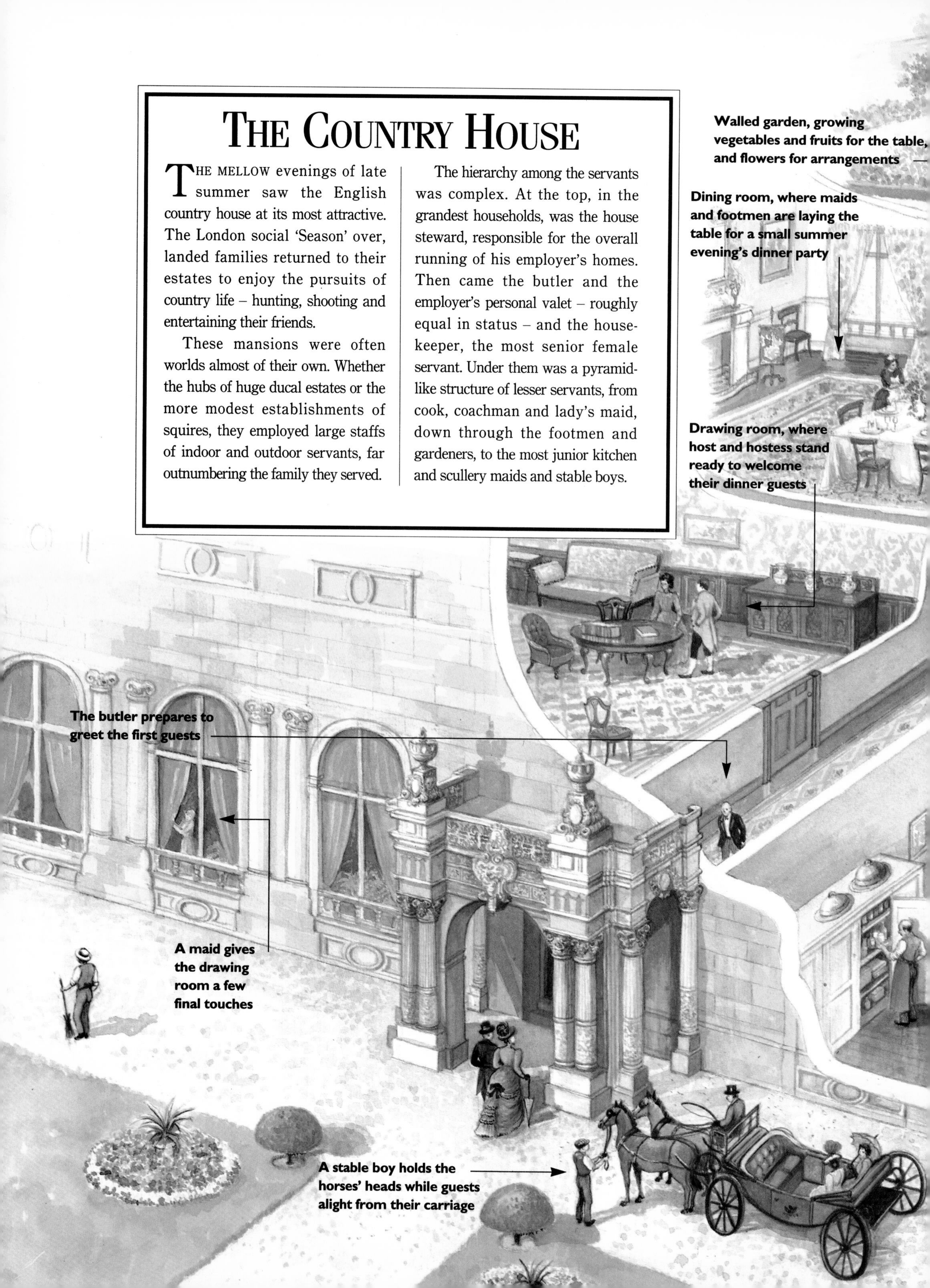

Walled garden, growing vegetables and fruits for the table, and flowers for arrangements
Dining room, where maids and footmen are laying the table for a small summer evening's dinner party
Drawing room, where host and hostess stand ready to welcome their dinner guests
The butler prepares to greet the first guests
A maid gives the drawing room a few final touches
A stable boy holds the horses' heads while guests alight from their carriage

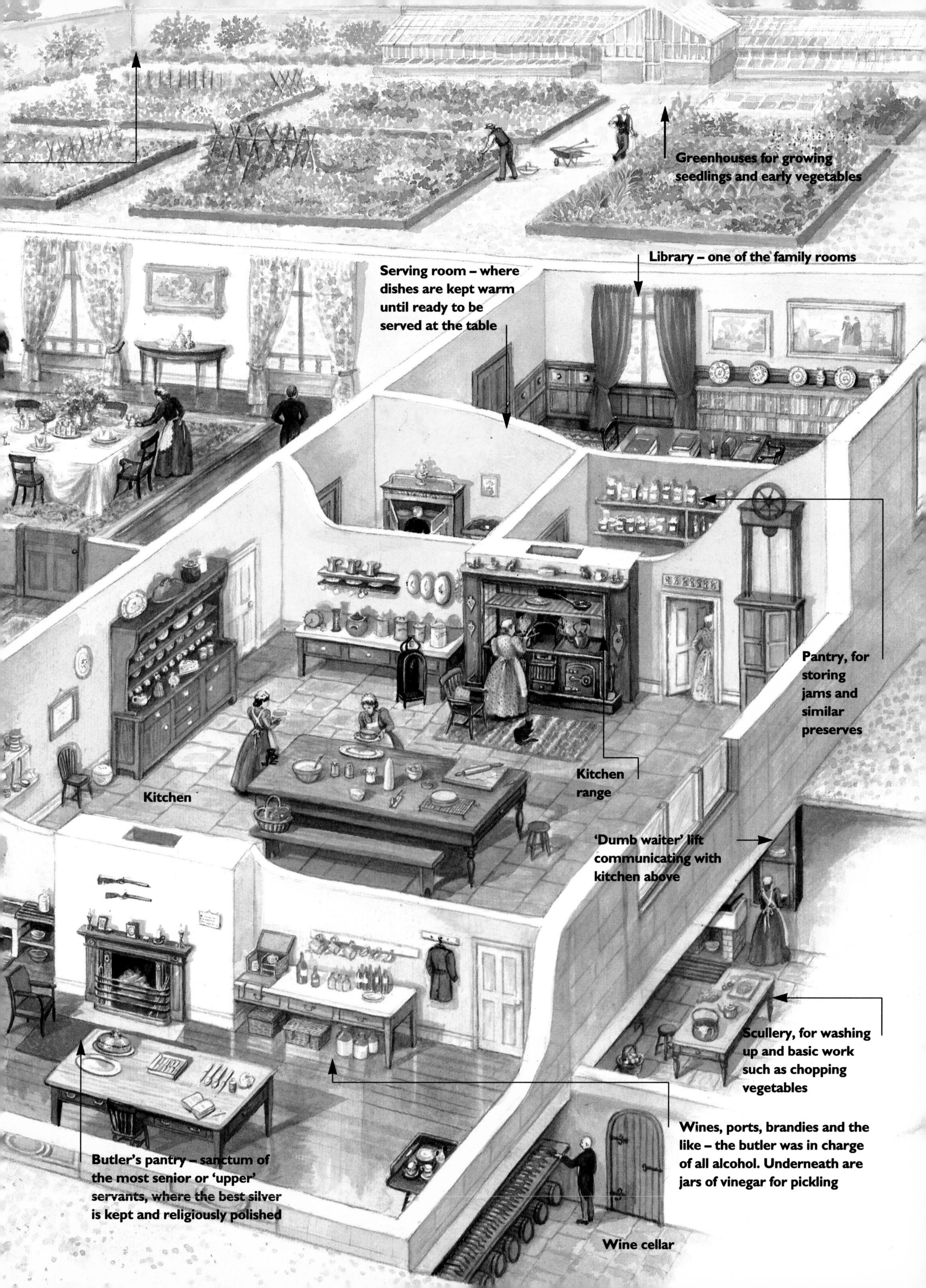
Greenhouses for growing seedlings and early vegetables
Library – one of the family rooms
Serving room – where dishes are kept warm until ready to be served at the table
Pantry, for storing jams and similar preserves
Kitchen
Kitchen range
'Dumb waiter' lift communicating with kitchen above
Scullery, for washing up and basic work such as chopping vegetables
Wines, ports, brandies and the like – the butler was in charge of all alcohol. Underneath are jars of vinegar for pickling
Butler's pantry – sanctum of the most senior or 'upper' servants, where the best silver is kept and religiously polished
Wine cellar

LAND OF OPPORTUNITIES **A poster of 1881 depicts the many wonders of the American West, especially the opportunities for farmers, hunters and prospectors.**

of admiration for the natural resources of the country. Every river, every valley, every mountain, every pass, every hill, every plateau is useful for some purpose. The mountains hide immense treasures of precious minerals, and they are covered with forests. The river valleys, the mountain parks and passes, and the treeless prairies abound with grasses. The soil makes the plowman rich, and other natural resources offer many opportunities for industrial undertakings.'

In fact, life even in the good years was never quite as easy as Richthofen suggested. The United States' great westward expansion onto the Plains – hitherto the more or less uncontested domain of buffaloes and the Indian tribes who lived by hunting them – was officially inaugurated in 1862 when President Abraham Lincoln signed the Homesteaders' Act. The Federal Government agreed to grant 160 acres of public land in the West to settlers prepared to pay a small fee and bind themselves to a few basic conditions. But the Act, designed to populate the West with small 'yeoman' farmers, was never an unqualified success and in the end the railroad companies and a minority of large-scale 'bonanza' farmers acquired much of the best land. Even so, thousands of smaller settlers did pour in, both from the East and Europe, especially Ireland, Britain, Germany and Scandinavia. Most survived, while some of them even managed to prosper.

They had plenty to contend with. The small settlers often found themselves with the driest land,

A DAY IN THE LIFE OF

A Parson on the Welsh Borders

WITH THE SQUIRE, the parson was one of the key figures in many villages of Victorian Britain. Francis Kilvert was vicar of Bredwardine in Herefordshire on the English-Welsh borders and kept a vivid diary of his daily round:

'*Friday, 23 April* [1875] To-day we laid Alice Grimshaw to sleep in the Churchyard at four o'clock in the afternoon. She was carried by young men to her grave. As I waited in the Church for the funeral the whole air without and within the Church was filled with the ceaseless singing of birds. All the place was in a beautiful and holy charm ... The funeral was very quiet and well ordered, but when we came to the grave, it was too short to receive the coffin. A cross and a wreath of primroses and daisies made by Mary Cole's nice children rested one at the head, the other at the foot of the open grave. Mary Cole said her girls were very "good children for flowering anyone", and the primroses and "pure daisies" she thought were so beautiful for the graves.'

PARSON ON HORSEBACK **Country parsons needed sturdy mounts to visit scattered parishioners.**

Forests and Plains Settlers establish their homestead amidst the forests of Washington State in the American Northwest. The prairies of Minnesota in the Midwest, meanwhile, present a bleaker, more open scene.

farthest from any river or creek and also from the nearest railroad. Summers were baking hot, winters bitterly cold, with added hazards to be feared in the form of tornadoes, dust storms, prairie fires and even occasional plagues of grasshoppers. Trees were scarce on the Plains, and so cow and buffalo 'chips' (dung) had to be laboriously gathered to use as fuel; corn and wheat stalks were also used.

Until the mid-1880s, good years on the whole balanced out the bad ones. Despite that, nothing could ever be taken for granted and there was little relief from sheer hard grind – especially for the women who were often expected to help with some of the outdoor farm work on top of the usual domestic tasks.

Homes, meanwhile, had to be built from scratch and were frequently primitive, notably in the early years when two kinds of structure were most widely favoured: the 'dug-out' and the 'sod house'. The dug-out, as its name implied, was simply carved out of a slope or hillside with makeshift walls constructed around the front and sides; a sod house was built using 12-inch blocks of sod (turf) that had been cut out of the ground and then left to dry.

The use of dug-outs was not confined to homesteaders. In 1867 Alice Blackwell Baldwin, the newly married wife of an army officer, arrived with her husband at Fort Harker in Kansas and discovered to her horror that they had been consigned a dug-out to live in: 'The walls of the kitchen were stayed and supported by logs,' she recalled later, 'while the ceiling was of the same material and covered with dirt.'

By comparison, some sod-built homes (sod was also used to build churches and courthouses) could seem veritably luxurious, as another Kansas-dweller testified: 'At first these sod houses are unplastered, and this thought perfectly allright, but such a house is

FRONTIER GOLD

Gold drew many pioneers to the frontier life, and out of it grew communities such as Gulgong in Australia.

FARMING was inevitably a long-term investment. But for those hopeful of quicker returns, there was an alternative lure to draw them into the wilds of untamed country. When gold was discovered in a mill race belonging to the Swiss-born settler John Augustus Sutter in central California, it triggered a stampede of a kind that would be repeated several times in the Victorian age.

Sutter's gold was found in January 1848, and during the course of the following year, over 80,000 eager prospectors – the 'forty-niners' – braved the still primitive land and sea routes to California. It was a minority who struck lucky and made large fortunes, but hope lived on. Gold was later discovered in Australia in the 1850s and after, South Africa and the Canadian Yukon in the 80s, and the Klondike (also in the Yukon) in the 90s, and each find – not to mention similar discoveries elsewhere, of diamonds and silver – set off fevered 'rushes', with gold-hungry adventurers pouring in from all parts of Europe, America and even China.

Life in the communities that sprang up on the goldfields was, not surprisingly, rough and often violent. Villages and towns mushroomed almost overnight, and living conditions in them were usually crude. Tempers frayed easily, and in many gold towns (especially at the height of gold rushes) bloody fights, sometimes ending in murder, were regular events. Where men worked so hard, they liked to play hard as well, so that bars, gambling halls and brothels sprang up with the gold towns and did brisk business.

And yet, even in these rough circumstances, the Victorian instinct for home-making often managed to assert itself. In Australia, for example, Gulgong grew up following strikes of gold and silver on the New South Wales fields in the early 1870s. This was when the British novelist Anthony Trollope visited it – in October 1871 – a matter of months after the first strike, and it was already a thriving place, with several thousand inhabitants and some pretensions to respectability.

Buildings, including the hotel where Trollope stayed, were certainly rough and ready, but new, more permanent ones were going up all around, and everything 'needful

MAKING NEW HOMES Many Gulgong homes were primitive affairs, with walls of lath and daub, and roofs of tree bark. An exception was this delicately carpentered cottage on Belmore Street.

MEAT AT ITS FINEST James Leggatt was a Londoner by birth, and reputed to sell the best meat on the Gulgong goldfield. As well as joints, he sold cows' heads, calves' heads, tongues and pigs' trotters.

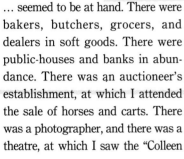

SHIFTING POPULATION Boarding houses abounded for travelling miners. This house was run by a Chinese family, banned by a rather discriminatory law of 1864 from taking part in the actual mining.

… seemed to be at hand. There were bakers, butchers, grocers, and dealers in soft goods. There were public-houses and banks in abundance. There was an auctioneer's establishment, at which I attended the sale of horses and carts. There was a photographer, and there was a theatre, at which I saw the "Colleen Bawn" acted with a great deal of spirit, and a considerable amount of histrionic talent.'

As for the people, Trollope was equally impressed. They came from many different parts of the globe – Italy, America, Germany and Scotland – but worked readily together and seemed honest in their dealings with one another. Furthermore, he observed, 'Of the courtesy of all these men it is impossible to speak too highly … The Australian miner when he is in work never drinks, – and seems to feel a pride in his courtesy. It must be understood that his is not a submissive deportment, prone to the touching of hats and a silent reverence of his betters, – but a manly bearing, which enables him to express himself freely, but which never verges on distasteful familiarity.'

Not that Gulgong was entirely lacking in some of the snobberies – as well as the refinements – of more genteel society. A few nights before Trollope arrived, there had been 'a most successful public ball. But I was distressed to find that there had been some heart-burning. Where was the line to be drawn in reference to the ladies? The postmistress would not attend the ball unless barmaids were excluded. The barmaids, – I think very properly, – were admitted, and the postmistress, who enjoyed the reputation of being the beauty of [Gulgong], remained at home.'

RED FLAG FLYING The flag shows that this shaft has 'bottomed on gold'. On the left, carts are being loaded with gold-bearing stone – known as 'payable wash'. On the right is a pile of valueless 'mullock'.

CAFÉ LIFE Tired miners often liked to eat out. Trollope when he visited was entertained to an 'oyster supper' at a restaurant, and noted afterwards that 'the comforts of life have not been altogether neglected at [Gulgong]'.

somewhat cold in the winter as the crevices between the sods admit some cold air; so some of the houses are plastered with a kind of "native lime!" made of sand and a very sticky native clay. This plaster is very good unless it happens to get wet. In a few of the houses this plaster is whitewashed, and this helps the looks very much. Some sod houses are mighty comfortable places to go into in cold weather, and it don't take much fire to keep them warm.'

Feudal Leftovers

While life may have been hard for the homesteaders, especially in the years of depression at the end of the century, at least many of them retained a measure of independence. Others were less fortunate. At the start of Queen Victoria's reign feudal serfdom, for example, survived in parts of Europe, notably the Russian and Habsburg empires, while slavery remained in force in the American South. Things changed, of course: serfdom (which bound a serf to a particular estate with statutory ties that were not too far removed from slavery) vanished from the Habsburg lands in the revolutionary year of 1848 and from Russia in 1861; slavery was abolished in the United States with the defeat of the South in the Civil War in 1865.

All the same, what replaced the former conditions was not always much better. In the South, above all, they often gave way to the much-hated sharecropping system. Plantation owners established a number of former slaves on plots of land, or 'shares', of 50 acres or so, and usually provided them with homes, a few rudimentary tools, seed, fertilisers and a mule or two. In return, the sharecroppers and their families worked the land and provided their own food and clothing. At the end of the year, landlord and sharecropper would share the crop – usually cotton – and its proceeds.

Although on the face of it a plausible-seeming scheme, sharecropping rarely worked. The sharecroppers found it hard to make a living and most fell ever more heavily into debt with their landlords and the local storekeepers. The landlords themselves, meanwhile, were not usually a great deal better off and generally kept their tenants on a tight rein with contracts that had to be renewed annually –

EYEWITNESS

Life on the American Cowboy Trail

Every year American cattlemen drove their herds hundreds, or even thousands, of miles across the Western Plains to railheads from which they would be shipped to the markets of the Midwest. Here, the former cowboy Andy Adams recalls a poignant moment near the end of one drive in 1882:

❛ Another day's easy travel brought us to within a mile of the railroad terminus; but it also brought us to one of the hardest experiences of our trip, for each of us knew, as we unsaddled our horses, that we were doing it for the last time. Although we were in the best of spirits over the successful conclusion of the drive; although we were glad to be free from hard duty and looked forward eagerly to the journey home, there was still a feeling of regret in our hearts which we could not dispel ... at no time in my life, before or since, have I felt so keenly the parting between man and horse as I did that September morning in Montana. For on the trail an affection springs up between a man and his mount which is almost human. Every privation which he endures his horse endures with him, – carrying him through falling weather, swimming rivers by day and riding in the lead of stampedes by night, always faithful, always willing, and always patiently enduring every hardship, from exhausting hours under saddle to the sufferings of a dry drive. ❜

Life in the Saddle
For the cowboy, the horse was definitely a man's best friend.

PLANTATION LIFE Victory over the Confederacy at the end of the Civil War meant that slavery was abolished throughout the United States from 1865. But for most of the black people working on the plantations of the South (left and background), cotton picking and other back-breaking tasks were still their everyday lot.

a sharecropper who failed to toe the line could thus be thrown off his land at the end of a year.

Even in places with a happier recent history, relations between those who owned the land or rented it on a large scale and those who laboured it could often be strained. In the year of Queen Victoria's death the British writer William Harbutt Dawson commented of some German farms, for example, that 'the relationship between the farmer and his hands is ... far from being as sympathetic as in earlier days, and the tendency, as in England, is more and more for the farmer to cut himself off from his dependents'. As large-scale farming was becoming more efficient, in other words, so the old paternal relationship between a farmer or landowner and his workers was giving way to a more strictly economic one.

Farm servants who, in both Britain and Germany, had once been like family members, eating and living with their masters, now became simply wage labourers. In parts of eastern Germany this led some large farmers to avoid using local German workers altogether and to employ cheaper Polish labour instead – in conditions which according to Dawson were 'more suggestive of slave plantations than of a modern free labour relationship'.

On top of that, while feudalism had officially been abolished in Germany, some of its less attractive attitudes seemed to remain in force. Dawson noted in particular a residual and distinctly feudal arrogance among the 'landed classes', many of whose members continued to be 'firmly convinced ... that the tillers of the soil absolutely exist for them, and that a man who is born an agricultural labourer should in duty remain such and train his sons and daughters to follow in his footsteps ...'

Although British landowners, by contrast, had a more liberal and benevolent reputation, conditions for many British labourers were scarcely idyllic. Hours were extremely long (from well before dawn to well after nightfall at certain times of the year); pay – usually given partly in kind and partly in cash – was low, and continuity of work by no means assured, especially for the humblest day labourers.

Admittedly housing was generally free, but this too could vary greatly. Improving landlords such as the wealthy Dukes of Bedford or Westminster built exemplary cottages for their estate workers. Many others, however, were less caring. A report in 1842 described some particularly grim farm housing in Dorset in the West of England where many cottages were 'mere mud hovels, and situated in low and damp places with cesspools or accumulations of filth close

HARVEST HOME **Evening draws in and the harvest has been safely gathered in an idyllic English scene by the painter C.H. Hart. An Italian painting shows peasants on the road with a flock of sheep and donkeys with nosebags. Both reflect a romanticised view of country life, common with the Victorians.**

to the doors ... Persons living in such cottages are generally very poor, very dirty, and usually in rags, living almost wholly on bread and potatoes, scarcely ever tasting animal food, and consequently highly susceptible of disease ...'

Moreover, British landowners also showed a certain residual feudalism, notably by enforcing draconian game laws. These could (and often did) condemn a man to two years' hard labour – or even, until the mid-century, seven years' transportation – for an offence such as the night-time poaching of a landowner's pheasants or partridges.

Country ways were thus for the most part hard. But of course they had their beauty too, and the Victorians (especially, no doubt, middle-class, urban Victorians) were generally ready to acknowledge that. In part this reflected a growing appreciation of natural beauty and the pleasures of outdoor life – especially in America where the first national parks, Yellowstone and Yosemite, were set up in 1872 and 1890. It was also, as so often in the Victorian age, fuelled by apprehension in the face of a changing world and by a nostalgic sense of the supposed simplicity of rural life.

In late Victorian America this theme gained added force when blended with another potent idea, that of the frontier spirit whose rugged values (as perceived by many Americans) were best summed up by the historian Frederick Jackson Turner: 'that coarseness and strength combined with acuteness and inquisitiveness; that practical, inventive turn of mind, quick to find expedients; that masterful grasp of material things ... ; that restless, nervous energy; that dominant individualism, working for good and for evil, and withal that buoyancy and exuberance which comes from freedom'.

Needless to say, there was a strong element of romanticism in all this. On the other hand, it was also true that parts at least of the Victorian countryside did retain a strong appeal and colour. Right to the end of the century, for example, some German peasants liked to wear their traditional costumes including such strange creations as the heavy pompom headdresses favoured by the women of Baden. Harvest festivities in Württemberg lasted several days and included events such as pitcher-carrying contests in which competitors had to carry a full pitcher of water on their heads over a fixed distance, without either using their hands to hold the pitcher or spilling any of the water. In these and other ways, country living seemed for many people to enshrine qualities of quiet strength and endurance that had been lost elsewhere in the modern world.

MIND, BODY AND SPIRIT

Life in the Victorian world changed in more than just technology and economics. The Victorians' crusading zeal led them to transform schooling systems, fight (especially in the United States) for fairer opportunities for women, champion the poor and spread the Christian gospel worldwide. At the same time, the practice of medicine was changed beyond all recognition, with better nursing, the use of anaesthetics and revolutionary discoveries about how disease was spread.

THE QUEST FOR SELF-IMPROVEMENT

Better schools in many countries meant more people who could read and write – and hence the growth, among other things, of the popular press. Women, too, started to fight for better access to higher education and the professions.

THE DESIRE to 'improve oneself' – to stock one's mind with knowledge and make the best of oneself socially, financially and in every other way – was deeply ingrained in many Victorians. 'From the time that I can remember having any thoughts about anything, I recall that I had an intense longing to learn to read,' wrote the former slave Booker T. Washington who grew up in the American South during the Civil War of the 1860s. 'I determined, when quite a small child that, if I accomplished nothing else in life, I would in some way get enough education to enable me to read common books and newspapers.'

In the event, he accomplished a good deal more than that. He worked his way through college as a night watchman, and in 1881 (aged just 25) embarked on his life's work as first president of the Tuskegee Institute in Alabama, a pioneering technical college for black Americans. From then until his death in 1915, he was one of the United States' most respected black leaders, and was even received at the White House in 1901, an unheard-of invitation for a black.

NEW HORIZONS

For many people and in many areas of life, the Victorian age was similarly one of expanding horizons and rising aspirations. Despite its dark underside, from the slavery of the pre-Civil War American South to the squalor and social injustices of the industrial cities, the period also saw revolutionary changes in fields as diverse as education and women's rights, religion and healthcare.

Education and the ability to read and write, for instance, were issues which opened up new opportunities and experiences for countless people. Industrial economies benefited by and large from

EYEWITNESS

'THE INTENSE DESIRE FOR AN EDUCATION'

FOR THE BLACK PEOPLE of the defeated South, emancipation at the end of the American Civil War meant the freedom to learn to read – as one of their leaders, Booker T. Washington, recalled:

❛ Few people who were not right in the midst of the scenes can form any exact idea of the intense desire which the people of my race showed for an education. As I have stated, it was a whole race trying to go to school. Few were too young, and none too old, to make the attempt to learn. As fast as any kind of teachers could be secured, not only were day-schools filled, but night-schools as well. The great ambition of the older people was to try to learn to read the Bible before they died. With this end in view, men and women who were fifty or seventy-five years old would often be found in the night-school. Sunday-schools were formed soon after freedom, but the principal book studied in the Sunday-school was the spelling-book. Day-school, night-school, Sunday-school, were always crowded, and often many had to be turned away for want of room. ❜

PIONEER Booker T. Washington was a reformer of black education.

Social Order The English artist Ford Madox Brown's 'Work' vividly depicts the social pyramid – gentry on horseback at the top, workers at the bottom.

literate work forces, and all across the Victorian world from the United States with its 'common schools' (state-funded primary schools, founded under the leadership of figures such as the pioneering Massachusetts secretary of education, Horace Mann) to Germany with its Volkschulen, different countries started gradually to provide free elementary schooling for all.

The results were clear enough from the literacy figures. The high standards of German schools (particularly the Prussian ones) had long been famous, so that even at the start of Victoria's reign the large majority of German people could read and write. By 1900 illiteracy in the German Empire stood at a minute 0.05 per cent. Britain and France, meanwhile, had many fine secondary schools, mostly for the middle classes – the British grammar and public (that is, private boarding) schools and French lycées – but both lagged behind in providing elementary education for the poor. As a result, up to a half of all British

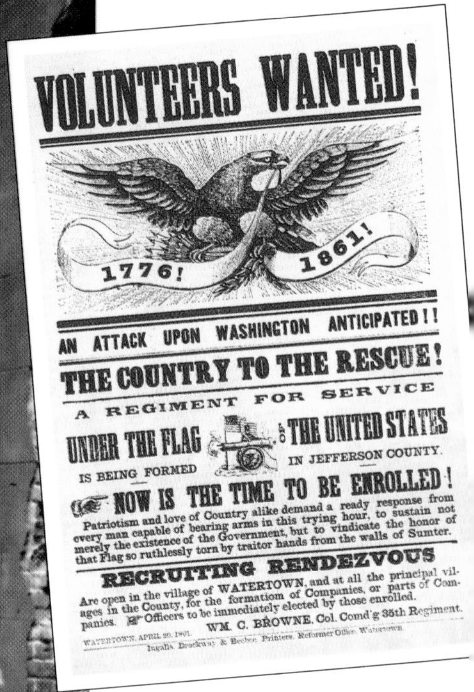
VOLUNTEERS WANTED!
1776!
1861!
AN ATTACK UPON WASHINGTON ANTICIPATED!!
THE COUNTRY TO THE RESCUE!
A REGIMENT FOR SERVICE
UNDER THE FLAG
OF THE UNITED STATES
IS BEING FORMED
IN JEFFERSON COUNTY.
NOW IS THE TIME TO BE ENROLLED!
Patriotism and love of Country alike demand a ready response from every man capable of bearing arms in this trying hour, to sustain not merely the existence of the Government, but to vindicate the honor of that Flag so ruthlessly torn by traitor hands from the walls of Sumter.
RECRUITING RENDEZVOUS
Are open in the village of WATERTOWN, and at all the principal villages in the County, for the formatiom of Companies, or parts of Companies. Officers to be immediately elected by those enrolled.
WM. C. BROWNE, Col. Comd'g 35th Regiment.

CHAOS AND DESOLATION War, as well as peace, was a reality for many Victorians. Here, four black children sit amidst the ruins of Charleston, South Carolina, devastated during the Civil War. A Union poster calls for volunteers to help to defend Washington.

women and nearly a third of British men could still neither read nor write in the 1860s; in France, more than half the population were still illiterate in the 1870s. Both countries, however, made rapid advances after that, with the French finally establishing a full nationwide system of free primary schools between 1878 and 1881 and the English over a longer period between 1870 and 1891.

The newly literate majorities asserted themselves in a number of ways, one of which was the growth of the popular press. In France the daily *Petit Journal* had led the way from as early as 1863 with a spicy mix of scandal, murder and gossip, but with the growth of literacy in the 1880s, it produced its first weekly colour supplement and on one occasion in 1887 sold more than a million copies.

Across the Atlantic, meanwhile, the Hungarian-born Joseph Pulitzer and later the Californian mining heir William Randolph Hearst were establishing their own distinctive brands of popular journalism. In the 1880s and 90s, the use of sensational headlines, pictures and a new campaigning style was employed in Hearst's crusade against Spanish rule in Cuba, believed by many to have played a crucial role in precipitating the Spanish-American War of 1898. In Britain, Alfred Harmsworth (later Lord Northcliffe) followed suit, founding the first British mass-circulation paper, the *Daily Mail*, in 1896.

At the same time, nationalism and an increased concern for people's rights of various kinds also had their parts to play. An age which saw the unification of Italy (in 1870) and Germany (in 1871), the confident forward march of the British and French empires, and the huge growth through immigration and westward expansion of the United States, was also clearly an age that set great store by patriotism. In promoting that – and thus helping to knit together nations like Germany, Italy and the United States, and to inspire older ones such as Britain and France – the schools in particular were expected to pull their weight: hence, among other things, a growing emphasis on history, with the glorification of national heroes, such as the Elizabethan buccaneer Sir Francis Drake in Britain and contemporary heroes such as President Lincoln in America.

Better education helped to spur different concerns: the anti-slavery movement, especially among middle-class Northerners in pre-Civil War America; the growing women's movement, strongest at first in the United States, then spreading to Europe; and the emerging trades union and workers' movements. Ordinary people's increasing concerns with national, economic and political rights were key forces behind the revolutions of 1848 and the turbulent events of 1870–71: Prussia's invasion of France and the subsequent turmoil of the Paris Commune when a revolutionary government with strong socialist elements took control of the French capital for just over ten weeks. A deeply felt concern for those less fortunate than themselves also led countless middle- and upper-class Victorians to dedicate themselves to a huge range of charitable and philanthropic causes, from better housing for the poor to animal welfare, and from prison reform to the care of orphans.

Tabloid Teasers
The French *Petit Journal*, with a weekly colour supplement, led the way in popular journalism. The cry of the newsboy became increasingly common on the streets.

Not all sentiments were so noble. One of the age's less attractive characteristics was seen in the Dreyfus affair in France. In 1894 a young Jewish army officer, Alfred Dreyfus, was wrongly convicted of selling military secrets to the Germans and sentenced to life imprisonment on the dreaded Devil's Island, off the coast of France's South American colony Guiana. The trial was highly irregular and clearly motivated by widespread anti-Semitism in both the army and the general population. Fortunately, Dreyfus was steadfastly championed by his wealthy family and later by a group of journalists and intellectuals, including the novelist Emile Zola. He was pardoned in 1899, although he was not fully rehabilitated until 1906 when a court finally reversed his earlier convictions.

Schooldays – The Rule of the Rod

The expansion of education was impressive, but like so much else in the Victorian age it had its dark side. In Britain, for example, the public schools inspired an almost fanatical loyalty from former pupils. But they were also infamously cruel; bullying of younger boys and 'fagging' whereby younger boys (with the full sanction of the school authorities) acted as unpaid servants to often tyrannical older boys were commonplace. They and the preparatory schools (for boys under 13) were also notorious for the frequent brutality of their discipline. One sadistic Anglican clergyman, the Revd H.W. Sneyd-

Cinq Centimes
L'AURORE
Littéraire, Artistique, Sociale
J'Accuse...!
LETTRE AU PRÉSIDENT DE LA RÉPUBLIQUE
Par ÉMILE ZOLA
LETTRE A M. FÉLIX FAURE
Président de la République

I Accuse ... ! Emile Zola published a long letter in defence of Alfred Dreyfus.

Crime and Punishment

As the cities grew, so did crime – despite numerous reforms, such as new model prisons.

Jail Food **Discipline was all, as convicts marched into dinner in New York's Sing Sing Prison.**

TRAINING for a life of crime started young on the streets of Victorian cities, as the British journalist Henry Mayhew observed during his investigations in London's slum areas in the 1840s. 'A coat is suspended on the wall with a bell attached to it,' he wrote of one training session he witnessed, 'and the boy attempts to take the handkerchief from the pocket without the bell ringing ...'

Rising crime was an alarming feature of the Victorian age, associated as contemporary observers never failed to emphasise with the growth of the cities and industrialism. Opportunistic 'sneak thieves' roamed the streets in increasing numbers, lifting what they could from shops or unwary householders, while skilled house-breakers and pickpockets (ranging from barefoot urchins to apparent 'swells' blending easily with the company at the most elegant public meeting places) plied their respective crafts. Footpads preyed on night-time walkers, while in the European (and particularly British) country-side gangs of poachers often fought violently with the gamekeepers of wealthy landowners.

It was a serious problem, and one that the Victorians tackled with characteristic earnestness and mixed results. Certainly, severity on its own seemed no answer. Not long before Queen Victoria came to the throne a person could (theoretically, at least) be sentenced to death in Britain for the modest offence of stealing goods worth more than £2, or – strangely – for damaging Westminster Bridge in London. Transportation to Australia was another frequent punishment, applied with an equally heavy hand: Henry Mayhew once interviewed a man who had been sentenced to 14 years' transportation to Australia for passing off three forged £5 notes. The French in similar fashion used Devil's Island as a grim penal settlement.

The prisons were inhumanely squalid, with men, women and

HUNTINGDON COUNTY GAOL,
6th Jany 1877

Particulars of a Person convicted of a Crime specified in the 20th Section of the Prevention of Crimes Act, 1871.

Name and Aliases: Dennis Fairey

Description when liberated.
Age (on discharge): 9 years
Height: 3/4 9
Hair: Lt Brown
Eyes: Blue
Complexion: Pale
Where born: Ellington Hunts
Married or single: Single
Trade or occupation: School Boy
Any other distinguishing mark: None

Photograph of Prisoner.

Address at time of apprehension: Huntingdon

Whether summarily disposed of or tried by a Jury: Summarily

Place and date of conviction: Huntingdon 19th Decr 1876.

Offence for which convicted: Stealing a loaf of bread and a quantity of oranges

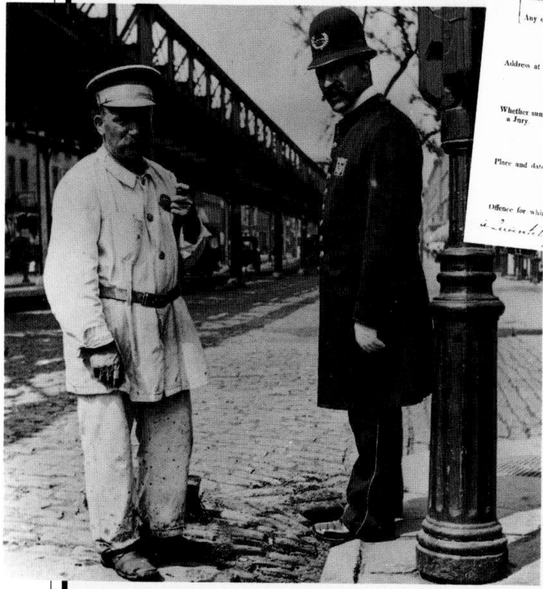

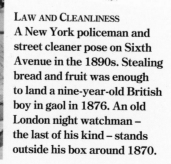

Law and Cleanliness
A New York policeman and street cleaner pose on Sixth Avenue in the 1890s. Stealing bread and fruit was enough to land a nine-year-old British boy in gaol in 1876. An old London night watchman – the last of his kind – stands outside his box around 1870.

children all herded together, regardless for the most part of the nature of their crimes, in filthy open galleries, but they were also flourishing breeding grounds for further crime, where inmates picked up new habits and skills. In the early years of the 19th century, the Americans had developed two differing systems, whose most revolutionary feature was the idea that prisoners should be kept in individual cells. According to the so-called 'separate system', prisoners remained more or less permanently in their cells (each with an exercise yard attached) and had no contact with anyone other than warders. In the 'silent system', they were given tasks to do alongside each other, but they were not to talk to each other – thus avoiding the problem of contagion in crime.

In fact, despite obvious psychological pressures, both systems represented a huge improvement on what went before and both were widely copied throughout the world. London's Pentonville Prison, opened in 1842, was modelled on the American system and included exemplary arrangements for its inmates such as heating, a water closet and basin in each cell, a table, a stool and gas lighting. It and others like it were model establishments ... the only trouble was, they did not work. Crime went on rising, and the authorities resorted to a stream of new experiments. The idea of hard labour as a deterrent – either useful labour such as road-building, or deliberately pointless tasks such as the infamous treadmill – became popular in the 1860s. The French introduced the parole system for good behaviour; the Austrians and Spanish started giving prisoners occupational training. Capital punishment remained in most places (though in 1868 the British abolished the gruesome spectacle of public hangings). In America, the National Prison Association, founded in 1870, called for a range of measures including the use of professionally trained prison officers.

In due course, many of these reforms became standard features of enlightened prison administration through much of the world – but it is doubtful if they made much of a dent in the crime figures.

As Quiet as a Prison Silence reigns in London's Brixton Prison during the 1860s. Warders keep the women prisoners busy with various sewing tasks.

Policeman's Lot A British 'bobby' practises his cutlass drill. Three prisoners at Derby gaol in the English Midlands pose for the camera of the prison's deputy governor.

THE THRASHING **An English schoolmaster has a suitably sadistic leer as he canes a pupil. Children drawn by the French cartoonist Honoré Daumier seem rather less awestruck.**

Kynnersley summoned wrong-doers to his study after assembly. They were made to pull their trousers down and kneel in front of a special block. 'The swishing', recalled the future art critic Roger Fry, one of whose duties as a senior boy at the school in the 1870s was to help to hold the offenders down, 'was given with the master's full strength and it took only two or three strokes for blood to form everywhere and it continued for 15 or 20 strokes when the wretched boy's bottom was a mass of blood.'

In countries such as Britain, many church and charity schools struggled hard to provide elementary schooling for the poor, but it was a tough fight. A shortage of qualified teachers meant that they often had to rely heavily on the rote learning of textbooks, frequently backed up again with ferocious discipline. The lack of teachers also obliged many schools throughout Europe and America to use the so-called Lancasterian system, devised by the Englishman Joseph Lancaster (another notorious beater) in the early 19th century. This involved bringing together anything between 200 and 1000 children and arranging them in neat rows in one large classroom. The teacher then instructed a group of 'monitors' or 'prefects' (one from each row) who afterwards went back to their rows to pass on what they had learnt.

Such methods were reasonably effective at imparting the basics of what the English-speaking world already knew as the 'three Rs', reading, writing and arithmetic, but they were scarcely inspiring. On the other hand, neither did they succeed in discouraging most people's faith in education. Many Victorians, of all social classes, remained determined to get the best possible schooling for their children, and were prepared to make big sacrifices. Middle-class parents saved hard, where necessary, to pay the fees for high schools (in America), lycées (in France), gymnasiums (in Germany) and public schools (in Britain) – with the British paying most, around £200 to keep one boy for a year at a public school such as Harrow in the

SCHOOLS FOR GIRLS **Germany lagged behind many other countries in providing schools for girls such as these, photographed in 1900.**

1870s, compared with the equivalent of £40 at a French lycée. Working-class parents were also prepared to go to great lengths to find the few cents or pennies needed to pay for their children. They would even do the laundry or other work for the school-master and his family in return for free lessons.

While old ways persisted, many new, usually more enlightened ideas emerged. The great New England reformer Horace Mann writing in 1844 was clearly unimpressed by the discipline of Sneyd-Kynnersley and his kind: 'What a damning sentence does a teacher pronounce upon himself, when he affirms that he has no resources in his own attachments, his own deportment, his own skill, his own character, but only in the cowhide and birch; and in the strong arm that wields them.' The highly influential Dr Thomas Arnold, headmaster of the English public school Rugby until his death in 1842, was equally crisp in demanding the highest intellectual standards from teachers.

FIRST STEPS IN PAINTING
An American publication gives children their first lessons in how to draw and paint.

On the continent of Europe, meanwhile, even more fundamental changes were taking place. In Switzerland Johann Friedrich Pestalozzi's approach was the very opposite of rote-learning, and based on the modern-sounding belief that children acquire knowledge best through their 'own investigation', that someone is 'much more truly educated through that which he does than through that which he learns' from someone else. Pestalozzi died in 1827, but his ideas were widely adopted, particularly in the German states. Other similarly influential figures included the Germans Friedrich Froebel, founder of the Kindergarten movement, and Johann Friedrich Herbart, whose achievements included systematic teacher training.

People like Pestalozzi and Froebel heralded much of modern educational theory, but even comparatively advanced Victorian schools remained firmly rooted in their time. The job of elementary schools, in the view of many people, was essentially to provide literate workers; that of the secondary schools to provide reliable administrators; and the most prestigious British and American schools concentrated on turning out 'gentlemen'. In the words of Squire Brown in the best-selling novel *Tom Brown's Schooldays* (1857), when pondering what to tell his son before sending him to Rugby: 'I

TOFFS IN TOPPERS
Tophatted pupils at Durham School in England loll with the ease that came from a privileged 'public school' education.

EYEWITNESS

THE IMPORTANCE OF BEING A GENTLEMAN

THE CONCEPT of the 'gentleman' was an essentially English invention, which left its mark on other Victorian cultures, especially the United States. Here, the Frenchman Hippolyte Taine attempts to describe it:

❛ I try to grasp the true meaning of this vital word, *a gentleman*; it is constantly cropping up, and encloses a host of ideas, all of them totally English. The key question about a man is always put in these words: "Is he a gentleman?" Similarly, with a woman it is: "Is she a lady?" … For [the English], a true gentleman is a true noble, a man fit to command, upright, impartial, capable of exposing himself and even of sacrificing himself for those he leads, not only a man of honour, but a man of conscience, in whom generous instincts have been confirmed by sound thinking, who behaves well naturally and behaves even better for his principles. – In this idealised portrait, you will recognise the model leader; add to it the typically English nuances of self-control, an unfailingly cool head, perseverance in adversity, natural seriousness, dignity of manner, the shunning of all affectation and bragging; and you will have the perfect superior who … rallies [people's] aspirations or their obedience. ❜

MILITARY BEARING Napoleon's conqueror, the old Duke of Wellington, who died in 1852, was a model for all gentlemen.

won't tell him to read his Bible, and love and serve God; if he don't do that for his mother's sake and teaching, he won't for mine … Shall I tell him to mind his work, and say he's sent to school to make himself a good scholar? Well, but he isn't sent to school for that – at any rate, not for that mainly. I don't care a straw for Greek particles … no more does his mother. What is he sent to school for? Well, partly because he wanted to go. If he'll only turn out a brave, helpful, truth-telling Englishman, and a gentleman, and a Christian, that's all I want.'

RIGHTS FOR WOMEN

In July 1848, as revolution swept across Europe, 150 women and 40 men gathered in the village of Seneca Falls in upstate New York to discuss the social, civil and religious rights of women, and came up with a new and startling declaration of independence. 'We hold these truths to be self-evident,' it announced: 'that all men and women are created equal … The history of mankind is a history of repeated injuries and usurpations on the part of man towards woman, having in direct object the establishment of an absolute tyranny over her. To prove this, let facts be submitted to the candid world.' What followed included the facts that American women (in common with women elsewhere) had no right to vote, had extremely limited rights to own property, suffered from unfair divorce legislation and many other inequalities in the eyes of the law.

For women who could not surrender themselves entirely to the Victorian cult of motherhood, life was extremely circumscribed. For most, their schooling was limited and convention forbade them from work. The Englishwoman Florence Nightingale, pioneer of modern nursing, aptly compared their position to the moon: 'the Earth never sees but one side of her; the other side remains for ever unknown.'

DEMURE IN BLACK Necessity forced some women to become governesses. Others travel in a women's car (background) on a New York train.

Philanthropy and good deeds offered a possible opening, and large numbers of well-to-do wives, keen for a field of activity beyond the home, threw themselves enthusiastically into charitable and other causes. They included the two organisers of the Seneca Falls convention, Elizabeth Cady Stanton and Lucretia Mott, both of whom were anti-slavery campaigners before they championed women's rights.

But for the less prosperous, things were a lot tougher. For middle-class women with the talent, one attractive option was writing (the English-woman Fanny Trollope, mother of the novelist Anthony, supported her family in this way). The rest were usually left with the single outlet of teaching (regardless of whether they had any aptitude for it), and this more often than not meant acting as governess to the children of a wealthier family.

It was a bleak destiny, as the Englishman Edward Carpenter recalled when looking back on his youth in the 1860s. He had six sisters and their father lived in constant 'dread lest he should not be able at his death to leave the girls a competent income'. If he had the smallest problem with his investments 'he would come down to breakfast looking a picture of misery', crying out that ' "the girls would have to go out as governesses." ' Silence and gloom would descend on the household.

To remedy this situation, one crucial right was to offer more women a decent education and thus more rewarding forms of work. Indeed, this was far more important in many women's eyes than the right to vote (which only New Zealand women succeeded in achieving for national elections during the Victorian age, in 1893). There was some opposition to the notion; the American health writer, S. Weir Mitchell, stated categorically that too much education was bad for a girl, that her 'future womanly usefulness' (by which he meant her ability to bear children and bring them up) was 'endangered by steady use of her brain'.

But, on the whole, women's campaigners made slow but steady progress. As early as 1821, the American Emma Willard had founded Troy Female Seminary in New York state, teaching a secondary curriculum that would have been wide-ranging even by the standards of many contemporary boys' schools; it included science, mathematics, geography and history as well as the inevitable classics. Then in

REMINGTON TYPE The typewriter gave rise to a new kind of female worker.

LEADING THE WAY Elizabeth Blackwell became the first woman to receive an American medical degree in 1849.

FAITH IN BUMPS

It was the shape of people's skulls that determined their personalities, according to some Victorians. Followers of the so-called science of phrenology, invented in the early 19th century by the Viennese doctor Franz Joseph Gall, believed that each different aspect of a person's thoughts and feelings – veneration, self-esteem, firmness and so on – had its own organ in the brain. By studying the 'bumps' on the head, you could tell the size of the various organs and thus the balance of somebody's personality.

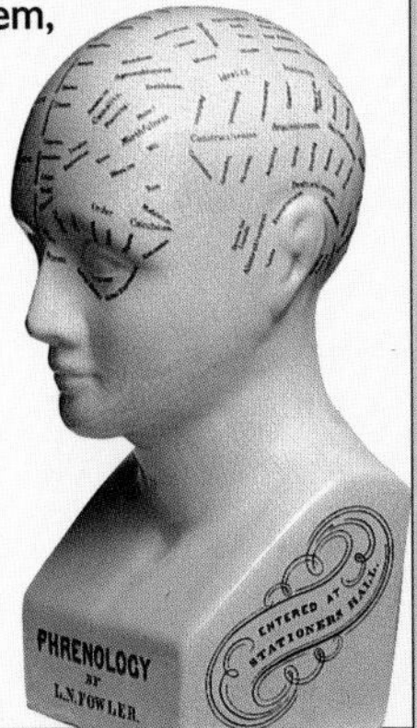

SKULL BONES A ceramic head shows the bumps.

WORKING WOMEN Life was very different for working-class girls in the coal mines around Wigan in the North of England, and for middle-class girls at the North London Collegiate School.

1833, Oberlin College in Ohio started taking female students, and after that several other institutes of higher education began to follow suit. In 1861 Vassar, the United States' first all-women college, was founded. By 1900 some 70 per cent of American colleges and universities were open to women.

In Britain, progress was more modest. Even so, Cheltenham Ladies' College and the North London Collegiate School were founded in the 1850s to give the daughters of the middle classes the chance of a modern education, and in 1869 and 1871 the women's colleges of Girton and Newnham were opened at Cambridge. France opened its universities to women in 1880, and in the same year set up the first comprehensive system of girls' lycées. The women's movement was slower off the mark in Germany. It founded the first girls' grammar schools only in 1889, and it was not until 1908 that Prussia finally opened its universities to women.

The next challenge was to prise open the professions, and here medicine was among the first to yield, though not without pressure. In 1847 the English-born American Elizabeth Blackwell, after several years of studying medicine privately and after being turned down by a number of medical schools, was finally accepted by the Geneva Medical College in New York state. Two years later she became the first modern woman to qualify as a doctor.

The world was indeed changing, and new opportunities were also opening for thousands more women. Shops and the new department stores needed more and more female workers who were numerate as well as literate, as did many factories, such as the food-processing plants of the American Mid-West or the textile mills of New England.

At the same time, the emergence of a new category of female worker was heralded in 1873 when the American gun-makers E. Remington and Sons started manufacturing a very different product: the typewriter. By the mid-1880s they were turning out 1500 typewriters a month and the new machines, along with the expansion of many businesses and institutions such as savings banks and national post offices, led to a revolution in the way offices were run. Many elementary bookkeeping and other similar tasks that had previously been carried out by young men who would later hope to rise in the management of the business were now done by female clerical staff.

Women were becoming a key part of office life, albeit with little or no prospect of ever rising to senior positions. Some observers, including many women, found even this modest development worrying – it 'is

Life in Bohemia: The World of Artists and Paupers

The death of the Parisian flower girl Lucile Louvet in April 1848 had the ring of romantic tragedy. Penniless, abandoned by a rich lover and suffering tuberculosis, the 24-year-old Lucile had a few months previously thrown herself on the mercy of another former lover, the struggling young writer Henri Murger. Through the worst of the winter weather Murger did his utmost to support himself and his dying mistress with the slender earnings of his pen. At the beginning of March, Lucile was admitted to the Hospital of Nôtre Dame de Pitié. She sank slowly, until one evening as Murger sat drinking in a café a friend broke to him the news that she had died the previous evening. In fact, it was a ghastly mistake: it was a young woman in a neighbouring bed who had died. Murger discovered the error and rushed to the hospital ... but too late. By this time Lucile really had died and her body was already being prepared for dissection by medical students.

Not all the aspiring young artists, sculptors, musicians, poets and their friends who met in the cafés and cheap hotels and lodging houses of the great Victorian capitals lived lives of such poverty as Lucile Louvet and the young Murger. But many did, especially in Paris in the decades of the mid-century – a time when the term Bohemian (previously used of gypsies) was first coined for those who, in the name of art, refused to worship at the middle-class shrines of social respectability and financial prosperity. Here, in favourite meeting places such as the Café Momus behind the Louvre, figures including the poet Charles Baudelaire, the early photographer Nadar, the writer Gérard de Nerval and the painter Gustave Courbet, would meet to drink and talk, interspersing such bouts with sessions of intense creative activity, but with rarely more than a few francs between them.

Murger later won fame and fortune with his largely autobiographical novel *Scènes de la vie de Bohême* (*Scenes from Bohemian Life*), in which among other episodes he gave Lucile the name Mimi and wrote a moving, scarcely embellished account of her death. The novel (published in 1849) was adapted for the stage and, later in the century, was transformed into Puccini's opera *La Bohème*.

Café Society **Café meeting places were central to the Bohemian life, chronicled by Henri Murger (right).**

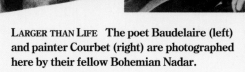

Larger than Life **The poet Baudelaire (left) and painter Courbet (right) are photographed here by their fellow Bohemian Nadar.**

Carriages at the Door **An imposing building on the Boulevard des Capucines housed Nadar's studio.**

THE AGE OF PHILANTHROPY

As industrialisation enabled fortunes to be amassed, people of conscience strove to improve the lot of the poor and homeless.

HOUSING
The Earl of Shaftesbury campaigned for better housing for inner-city workers. The homeless were housed in workhouses.

IN HIS ESSAY 'The Gospel of Wealth', Andrew Carnegie wrote of the obligation on the rich to distribute their surplus wealth for the general good. Carnegie himself had been born in a poor home in Scotland in 1835 and was almost entirely self-educated. As a child, he had emigrated with his family to the United States and worked in a cotton factory before training himself as a telegraph operator. By the age of 30, he had bought a farm in Pennsylvania that yielded oil, and he used the money from that to found an iron-and-steel company that was to make him one of the world's richest men.

Conscious of what a hard-earned education had done for him, he began to spend much of his huge fortune on building and stocking public libraries in the United States, Great Britain and elsewhere in the English-speaking world, and on founding institutes of higher learning.

BEFORE AND AFTER
A boy is rescued off the street thanks to Barnardo's Homes for destitute boys.

Among other such philanthropic businessmen was the American George Peabody, who set up a business in London in 1837. He donated the sum of £350,000 for housing schemes 'to ameliorate the condition of the poor . . . and to promote their comfort and happiness'. Similarly, the Quaker-run Cadbury chocolate company, concerned for the well-being of its workers, provided purpose-built estates for them.

Carnegie's view of the obligations of wealth seems a natural one for people of conscience in an age when the gulf between the rich and the very poor was almost unimaginably wide. Yet, so far apart did they live that it was quite possible for many rich people not to know anything about 'the prodigious misery and ignorance of the swarming masses of mankind' – as Charles Dickens described it.

In 1835 Dickens, at 23 already a successful novelist, met the hugely wealthy heiress Angela Burdett-Coutts, then 21, and the two began a friendship that was to last for life. She had already determined to devote her fortune to aiding the less fortunate, but it was Dickens who gave direction to her charity by describing for her the wretchedness of the lives of the London poor in places where no respectable Victorian woman could set foot.

He wrote to her about the Ragged Schools, where poor volunteers struggled in the most squalid conditions to bring the rudiments of education to the urchins of London's East End;

HOMES FOR WORKERS **Peabody Square, Blackfriars Road, London, was built in 1872. It was one of the blocks of model residences for working-class families that were built with donations from George Peabody.**

she provided money for better accommodation. He wrote about the lives of London's thousands of prostitutes; she paid for a special hostel for 'Fallen Women', with rules devised by Dickens, where the women would be 'tempted to virtue'. He described the filthy, overcrowded conditions in which the poor lived; she paid for slum clearance and model apartment buildings. Together, Dickens and Angela Burdett-Coutts – who became Baroness Burdett-Coutts in 1871 – at least did something to alleviate 'the misery and ignorance of the swarming masses'.

It was experience of those Ragged Schools that altered the life of Thomas Barnardo, who had come from Dublin to London in 1866 to train as a medical missionary, intending to work in China. During his training he became the superintendent of a Ragged School in the East End and saw that his help was needed nearer home. He founded the first Dr Barnardo's Home for destitute boys in 1870; it was the first such refuge to offer unlimited admission for care and education. The first for girls was started in 1876. By the time of his death he had opened more than 90 Barnardo's Homes.

Barnardo received financial help from Anthony Ashley Cooper, 7th Earl of Shaftesbury, one of the most effective British reformers of his day. He was an MP from 1826, and in 1833 became leader of the movement to legislate for a ten-hour day in textile mills (the Ten Hour Act was passed in 1847). Other achievements included an Act to exclude women, and girls and boys under the age of 13, from work in coal mines; he had received reports of boy mineworkers as young as four years old. He also pressed the government to sponsor low-cost housing projects for workers and to improve the housing that already existed. During his lifetime he was accused of ignoring the destitution of rural labourers, but his work for the poor of the industrial towns was valued highly enough to be commemorated in the statue of Eros in London's Piccadilly Circus.

SWEETENER **The Bourneville Estate was built in 1878 to provide decent-quality housing for the workers of the Cadbury chocolate company.**

EVOLUTION Darwin's theory of evolution claimed that apes and men had a common ancestor. This caused howls of outrage – as in this British cartoon playing on Darwin's own somewhat ape-like features.

a plain, simple fact that women have shown themselves naturally incompetent to fill a great many of the business positions which they have sought to occupy,' protested the American *Ladies' Home Journal* in 1900. But others were more welcoming, including the New Yorker A.D. Noyes who saw the 1890s as a turning point. 'The nineties saw ... the entry of women into the field of practical employment,' he wrote. 'It was not long before the nineties that the appearance of well-dressed young women in the stream of humanity moving up and down Wall Street and lower Broadway would occasion curious glances from male pedestrians, who considered that part of the city as their own preserve. In the nineties, women's participation in active downtown life began to be taken as a matter of course.'

SUNDAY SOLEMNITY

'I almost forgot that it was Sunday this morning,' a high-spirited 11-year-old, Caroline Richards, growing up with her grandparents in rural New York state, noted in her diary in 1854, 'and talked and laughed just as I do week days.'

Times were changing when it came to religion. In intellectual and scientific circles at least, atheism (long regarded as a kind of spiritual leprosy) was slowly becoming acceptable, and bombshells such as the British naturalist Charles Darwin's *Origin of Species* (published in 1859) took their toll – in the book Darwin first systematically expounded the theory of evolution, thus casting doubt on the traditional Christian vision of creation and provoking bitter controversy among theologians, churchmen and many devout lay people. And yet for most ordinary people the effect of these developments remained strictly limited. Indeed, it was an age of extreme energy, vision and dedication in most churches, with ardent young men and women giving up promising careers to go and serve as missionaries in far-off, sometimes unexplored lands – the Scotsman David Livingstone in Africa being one famous example. Newly founded organisations such as the Salvation Army and the Young Men's Christian Association (YMCA) brought practical as well as spiritual succour to those caught in the bleak terrain of the growing cities.

SERMON SLEEPINESS For one girl in an American church, painted in 1886, the sermon has clearly been too much.

In Catholic Europe, meanwhile, as well as among the United States' growing Catholic population – due to increased immigration from Ireland and continental Europe – the ever-more conservative Pope Pius IX sought to meet the times and impose his idea of order with a *Syllabus of Errors* published in 1864. It denounced a list of 80 'errors' ranging from civil marriage and secular education to the idea that 'the Roman Pontiff can and ought to reconcile himself and come to terms with progress, liberalism and modern civilisation'. Six years later he promulgated for the first time the notion of papal infallibility.

At the same time, the Victorian age was also for Catholics a renewed age of saints: figures such as Bernadette of Lourdes in the French Pyrenees and the delicate Carmelite nun from Normandy, Thérèse of

Lisieux, who died of tuberculosis in 1897 aged only 24. The exemplary lives of both, though short, inspired devotion among Catholics and the shrine at Lourdes (where the 14-year-old Bernadette was said to have received several visions of the Virgin Mary in 1858) became one of the most popular centres of pilgrimage among Victorian Catholics. The railway companies laid on special trains and these, combined with reports of miraculous healings among those who made the pilgrimage, drew thousands to Lourdes – between 300,000 and 400,000 a year by the turn of the century.

In devout households, this commitment to the Christian faith was inextricably woven into the texture of daily living. Grace preceded meals and the ritual of family prayers each morning,

IN DARKEST ENGLAND For the men and women of the Salvation Army, the mission field began among the poor of Britain's own cities and countryside.

A DAY IN THE LIFE OF

A LONDON STREET BEGGAR

HENRY MAYHEW'S *London Labour and the London Poor* was published in book form in the early 1850s. Here is one of his interviews, with a 13-year-old boy beggar:

'I came to London to beg, thinking I could get more there than anywhere else, hearing that London was such a good place. I begged; but sometimes wouldn't get a farthing in a day; often walking about the streets all night. I have been begging about all the time till now. I am very weak – starving to death. I never stole anything: I always kept my hands to myself. A boy wanted me to go with him to pick a gentleman's pocket. We was mates for two days, and then he asked me to go picking pockets; but I wouldn't. I know it's wrong, though I can neither read nor write. The boy asked me to do it to get into prison, as that would be better than the streets. He picked pockets to get into prison. He was starving about the streets like me. I never slept in a bed since I've been in London: I am sure I haven't: I generally slept under the dry arches in West-street, where they're building houses – I mean the arches for the cellars.'

A PENNY, KIND SIR ... A London crossing sweeper begs his dues from a passing gentleman.

Warmth on the Street
New York street 'arabs' huddle over the steam-vent of a newspaper press, to catch the warm air rising through it. A Sunday school teacher, meanwhile, stands prepared to instruct a different group of ragged charges.

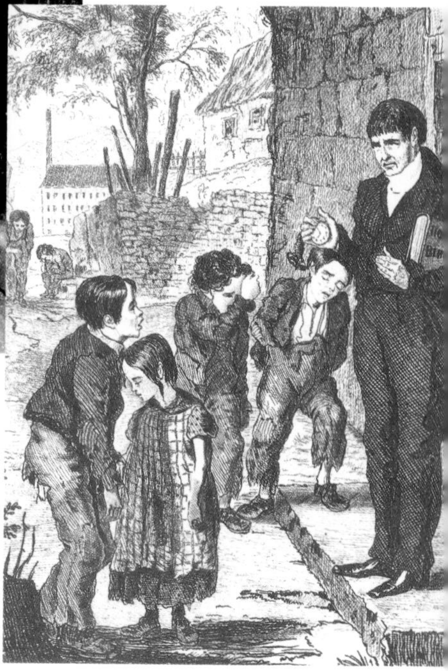

led by the father and usually with the servants in attendance, was a standard feature in middle-class homes. And things were often taken further than that. The young Caroline Richards with her grandparents in New York state had to read three chapters of the Bible before going to school and five on Sundays – which took her through the whole Bible in roughly a year. She had a prayer meeting on Wednesday evenings, Sunday school at nine in the morning followed by two church services, one in the morning and one in the evening – 'I never knew any one who liked to go to church as much as Grandmother does' is one engagingly wry comment from her diary.

As for more worldly pastimes, an acquaintance once told Caroline that her grandparents had first met at a village dance. She asked her grandmother if this was true and received a crisp reply: 'she said she never had danced since she became a professing Christian and that was more than fifty years ago.' Though by no means unattractive, the grandmother's Christianity was markedly austere, its values best summed up perhaps in the motto she passed on to Caroline – 'To be happy and live long the three grand essentials are: Be busy, love somebody and have high aims.'

Winning souls, at home as well as on foreign missions, was yet another priority. Sunday schools (originally conceived in the 18th century) remained an important and expanding part of church life and their schedules were liberally dotted with 'decision days' when children were encouraged to make definitive commitments to Christ. In the Anglo-Saxon world in particular, 'revival' missions were a regular and often spectacular feature. Here, the American Dwight L. Moody, a former businessman (in the shoe trade) who had switched to full-time Christian work when living in Chicago in 1861, was among the most inspired practitioners. Wherever he went huge crowds filled the halls that he hired with the backing of sympathetic business contacts, including the circus-owner P.T. Barnum whose New York Hippodrome was one of the venues.

Moody, who was never ordained, prided himself on his businesslike methods, but he was not afraid to tap the emotions. Sentimental songs such as *Room Among the Angels* and *One More Day's Work for*

SPREADING THE WORD Two intrepid women missionaries set out with 'native' bearers to take the Christian gospel into the heart of West Africa.

Jesus, One Less of Life for Me were a regular part of the meetings and he often wept as he preached. It was emotive, but also sincere (no breath of scandal ever touched Moody), and supremely powerful as no less a figure than the son of an Archbishop of Canterbury was ready to confess. The British writer A.C. Benson was an undergraduate at Oxford when he heard Moody on one of his visits to England. He remembered the preacher as being 'a heavy-looking, commonplace man, with a sturdy figure and no grace of look or gestures'. For all that, 'he had not spoken half-a-dozen sentences before I felt as though he and I were alone in the world.'

A DAY IN THE LIFE OF

A MISSIONARY ON THE YANGTZE RIVER

THE ENGLISH METHODIST James Hudson Taylor was among the first Protestant missionaries to penetrate inland China. He often used a boat on the Yangtze River as a base for his activities, as on this day in May 1855:

'Got off at 6 A.M., and with the tide ran up the Yangtze till we reached the Pah-miao kiang or Creek of the Eight Temples, which we entered. Here, after seeking the Lord's blessing, I landed, and was quickly surrounded by sixty or eighty people who had never seen a foreigner before. To them I preached the glad tidings of salvation before proceeding to a town called Liu-ho-chen. The road was miserably dirty, and though the distance was only two miles it seemed like four at least …

'Faint and weary, having had no food since breakfast, I arrived at Huang-king at 4 P.M., and prayed God to enable me to distribute my books to the best advantage and to give me a word to speak to the people.

'The prayer was indeed answered, and I found the place so large that had I had four times as many books with me they would have been barely enough to supply all the applicants who could read.'

Hudson Taylor got back to his boat at 8pm 'very tired and ready for dinner'.

MISSIONARY CALLING The huge population of China offered a tempting prize for Christian missionaries. The Englishman James Hudson Taylor was a pioneer among them, first arriving in China in 1854.

THE HEALING ARTS

At the start of the Victorian age, a slug of whisky was the best pain-killer a surgeon could offer his patients before an operation. By the end, anaesthetics were in widespread use, and the foundations of modern medical science had been firmly laid.

MEDICINE LIKE EDUCATION had its horror stories, of ignorance, incompetence and sheer bad practice. In a small town in late Victorian Illinois, for example, one of the doctors was called 'Dr Dictionary' – because he boasted of knowing the 'Devil's Dictionary' of swearwords off by heart. He was once called to a local woman who had accidentally sliced through an artery in her arm with some broken glass. 'Dr Dictionary', not knowing how to deal with this problem, poured a little of a favourite cure-all, tannic acid, over the wound and told the woman to lie still for a while. 'The patient, after the doctor's departure, did lie very quiet,' recalled another local doctor, Thomas Shastid. 'She lay very quiet for a very long time – until, in fact, her son, becoming suspicious, investigated her quietness and found she was going to be quiet from that time on.'

In medicine, as in so much else, the Victorian age was one of change. At the start of the age surgery was still one of the grimmest of ordeals. In the absence of anaesthetics, patients were usually strapped to the operating table and plied with opium or a spirit such as whisky to provide at least some measure of numbing relief from the appalling pain.

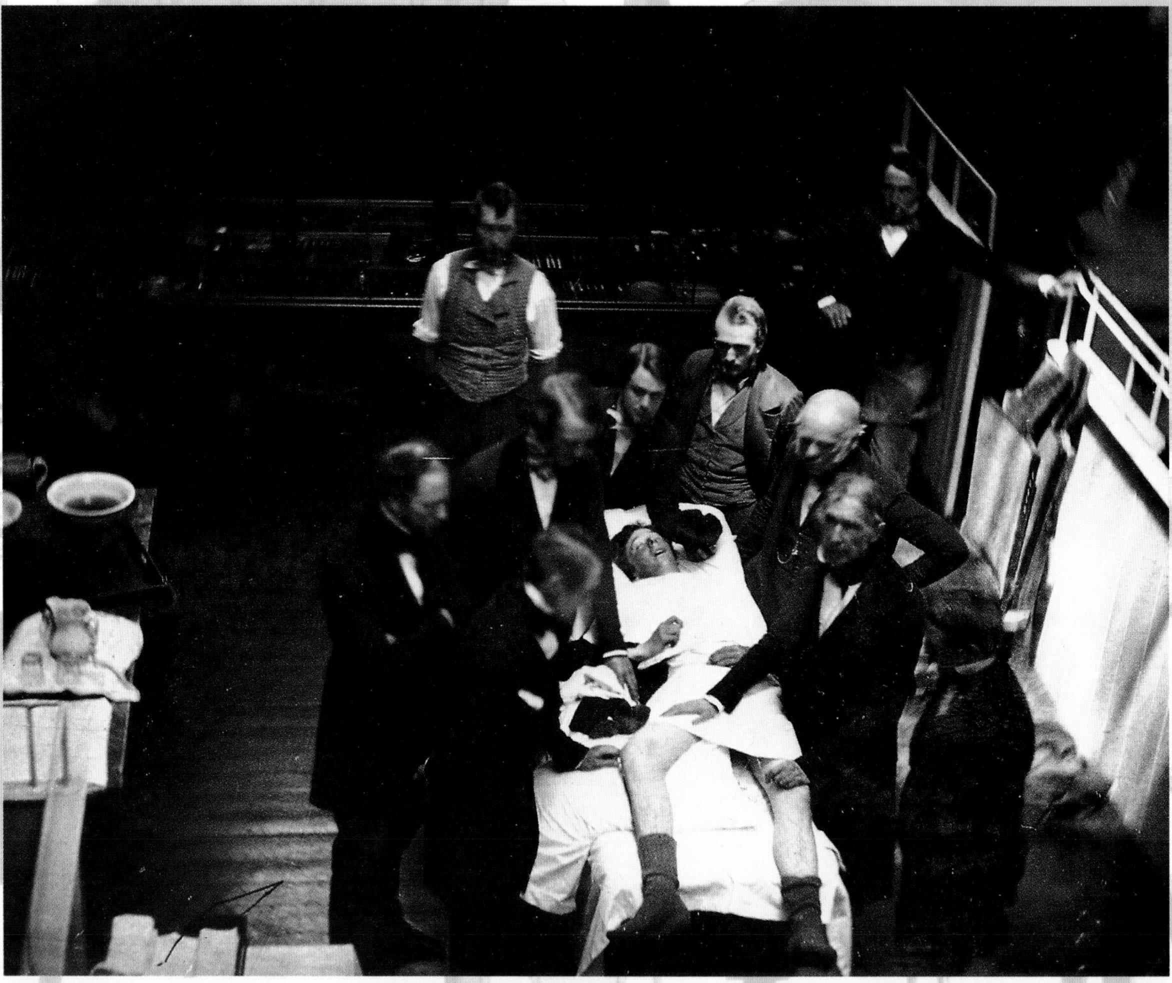

LAID OUT BY ETHER Doctors at the Massachusetts General Hospital examine a patient anaesthetised by ether. An American catalogue (background) displays an array of medical instruments.

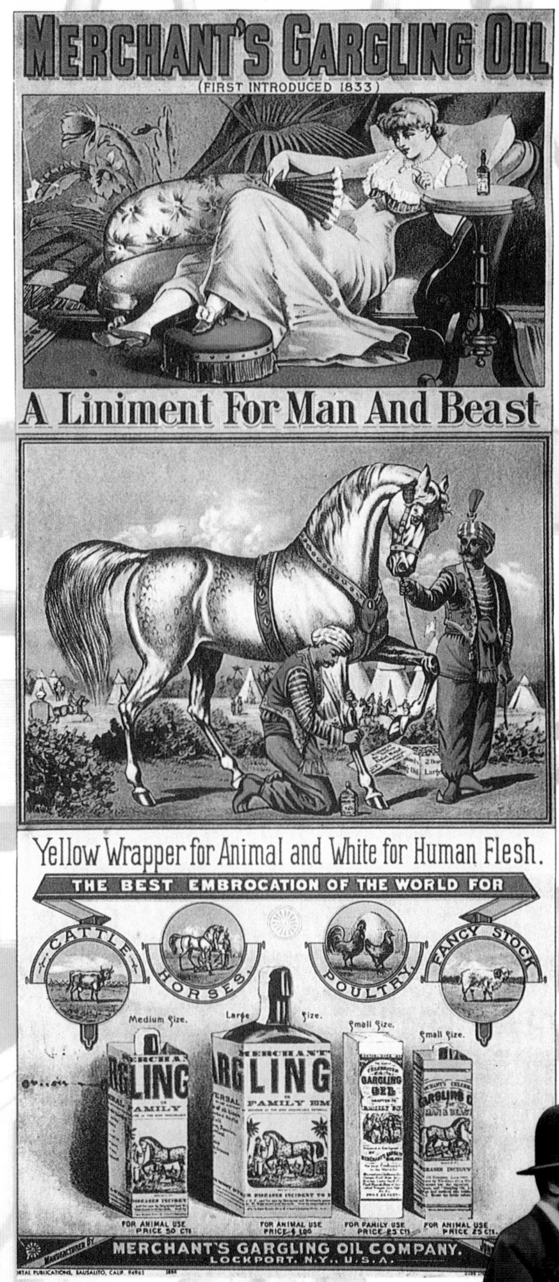

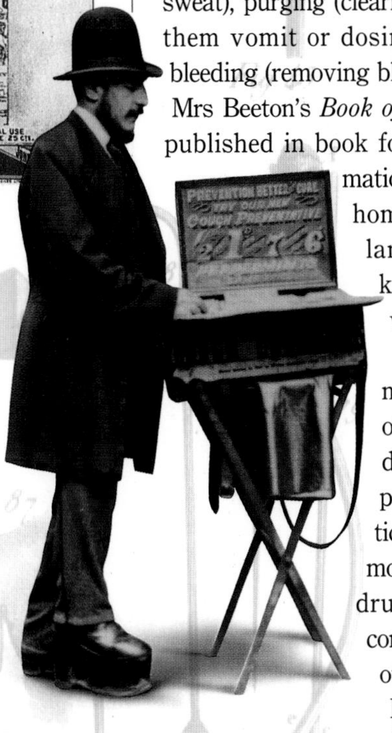

PATENT TONICS The American patent remedy Merchant's Gargling Oil – good for 'Man And Beast' – was nothing if not wide-ranging in its claims. A British 'street doctor' offers a peppermint-flavoured 'cough preventative'.

PASSING WOMEN

When the distinguished British army medical officer, Dr James Barry, died in 1865, the people preparing his body for burial had a rude shock: the doctor proved not to be a man at all, but a woman. Barry was in fact just one of a surprising number of women who negotiated social taboos that would have kept them out of work by reinventing themselves as men. They voted and married (though on what terms remains uncertain); some fought in the American Civil War; one, 'Marshall Hall', became a reasonably prominent New York politician. And most of them got away with it undetected, until death or an illness obliged them to undergo medical examination.

The surgeon then went to work as fast as he could – a good one could amputate a leg and seal the resulting wounds in three minutes. On top of that, there was the threat of gangrene. Few people yet realised the importance of hygiene, so that gangrene often spread from patient to patient at a terrifying rate, usually carried on the hands of the surgeon himself or one of the attendants. Many survived the operation only to die of gangrene later.

Nor were things much better in general medicine. Most doctors' understanding remained extremely primitive well into the Victorian age and their ways of treating illnesses as diverse as tuberculosis and common fevers relied heavily on practices that often dated back to the Middle Ages and beyond: sweating (wrapping patients in heavy blankets to make them sweat), purging (clearing out their insides by making them vomit or dosing them with laxatives) and bleeding (removing blood from them). Works such as Mrs Beeton's *Book of Household Management*, first published in book form in 1861, even gave information on how to bleed someone at home: you opened a vein with a lancet (a short-bladed surgical knife) and then let the required volume of blood drip out.

When it came to prescribing medicines, the picture was equally obscure. Few early Victorian doctors had any concept of using particular medicines for particular illnesses. On the contrary, most felt that if a drug or blend of drugs appeared to work for one condition, then why not for all the others? In London, the famous St Bartholomew's Hospital, for

HEALTH AND HYGIENE

Regular epidemics were a terrifying feature of Victorian life, and inspired numerous campaigns to improve public hygiene.

EPIDEMICS were a blight that no Victorian could safely ignore, least of all in the growing cities. Cholera, typhus, typhoid, yellow fever, diphtheria and smallpox, all were regular scourges, taking their tolls in hundreds or even thousands of lives; and few families escaped.

Fortunately, the fight against these diseases was among the most determined and, in the end, successful of Victorian medical campaigns. Even before people understood the causes of disease, certain factors were becoming clear: that there was more disease (and poor health generally) in the cities than in the countryside, and that there was a direct link between disease, on the one hand, and the filth of the poorest city areas, on the other. It was obviously a public, not simply a private, problem and under the leadership of figures such as John Griscom and Lemuel Shattuck in the United States, Edwin Chadwick in Britain and Rudolf Virchow in Prussia, campaigners battled vigorously for a new approach. A report of the British Poor Law Commission in 1838 argued the case for tackling it on a community basis, and ten years later the British Parliament responded by setting up a Board of Health to promote public hygiene. In 1865, the

COAL FOR FREE Coal from the city authorities helped to warm the poor in New York.

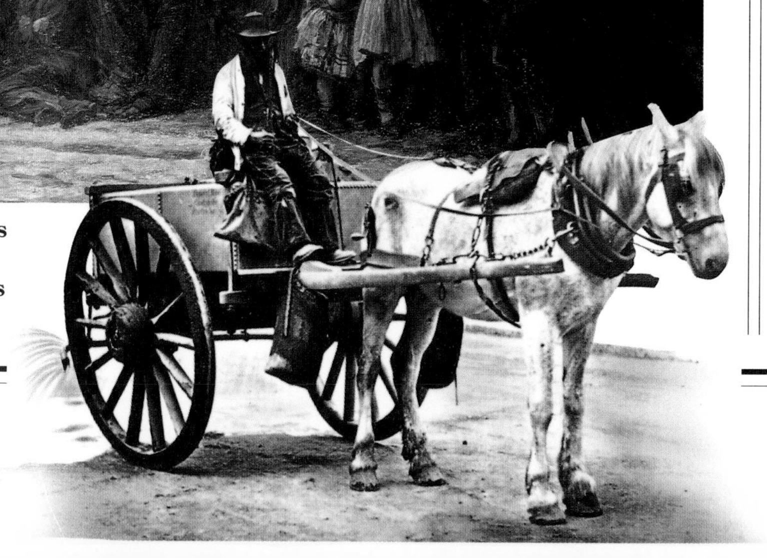

OUT PATIENTS A painting by Luke Fildes shows the poor and sick queuing for the out-patients ward of a London hospital. A water-cart sprays the London streets to help to keep them clean.

MON DIEU, A WASHSTAND!
British people poked fun – as in this cartoon – at foreigners' supposed lack of cleanliness. In London, however, pumps such as this were the only source of water for large areas.

university of Munich established the world's first chair of experimental hygiene. A year later New York City followed the British example by creating a public health board. Many city authorities built new sewers and drains, improved water supplies and organised efficient rubbish collection.

The results were impressive. The English town of Macclesfield, for example, had a mortality rate of 42 per thousand in 1847. The following year it began improving its sanitation, and 10 years later the mortality rate had almost halved to 26 per thousand. But this dealt with only one part of the issue. The problem of contagion and its causes remained, and here progress was at first patchy. In the case of cholera, for instance, one significant breakthrough came in 1855 when the London doctor John Snow published findings made during an outbreak the previous year. He contended – correctly – that the cholera infection was water-borne, citing among other cases that of London's Broad Street. He had established that all the infected households in one area drew their water from the Broad Street pump; when its handle was removed, the outbreak in that area ceased.

Although such theories were treated with some scepticism at the time, they eventually proved their worth, and across the Atlantic the building of the Panama Canal was evidence of their importance. In 1900 the Americans Walter Reed and James Carroll identified the *Aedes Aegypti* mosquito as the carrier of yellow fever. In Panama, plagued by the disease, the authorities set about eliminating the mosquito, with dramatic results: the death rate among the canal workers plunged from 176 per thousand to just six.

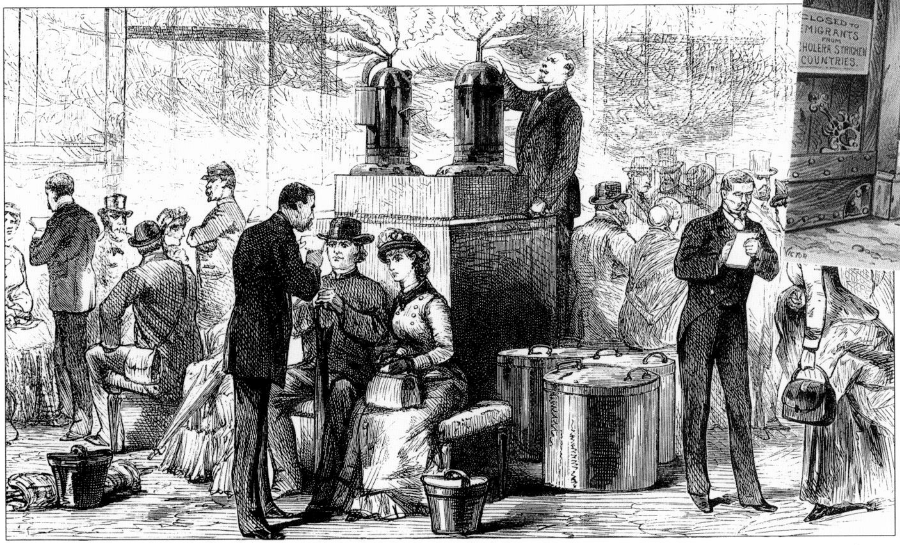

KILLER CHOLERA
Passengers are fumigated at a French railway station to stop the spread of cholera. An American cartoon plays on the fear of cholera being brought in by immigrants.

PIONEERS Florence Nightingale does her rounds of a military hospital during the Crimean War. The French chemist Louis Pasteur is shown in his laboratory.

CHAMPION NURSE Dorothea Dix helped to transform American nursing methods. She also championed better treatment for the mentally ill.

GERMAN GENIUS Robert Koch isolated the bacilli causing tuberculosis and cholera, and was a key pioneer in the science of bacteriology.

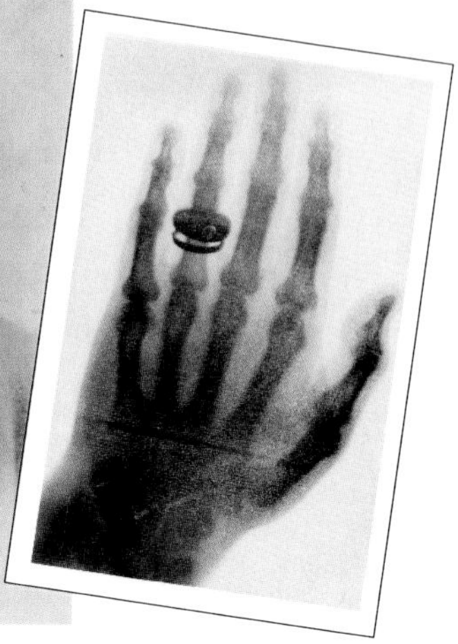

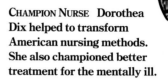

THE REVEALING X-RAY The German Wilhelm Conrad Röntgen discovered X-rays in 1895. His wife's rings stand out clearly in this early X-ray photograph.

example, had a large brown jug in its out-patients' department containing a brew of various purgatives, cod-liver oil, iron and other substances (including one now used against worms) with which patients were almost uniformly dosed, whatever their ailment. Ordinary people, meanwhile, throughout the Victorian age put huge faith in numerous cure-all 'patent' medicines, advertised in the press (often with a doctor's endorsement) or sold by wandering quacks. These were harmless enough in some cases, such as the British 'Beecham's pills', a simple mix of laxatives. But others were based almost entirely on opium or alcohol – such as the massively selling 'Lydia E. Pinkham's Vegetable Compound' in the United States, advertised as 'the greatest remedy in the world'.

In 1860 the New England doctor and man-of-letters Oliver Wendell Holmes put the case against early Victorian medicine trenchantly: 'I firmly believe that if the whole materia medica, *as now used*, could be sunk to the bottom of the sea, it would be all the better for mankind, – and all the worse for the fishes.' Many people would undoubtedly have agreed. Public faith in the medical profession had sunk extremely low and this was leading many (not just among the poor, who had rarely been in the habit of consulting expensive doctors anyway) to turn to various alternative healers: from homeopaths to the traditional 'wise women', bone-setters and urine healers of the countryside.

The Victorian Way of Death

Disease and the dangers of childbirth meant that death called all too frequently at Victorian homes, with the result that the procedures surrounding it were well oiled and clearly established. Blinds kept permanently lowered in the windows were the first sign to the outside world that a family had suffered a bereavement. The head of the family would then send black-bordered notes to inform relatives and close friends, and a day for the funeral would be fixed with the undertakers.

On that day, the mourners would gather first at the dead person's home where, in many cases, the undertakers issued them with special black gloves, hatbands and scarves. The men – but not usually the women – would then proceed to the church and cemetery. In wealthier circles this would take the form of a carriage procession, headed by the carriages of the immediate family, followed by those of more distant relatives and friends, with the rear brought up by a succession of empty carriages belonging to those unable to attend but wishing to show their respect to the memory of the deceased. After that came a period of mourning, in which men wore only black suits and neckties and women black dresses of simple materials such as stuff (a woollen fabric) or crepe.

It all involved a rigid set of formalities which bereaved people ignored at their social peril. But that did not imply a lack of feeling. On the contrary, many Victorians, lacking the comparative fatalism of earlier generations, seemed to feel the poignancy of death, like that of so many other areas of existence, with an exceptional intensity.

One result was the popularity of devices – often macabre-seeming to modern eyes – that somehow helped them to cope with their grief: lying in bed at night like Queen Victoria with a plaster cast of a dead spouse's hand; wearing jewellery made from the plaited hair of the beloved; building elaborate tombs or memorials; or even making a desperate attempt to contact the departed soul by using the services of a spiritualist medium.

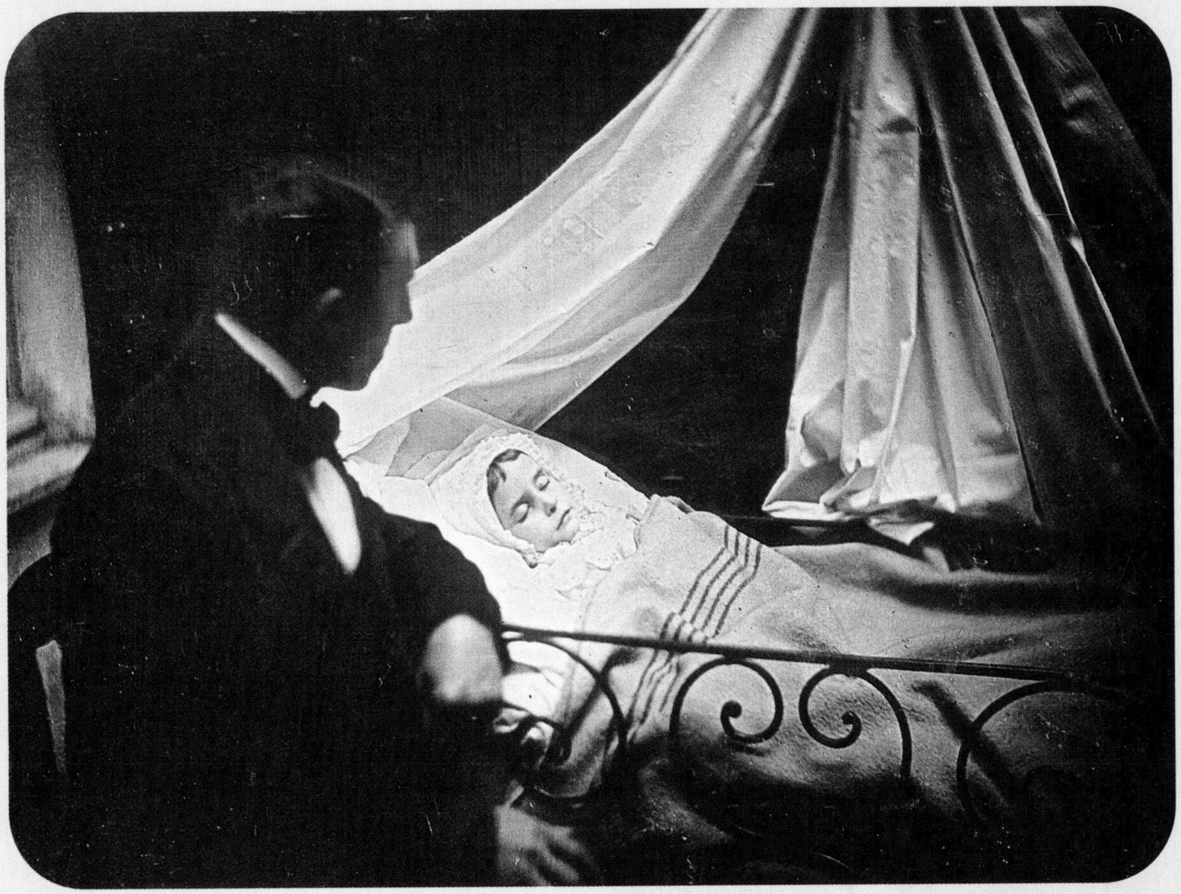

Eternal Sleep **A dead child photographed before burial, her grieving father sitting beside her.**

On the other hand, things were changing for the better. The Victorian revolution in medicine was well under way, transforming standards of treatment. As early as October 1846, the American dental surgeon William Thomas Morton had first successfully demonstrated the use of ether as an anaesthetic at the Massachusetts General Hospital. A year later in Scotland, James Young Simpson, professor of midwifery at Edinburgh University, had demonstrated chloroform for the same purpose.

The French chemist Louis Pasteur started to uncover the role of micro-organisms (bacteria, viruses and so on) in spreading disease, and building on these discoveries his friend Joseph Lister, professor of surgery at Glasgow, developed the science of antiseptics. In Germany, another contemporary, Robert Koch, isolated the micro-organisms causing diseases such as tuberculosis (or consumption).

Much else was changing. Thanks to the efforts of Florence Nightingale in England and her near-contemporary Dorothea Dix in America, nursing was becoming a career for properly qualified professional women, with the result that hospitals were being transformed – they would no longer be seen as places where poor people went to die, but where people of most classes went to recover. Among physicians, where most in the past had focussed on their patients' histories (sometimes carrying out examinations entirely by post), some now began to give more thorough physical examinations, employing the techniques of 'palpation' (feeling the patient's body) and 'percussion' (tapping it and listening for resonances inside). In 1895, the German Wilhelm Conrad Röntgen first demonstrated the medical use of the X-ray machine, and four years later the Bayer company, also in Germany, started selling the first aspirins. In Vienna, at the same time, Sigmund Freud was breaking new ground as he delved into the mysteries of the subconscious.

Anaesthetics and the new antiseptic techniques meant that surgeons, such as the much-respected American William Stewart Halsted, Professor of Surgery at the new Johns Hopkins Medical School in Baltimore, were able to carry out operations such as the removal of cancerous growths from the stomach. Physicians' powers of diagnosis improved considerably and with them popular faith in their abilities (tighter regulation of doctors also helped).

LIFE AT THE SURGERY
A doctor takes the pulse of a young lady patient in a painting by the British artist Arthur Miles.
A four-wheeled buggy stands ready outside the door of an Australian doctor's home.

Many of the terrifying epidemics that regularly afflicted even the most advanced Victorian countries were slowly being brought under control. But for more ordinary ailments doctors were still frustrated – by the lack of suitable drugs, above all. Late Victorian patients displayed a growing, at times almost blind, faith in their doctors' healing powers, as the American Arthur Hertzler recalled: 'I once examined an old lady's chest with my stethoscope, an instrument she had never seen and mistook for a means of treatment. After taking a few deep breaths she enthusiastically declared that she already felt greatly relieved ...' But good doctors, at least, were only too aware of their limits.

The Victorians at Play

The modern holiday was, to a large extent, a Victorian invention. It was the Victorians who acquired the habit of regular seaside breaks and who started taking package holidays abroad. They were also keen sportspeople who developed and codified a range of spectator sports, from baseball to cricket to football in all its various forms. Stage shows, from the solemnity of Shakespeare to the high-kicking fun of vaudeville, had their own numerous fans.

PLEASURES AND PASTIMES

The industrial timetable gradually imposed its own patterns of work and play. These resulted in the end of many old religious holidays and the introduction of new secular ones. The railways also had their effect, in allowing ordinary people to take cheap trips to the seaside and elsewhere.

THE THEATRE was among the most popular of Victorian entertainments. It could arouse the highest passions ... as in New York, on May 10, 1849. On that night, a long-standing feud between two highly esteemed Shakespearean actors – the Englishman William Charles Macready and the American Edwin Forrest – ended with 21 people shot dead and 33 wounded.

Macready, a regular visitor to America, was to appear as Macbeth at the Astor Place Opera House. Forrest's partisans, however, were far from happy. Already, three evenings earlier, they had pelted the English actor off the stage with a barrage of apples, eggs and chairs. On the 10th, they posted stickers around New York appealing to the nationalist feelings of their countrymen. 'Workingmen, shall Americans or English rule in this city?' the posters read. 'The crew of the British steamer have threatened all Americans who shall dare to express their opinion this night at the ENGLISH AUTOCRATIC *Opera House!* We advocate no violence, but a free expression of opinion to all public men. WASHINGTON FOREVER! Stand by your *Lawful Rights!*'

There was violence, however. The performance was interrupted by hecklers inside the theatre and stone-throwing crowds (estimated at several thousand strong) outside. Mounted police and militiamen were called and opened fire on the mob. Macready was lucky to escape with his life. He slipped out of the theatre in disguise and the next day made his way to Boston, and caught the next steamer back home to England.

The Victorians definitely took their entertainments seriously. One of the consequences of industrialisation

A DAY IN THE LIFE OF

A STROLLING PLAYER IN AMERICA

THE NEW YORK actor-manager Harry Watkins started his working life in the middle of the 19th century as a teenage regimental fife-player, but later switched successfully to the similarly vagabond life of the stage:

'Thursday 31st [*December*], *1846.* Last day of the Old Year. It leaves me in a flourishing state, not in the way of money but professionally speaking. Four months ago, I was playing small business in Louisville [Kentucky], servants, delivering messages, stage filler, etc. Now I am [in New Orleans] acting respectable parts, to the mortification of others who have been on the stage for ten years, and have to put up with subordinate parts to me, and I've only been in the profession for 14 months. They growl about it, but I don't mind. Played Hilairion in "Giselle," a pantomine part, being the first of its kind I ever played. I got along with it to my own satisfaction, and apparently to that of the audience ...

'Thursday 14th [*January, 1847*]. Today I am 22 and I've learned many hard lessons. I am poor in a hard profession, without friends to assist me, entirely dependent on my own exertions. Hoping for the best I shall take whatever comes ...'

VAGABONDS Young actors and entertainers were rarely able to stay long in one place.

High Brow, Low Brow **Working-class London children enjoy ice creams from a 'hokey-pokey' stall. Ladies and gentlemen enjoy the more refined pleasures of an art exhibition.**

and the growth of the cities was the dislocation of old communities and their traditional patterns of work, play and holiday. Old sports, such as cock-fighting and bear and bull-baiting, fell slowly out of favour, or were banned in parts of northern Europe and America, to be replaced by newly popular spectator sports, above all the various ball games: Association football, Rugby and American football, baseball, cricket and others. In a different area, vaudeville and music hall evolved from earlier bar-room or café entertainments, and in the last decade of Victoria's reign the first short, flickering motion pictures joined the bill.

The Coming of the Holiday

Holidays were transformed in the early years of the Industrial Revolution in most countries. Vast numbers of workers found themselves labouring inhumanly long hours with only irregular bouts of freedom when (to the exasperation of their employers) they simply took time off as it pleased them – to attend a local fair or sporting event, perhaps, or to maintain the tradition of 'Saint' or 'Blue' Monday, by which they took the day off to recover from the carousings of Sunday. This changed significantly over the course of the Victorian age. A key event in Britain was the Factory Act of 1850 which obliged textile mills to close at 2pm on Saturdays: thus was born the 'English week' of five-and-a-half days, which was rapidly copied elsewhere. In Protestant and some Roman Catholic countries, the number of religious holidays was often reduced, to be replaced in part by secular ones, such as the four British 'bank holidays', introduced at first for bank employees in 1871.

In Britain, employers took advantage of the annual 'wakes' festivities (religious celebrations commemorating the dedication of the local church) to shut down their factories for maintenance work. Their employees thus found themselves with seven days' official (though unpaid) holiday. In the 1870s, several British railway companies and government departments went a step further and gave their clerks a week's paid holiday each year. Again the pattern was repeated elsewhere, though it was far from universal. The Americans were most advanced in this respect, and by the end of the century one or even two weeks' annual paid vacation was well established in many businesses. Parisian department stores, on the other hand, had no such traditions. There, the custom was for employees to have one day's unpaid leave each year (on top of the various public and religious holidays, of course) – or, if they preferred, they could save up over six years and take a full week.

Free time combined with improved means of transport encouraged leisure. As early as the 1820s,

Summer's Rest **London's grime seems a world away for picnickers on Hampstead Heath.**

Beside the Seaside

As travel became easier and annual holidays more common, resorts developed to cater for all tastes and interests.

New Pastures The railways opened up new areas, such as the Alps, to tourists. The classical charms of Greece (left) appealed to others.

Most holiday resorts grew up for reasons of health. In the 18th century, well-to-do people 'took the waters' at spas, some of which, such as the English resort of Bath, Vichy in France, Baden-Baden in Germany and Marienbad (now in the Czech Republic), had been known for their waters since Roman times. Apart from the supposedly healthful properties of the spa water, these were elegant resorts, where the fashionable came to view each others' clothes and seek suitable marriage partners for their children. Bath had its heyday in the late 18th and early 19th centuries, but the Continental spas continued to flourish throughout the 19th century, adding casinos, formal gardens and elegant hotels to their attractions.

From the mid-18th century, doctors such as the Englishmen Richard Russell in Brighton and William Hutton in Blackpool had been advocating the therapeutic powers of seawater, both to drink and to bathe in. Their message bore fruit as seaside resorts supplemented or replaced the inland spas.

Fashionable seaside resorts grew up from former fishing villages on all the coasts of Europe. Deauville in Normandy was founded as a resort by the Duc de Mornay in 1866; while Biarritz, on France's Atlantic coast, rose to prominence after Napoleon III went there in 1854. At Nice, on the Riviera, the famous Promenade des Anglais was built by the English community there in 1822. Well-to-do Russians wintered elegantly at Yalta on the Black Sea or went further afield to the German spas, Monte Carlo or the Lido at Venice.

City-dwellers in Europe and North America lacked the good fortune of Australians in having magnificent beaches such as Sydney's Bondi on their doorsteps. It was cheap public transport in the shape of trains and steamboats that created the popular holiday resorts of Europe and the Eastern United States from the 1840s onwards. The third-class railway fare to Brighton was only 4s 2d in 1844, and by 1859 73,000 people went there in a single week. Blackpool, formerly a small

Sightseeing An early charabanc transports holiday-makers on the Isle of Man. People flocking to the new resorts needed to be ferried about in large numbers.

BATHING BELLES For bathing, women wore serge bloomers concealed by thick skirts. Above: On the beach it was thought improper to be seen in a bathing costume, and men, women and children dressed in only slightly less formal versions of their everyday attire.

watering place, grew as a resort for people from the industrial towns of Lancashire. Atlantic City, in New Jersey, became a major resort after a consortium of its citizens persuaded the Camden and Atlantic Railroad to make its eastern terminus there; its first boardwalk was built in 1870 and it introduced the rolling 'bath' chair, for conveying less nimble holidaymakers, in 1884. Germans began to flock to the bracing pleasures of the North Frisian islands, such as Sylt.

Some of the pleasures of 19th-century seaside resorts resembled those of today. Amusement piers were built at most of them; bands and minstrel shows entertained the visitors; vendors sold whelks or eels or saltwater taffy [toffee]. But bathing itself was a discreet activity, conducted from bathing machines that were drawn into the sea by horses, and men's and women's bathing areas were strictly segregated.

The smart coastal resorts of continental Europe offered splendid hotel accommodation, but food and lodgings at the popular resorts in Britain were notoriously bad, and often overcrowded. Most people preferred to rent houses or apartments, rather than staying at hotels or boarding-houses.

HOLIDAY PURSUITS Outdoor holidays spent walking and enjoying stunning scenery were popular, although some people preferred to try their luck in the casinos of fashionable resorts.

ON THE SANDS **Americans pose in a variety of seaside garb. A German girl snuggles up against the wind.**

many London clerks and artisans had picked up the habit of taking Sunday steamer trips down the Thames to Gravesend or Margate. By the 1840s the railways were making such excursions increasingly common. In the North of England, the Lancashire and Yorkshire Railway offered cheap Sunday return fares to the inhabitants of the big industrial cities. 'Sea Bathing for the Working Classes ...' it announced in its advertisements, though it was careful to add that 'Parties availing themselves of these trains will be enabled to bath and refresh themselves in ample time to attend a Place of Worship.'

Sea bathing was enjoyed with no less gusto by wealthy vacationers such as those at one of America's most exclusive resorts, Newport, Rhode Island. 'I do not believe that Franconi's Hippodrome [a popular New York variety theatre] ever presents a gayer, more grotesque and animated scene than I witnessed,' recorded one visitor in 1853. 'Hundreds of bathers, clad in garments of every shape and color – green, blue, orange and white – were gaily disporting themselves before me, and within a few yards of my window. The blooming girl, the matronized yet blushing maiden, the dignified mamma, were all playing, dancing, romping, and shouting together, as if they were alive with one feeling.'

In fact, it was the upper classes in the 18th century who first discovered the pleasures – as well as the supposed medical benefits – of sea bathing at English resorts such as Brighton, and class distinctions

SEASIDE FROLICS **German bathers splash lustily at the popular resort of Binz on the Baltic island of Rügen.**

BEACH BEAUTIES A line of unmarried girls have eyes only for a dandified male promenader out with his dog.

remained crucial in the Victorian age. On the one hand were 'popular' resorts with definite working-class appeal, such as Coney Island in the United States, and Blackpool in Britain; on the other were middle or upper-class resorts such as Newport in America, Bournemouth in England and Deauville in France. And each had its distinctive range of entertainment. At Coney Island these included shooting galleries, freak shows, dance halls and, after 1897, the delights of Steeplechase Park with attractions such as the Giant See-Saw. There were also minstrel and Punch and Judy shows, donkey or goat-carriage rides for the children, sailing trips and perhaps a German oompah band. At middle-class resorts, by contrast, (and these remained the majority throughout the Victorian age), things were a good deal more restrained. Visitors might enjoy donkey rides and music from the bandstand, but the emphasis was on more sedate and often 'improving' pleasures, such as exercise on the promenade or pier, visits to botanical gardens, trips to see local places of geological or fossil interest, or maybe a relaxing game of golf.

Indeed, combining health and self-improvement with pleasure loomed large in middle and upper-class holidaying. Spas boomed, notably the many German resorts such as Baden-Baden and others such as Vichy in France and Saratoga Springs in New York state. They combined supposedly health-restoring mineral waters with the more worldly delights of fashionable society, gambling, horse-racing and so on. Mountain resorts were also popular, as were sanatoriums for those who were ill, including places such as Battle Creek in Michigan which was run by the ferociously vegetarian Dr James Harvey Kellogg.

Travel abroad came within the reach of more members of the middle classes, especially the British and Americans. In the 1850s, the American writer Nathaniel Hawthorne, then serving as consul in Liverpool (the British destination of most transatlantic steamers), noted his young countrymen making a European tour in the gap between finishing education and starting work: 'It seemed to me that nothing was more common for a young American than deliberately to spend all his resources in an aesthetic peregrination about Europe, returning with pockets nearly empty to begin the world in earnest.' This travel habit spread to other age groups, the whole process made considerably easier for both American and British tourists by the English former woodworker and keen Baptist temperance campaigner, Thomas Cook. In 1841 Cook negotiated a deal with railway companies to allow 500 teetotal workers to travel at cheap rates to a temperance rally in the British Midlands, and laid the

COOK AT POMPEII A party of Cook's tourists are snapped amidst the ruins of Pompeii in 1868.

Toys and Games

Children's toys and games increased in variety and ingenuity throughout the Victorian age.

VICTORIAN CHILDREN were lucky to grow up in an age of technology. Ingenious mechanical toys, miniature replicas of the marvels of industry, a greater range of dolls – all made their way into nurseries in growing numbers and added to the fun of childhood. The Germans led the way in cheaper, machine-made toys. At the same time, there was the usual concern to combine pleasure with improvement. Magic lantern shows illustrated the stories of the Bible (especially at Christmas time) or scenes from the growing body of 'improving' children's classics.

MAGIC SLIDE SHOWS Magic lanterns could project hand-coloured scenes from romance and myth.

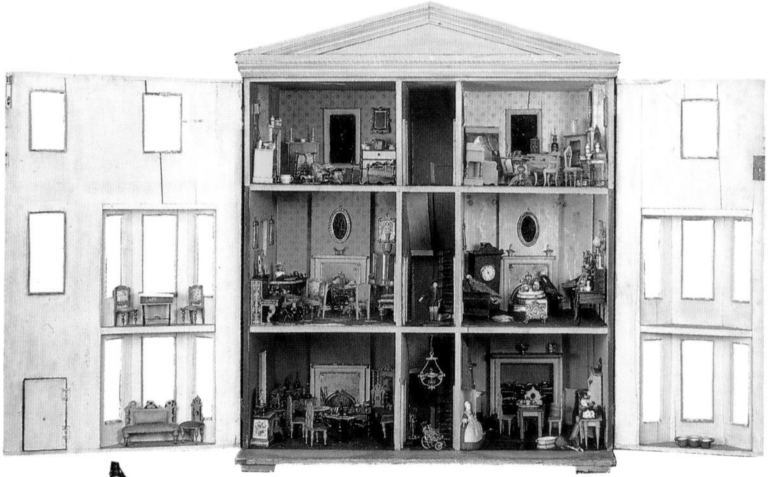

FIT FOR A QUEEN The Duchess of Teck gave this dolls' house to her daughter, Princess Mary, later to marry Queen Victoria's grandson, the future George V.

DRESSED UP TO THE NINES Beautifully dressed French dolls were popular, such as this one from around 1870.

TODDLER SAILORS For city children, a favourite treat was a trip to the nearest park. There, the fun might include a chance to sail model boats on a pond.

HOME AT THE RANGE A miniature range could furnish a dolls' house kitchen. It came complete with matching pots and pans, all made from the finest copper.

CLOCKWORK PIANO PLAYING This American doll sat at a piano which played a selection of tunes.

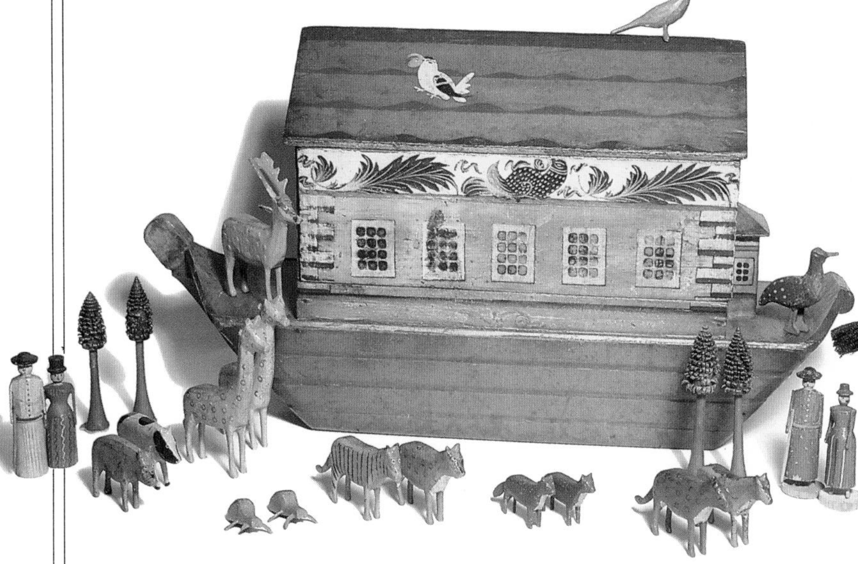

SPLENDID IN RED An English doll, with the usual porcelain face, is richly dressed in velvety red.

TOYS FOR THE SABBATH Playing with a Noah's Ark was considered suitable fun for Sundays. The carved and painted animals could be endlessly arranged and rearranged. Some, such as this, had figures for Noah and his family.

MECHANICAL WONDERS An American catalogue offers various clockwork toys, including a wind-up 'Visiting Statesman'.

LADY ROCKER No nursery was complete without its rocking horse. This American girl is riding side-saddle, in truly ladylike fashion.

MOVING PICTURES A whirl of the 'zoetrope' projected a succession of pictures to give the impression of movement.

RAILROAD RIDERS The Germans were among the first to make toy train sets.

Opening New Worlds: the Bicycle

The impact of the bicycle in the last decade of the Victorian age was enormous. The 'vehicle of the healthful happiness', as one manufacturer advertised it, gave thousands of young people a new freedom and mobility. Though by no means cheap – in France, a bicycle cost around 500 francs (three months' salary for a schoolteacher) – it was still less expensive and difficult to maintain than a horse. It also had a notable effect on fashion. 'A few years ago,' observed one American, 'no woman would dare venture in the street with a skirt that stopped above her ankles ... [The bicycle] has given to all American womankind the liberty of dress for which reformers have been sighing for generations.'

The bicycle dated, in fact, from 1839 near the start of Victoria's reign, when the Scottish blacksmith Kirkpatrick Macmillan devised a primitive machine of wood and iron propelled by two foot-driven cranks. This was later refined by the French father-and-son team of Pierre and Ernest Michaux whose 'velocipedes' (or 'boneshakers') set off a brief craze in the 1860s. In the 1870s the Englishman James Starley produced the heavy and somewhat precarious 'ordinary' (or 'penny-farthing', after the largest and smallest British coins), to be followed by his nephew John who in 1885 started manufacturing the considerably lighter and faster Rover 'safety bicycle'. This at last was the bicycle in its modern form. When the Belfast vet John Boyd Dunlop developed the pneumatic tyre (instead of solid rubber ones) in 1888, cycling clubs sprang up all over the Victorian world, and by the late 1890s a million bicycles were being manufactured each year in the United States alone.

In 1892 the tyre manufacturers Michelin sponsored a long-distance race from Paris to their headquarters at Clermont-Ferrand (the first Tour de France was held in 1903). And almost everywhere cycle touring became a popular summertime pursuit. Every Sunday trains would off-load thousands of young cyclists from the cities eager to explore the lanes and byways of the country-side. In France, in 1900, Michelin produced the first of its touring guides and maps.

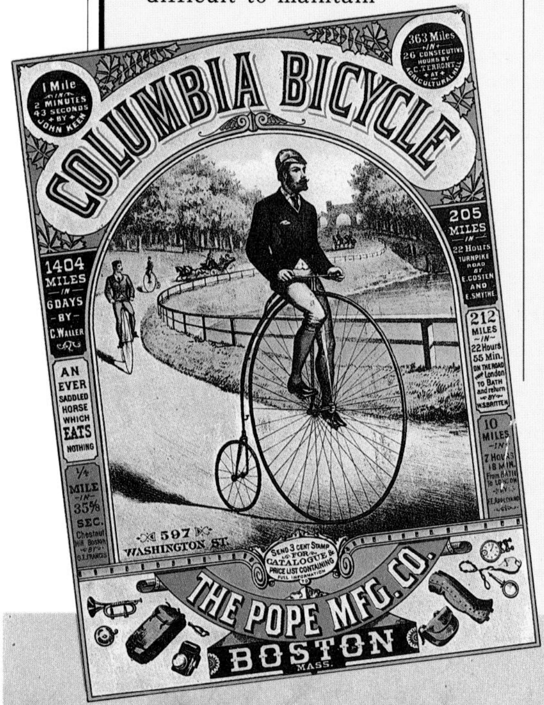

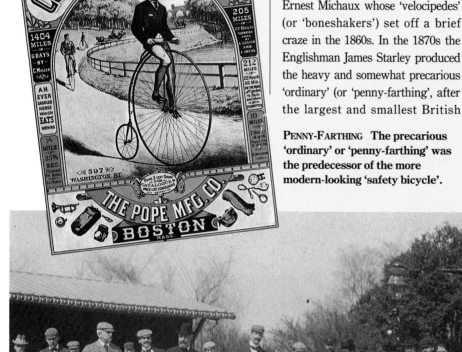

Penny-Farthing The precarious 'ordinary' or 'penny-farthing' was the predecessor of the more modern-looking 'safety bicycle'.

A Day Out Members of a New York bicycling club gather at the start of a healthy day on the road.

SPORT FOR ALL The fad for lawn tennis offered middle-class women a new sporting freedom from the 1870s onwards. Golf was a later addition to their repertoire. Baseball, however, remained a strictly male preserve.

foundations of the modern package holiday. Ten years later he was organising cheap fares for working people wishing to visit the Great Exhibition in London. Four years after that, the Paris International Exhibition saw him working on the Continent, organising similar fares for now mainly middle-class travellers to the French capital. For the rest of the 1850s he expanded the international side of his business, arranging and leading tours of sightseers to France, Switzerland and Italy. His son John, who took over in 1865, expanded the business, introducing such exotic items as Nile cruises. Inevitably, more enterprising travellers were scornful of Cook's tourists, one American in 1890 referring to that 'harbor of the intellectually destitute – Cook's nearest office ...' But the same observer was also obliged to admit the convenience of such a place – 'where a highly competent and obliging official maps out the whole [holiday], counts the cost, and assures [the travellers] that he will see them safely through the whole adventure'.

SPORT COMES OF AGE

If the Cook's tour was a symbol of the comfort and confidence of middle-class living, the ever-growing array of sports was no less representative of the Victorian age. As Mark Twain said of his country's most popular ballgame: 'Baseball is the very symbol, the outward and visible expression of the drive and push and rush and struggle of the raging, tearing, booming nineteenth century.'

The history of baseball was typical of a number of the sports that emerged during Queen Victoria's reign. Originally a rough-and-ready game with few set rules but owing much to English rounders, it became organised when a group of well-to-do New York enthusiasts set up the Knickerbocker Club and published a set of rules in 1845. They considered baseball a game for gentlemen-amateurs, but as its popularity spread so did its democratic appeal. It was played by off-duty Federal soldiers during the Civil War and in 1869 the first professional team was established: the Cincinnati Red Stockings. The team made a clean sweep of amateur opponents that

PURSUITS FOR LADIES Archery was long considered the most ladylike of sports.

The Photographer's Art

The pioneers of the new art of photography left a wealth of images of Victorian life.

Two Frenchmen and an Englishman made the vital breakthroughs in trying to fix chemically the images cast by light on reflecting surfaces. Several people attempted in the early 19th century, but the first to succeed were the Frenchmen Joseph-Nicéphore Niepce, who made the first ever photograph, and Louis-Jacques-Mandé Daguerre, who developed the daguerreotype. An Englishman, William Henry Fox Talbot, managed to fix images on paper to produce negatives. From these he could make large numbers of positives, unlike daguerreotypes which could not be reproduced.

For most of the century photography was a cumbersome process. It was gradually refined, however, until the 1880s when easily portable box cameras taking rolls of film made amateur photography possible for a large public for the first time.

Photographic First The first photograph was taken by Niepce in 1826, when he succeeded in fixing on a pewter plate a crude image of the barnyard on his country estate. The exposure time was 8 hours.

Daguerreotype Daguerre photographed in 1848, and his camera. With Niepce, he developed the process known as the daguerreotype (above right), which produced images on sheets of silvered copper plate.

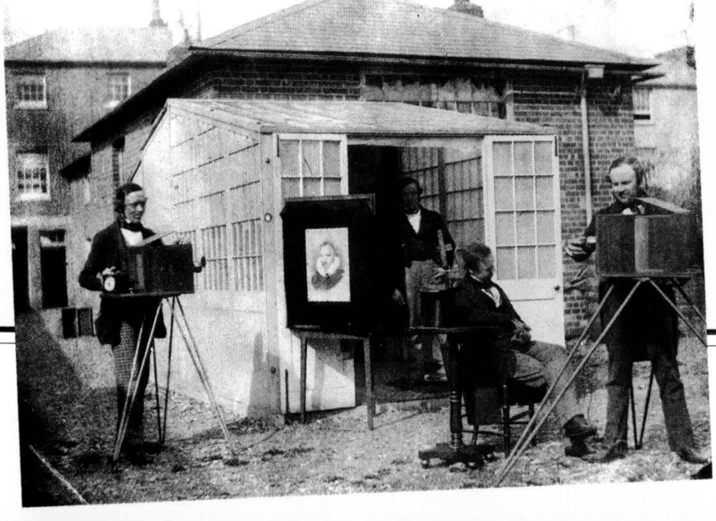

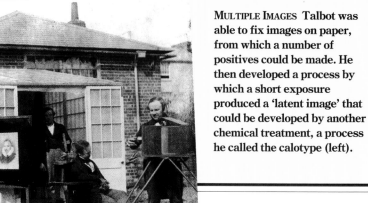

Multiple Images Talbot was able to fix images on paper, from which a number of positives could be made. He then developed a process by which a short exposure produced a 'latent image' that could be developed by another chemical treatment, a process he called the calotype (left).

PHOTOGRAPHY AS ART The Englishwoman Julia Margaret Cameron, photographed in about 1875. She produced many of the classic photographs of the mid-Victorian period.

DOCUMENTATION In the 1840s the Scottish partnership of David Octavius Hill and Robert Adamson took up Talbot's invention of the calotype and used it to record scenes of Scottish life.

PARIS FROM THE AIR The French photographer Nadar used a balloon to take the first aerial photograph in 1862, to the press's amusement.

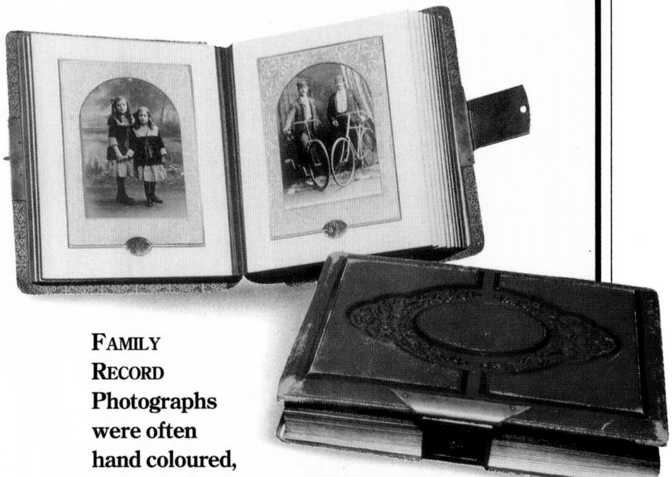

FAMILY RECORD Photographs were often hand coloured, and were kept in special albums that presented them like paintings.

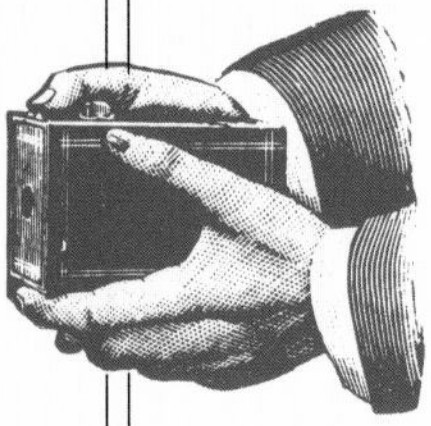

SNAPSHOT The most famous box camera was the Kodak, invented by George Eastman in 1888.

PORTABLE STUDIO A photographer waits for customers, around 1880. Simplification of the process made photographers more mobile.

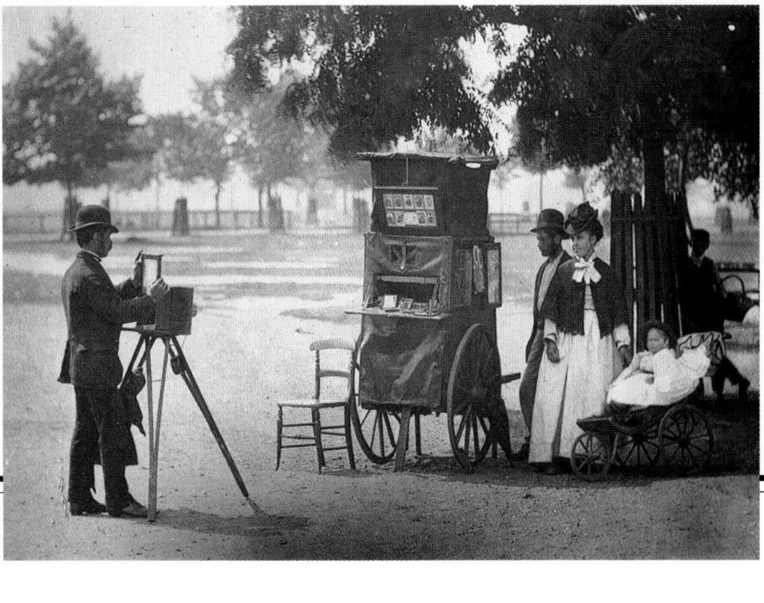

THE ART OF BOXING John L. Sullivan was an imposingly elegant figure in older age, but in his youth in the 1880s, he dominated the ring as the 'Boston Strong Boy'. A referee, also clad in full evening dress, imposes newly tightened rules in an American boxing match.

summer. After that professional baseball was unstoppable, and despite the protests of amateurs a National Association of Professional Base Ball Players was set up in 1871. Five years later this gave way to the National League of Professional Base Ball Clubs, forerunner of today's National League.

Enthusiasm for sports grew partly from a widespread concern in several countries at the manifest lack of health in much of the urban population – not just among the ill-fed and ill-housed poor, but also among the sedentary middle classes. In the caustic words of the American Oliver Wendell Holmes in 1858, 'such a set of black-coated, stiff-jointed, soft-muscled, paste-complexioned youth as we can boast in our Atlantic cities never before sprang from the loins of Anglo-Saxon lineage.' For some people too, concern with physical health combined with concern for people's spiritual wellbeing to produce the strange notion of 'muscular Christianity', so that looking after the body became a moral, even a religious duty. Gymnastics – pioneered by the Germans and Swedes – and the exercise routines known as calisthenics became immensely popular; devices such as the 'Parlor Rowing Machine' or the 'Parlor Gymnasium' (little more than a length of rubber with handles at either end) enabled people – women as well as men – to exercise in the privacy of their homes. Body-building too became a preoccupation for many men, and experts such as the German-born American Eugene Sandow became celebrities, distributing photographs of themselves as an encouragement to others.

Team and competitive sports had the advantage of character-building – hence their popularity in colleges and universities. It was thought that cricket, rugby, baseball, rowing and athletics helped train young men in the gentlemanly qualities of manliness, fair play and self-control in both victory and defeat. Even the bloody rough and tumble of boxing – a sport which had originated lower down the social scale – was refined with the introduction of gloves, and in 1867 with a new set of rules devised by the Englishman John Graham Chambers and named after the Scottish nobleman, the Marquess of Queensberry. It was encouraged by the colleges and universities, though its greatest heroes remained working-class figures such as the 'Boston Strong Boy' John L. Sullivan who dominated the heavyweight ring from 1882 to 1892. For young women, there were the suitably ladylike pursuits of archery, croquet, basketball, hockey and above all lawn tennis – popularised first by the British in the 1870s and then spread to the rest of the Victorian world.

These sports, like traditional favourites such as horse-racing, proved good to watch as well as play. As early as 1860 in pre-Civil War Brooklyn, a match between two rival baseball teams, the Excelsiors and the Atlantics, drew 15,000 spectators, and by the end of the century support for teams throughout America often reached fanatical levels. In Britain football (soccer), rather like baseball in America, was taken over by working-class professionals, and matches played in the growing number of stadiums also drew huge crowds. Cricket, boasting heroes such as the

KEEPING FIT German women keep fit with calisthenics. An American advertisement seeks to attract women to the wilier ploys of the billiard table.

redoubtable W.G. Grace, saw the institution of international 'test matches', the first of which was played in 1877 between an English and an Australian team in Melbourne, Australia, and resulted in a narrow Australian victory.

Indeed, the Victorian age saw the institution of many of the modern world's best-known sporting fixtures – Britain's Henley Regatta for rowing in 1839, for example, Wimbledon for tennis in 1877, the modern Olympic Games in 1896. The element of international rivalry provided much of the keenest excitement. When in 1851 the former dispatch boat *America* defeated British rivals in British waters to win what became the America's Cup, it was more than just a sporting triumph for the American yachtsmen – it was regarded as a symbol of the United States' emergence as a great nation.

ALL THE WORLD'S A STAGE

Spectator sport offered excitement, but for sheer scale and variety of spectacle Victorian theatre had few rivals. When the Frenchman Jules Verne's novel *Around the World in Eighty Days* was turned into a stage play in 1874, it required a colossal army of 1800 people in all, including actors, extras, stage-hands and orchestra. Some 800 costumes had to be made and special effects included bringing a railway train onto the stage, complete with a steam whistle, and an ocean liner blowing up in stormy seas. In the large metropolitan theatres, it was not uncommon to have 500 or 600 actors and extras on stage at one time, and creating special effects simply represented another irresistible challenge to Victorian technical ingenuity. Forest fires, earthquakes, snowstorms, shipwrecks, battles, horse races (with real horses), floods, volcanic eruptions, avalanches, ghostly hauntings – all were staged with the full trappings of verisimilitude.

The spectacular and the marvellous extended into other areas of entertainment too. At the most intellectual level it could be seen in the enthusiasm for museums, zoos and galleries – many of the most famous were Victorian foundations, including New York's American Museum of Natural History (1871) and Metropolitan Museum of Art (1872) and London's Natural History Museum (1881). It could be seen also in the offerings of Phineas T. Barnum, America's flamboyant showman and impresario. He started his career in 1835 by passing off an old woman as George

ENTER THE LIMELIGHT

The theatre's first spotlights were blocks of calcium (lime) heated until incandescent, when they produce beams of brilliant light. Limelight, originally invented in 1816 for lighthouses, was first used in the theatre in 1837 and by the 1860s was almost universal. It was ideal for creating the effect of sun- and moonlight, and had the advantage that its beams could be directed, unlike the old banks of candles. One result was to focus attention more seriously on the stage – theatres began to dim the houselights during performances and the real spectacle became the action on stage, rather than the rest of the audience. Although carbon-filament electric lamps began to appear in the 1880s, limelight mostly held its own until the end of the Victorian age.

IN THE GYM Young men fence, box, swing on bars and exercise with Indian clubs in an American gymnasium. A British group, meanwhile, enjoy the more sedate pleasures of croquet.

Washington's 161-year-old nurse. Between 1842 and 1868 his American Museum was New York's most popular attraction, bringing in a total of 82 million visitors to enjoy a varied fare of acrobatics, waxworks and technical and natural marvels, including an array of gruesome 'freak shows' (bearded women, armless wonders, thin men, fat ladies and so on). Many of his exhibits were undoubtedly fraudulent, but many were real enough, such as the 25-inch-tall celebrity Charles S. Stratton, better known as 'General Tom Thumb'. The public appetite for such wonders and oddities was insatiable – in Britain a similar crowd-puller was the unfortunate 'Elephant Man', John Merrick.

At the same time, a growing number of circuses – including Barnum's 'Greatest Show on Earth', founded when he was over 60 years old in partnership with James A. Bailey – was providing similarly colourful entertainment with animal acts, trapeze performances, acrobatics, fire-eaters, sword swallowers and snake enchantresses. In the 1880s 'Buffalo Bill' Cody opened his Wild West and Congress of Rough Riders of the World, an immensely popular show. He toured both America and Europe (Queen Victoria came to one performance), re-enacting traditional Indian ceremonies or attacks on stage coaches and including an act from the sharp-

THE CIRCUS COMES TO TOWN Townspeople in the English city of Bristol watch the pre-show parade of Barnum and Bailey's Circus on a European tour.

shooting Annie Oakley, 'Little Miss Sure Shot'.

The appetite for entertainment was fed in other ways. No self-respecting city was complete without its opera house, for instance – among the most astonishing of which was the Teatro Amazonas built in Manaus, the rubber boom-town deep in the Amazon jungle. The lurid plots of melodramas such as *Under Gaslight* or *The Girl I Left Behind Me* (about an Indian uprising) wrenched the heart strings in hundreds of theatregoers across the Victorian world. The age was also one of great stars commanding rapturous followings wherever they went: the French ballet-dancer Fanny Elssler, the 'Swedish Nightingale' Jenny Lind, the Australian-born opera-singer Dame Nellie Melba, the actress Lily Langtry (mistress of the Prince of Wales, later Edward VII), the great French actress Sarah Bernhardt, and the doughty English actor-managers Sir Henry Irving and Sir Herbert Beerbohm Tree.

And then, of course, there was the music hall or vaudeville, with its own gallery of stars, from the Scotsman Harry Lauder to the young W.C. Fields, and the Englishwoman Marie Lloyd to France's Yvette Guilbert with her trademark, long black gloves. The origins of vaudeville lay in fairly crude performances in the saloon bars of the American West and in the pubs and cafés of European cities. Audiences were a healthy mix of rich and poor, young and old, who sat and ate or drank while a series of performers acted out satirical or humorous sketches, acrobatic stunts, tight-rope extravaganzas, miniature ballets, magical turns or sang love songs and sentimental ballads of domestic tragedy. It was entertainment at its most rumbustious, though often extremely polished as well. In Paris, entertainment ranged from the strictly family fare of the Eden-Concert to the can-can dances and other performances of the Moulin Rouge and Folies-Bergère, which were definitely not suitable for children.

HIGH STRINGS Acrobatics join with violin-playing in a vaudeville act.

At the dawn of the Victorian age, the English writer Fanny Trollope had commented somewhat acidly on the solemnity of the British and Americans: 'We [the British] are by no means as gay as our lively neighbours on the other side of the Channel,' she observed in 1832, 'but compared with Americans, we are whirligigs and teetotums; every day is a holiday and every night a festival.' By the end of Victoria's long reign, however, things were very different. All across the Victorian world, places of entertainment from amusement parks to restaurants were making their mark on the lives of city-dwellers at least, while countless other developments were having their effect: the growth of a vigorous popular press, for example, and the arrival of new and daring dances (the waltz and polka both required partners to hold each other around the waist, and the tango was overtly seductive). The world had definitely changed. Where earlier generations of Victorians had found entertainment in attending lectures by celebrities like Charles Dickens, their successors found it in the controversial plays of the Norwegian dramatist Henrik Ibsen. The age of Victoria was giving way to the very different age of her son Edward.

RED MILL A poster by the artist Henri de Toulouse-Lautrec advertises one of Paris's best-known music halls. The hugely popular Iowa-born entertainer Lillian Russell wears her full gaudy finery.

Time Chart

1840s

News of the World

1840 In Britain, Queen Victoria marries Prince Albert of Saxe-Coburg-Gotha.

Frederick William III of Prussia dies after ruling for 43 years and is succeeded by Frederick William IV.

Karl Marx and Frederick Engels meet in Paris. (Engels publishes *The Condition of the Working Class in England* in 1845 and Marx writes the manifesto of the Communist League in 1847.)

1841 Lord Melbourne, the Whig Prime Minister of Britain, resigns and is replaced by the Tory Sir Robert Peel.

William Harrison, the 9th US President, dies after a month in office and is replaced by John Tyler.

1846 Austrian and Russian troops take Cracow, Poland, while the USA and Mexico go to war over New Mexico.

1848 The US-Mexican War ends with the US gaining California, Texas, New Mexico, Utah, Arizona and Nevada.

The French king Louis Philippe abdicates after a popular uprising, and Louis Napoleon is elected President of the French Republic. Uprisings take place in Vienna, Venice, Berlin, Rome, Parma, Milan and Czechoslovakia.

1849 Zachary Taylor is elected 12th US President.

The French restore Pope Pius IX to the Vatican.

COMMUNIST MANIFESTO Frederick Engels and Karl Marx lay the foundations for profound future industrial and social change.

Leisure and Learning

1840 The Belgian instrument-maker Adolphe Sax invents the saxophone.

1841 The first detective story, *The Murders in the Rue Morgue* by Edgar Allan Poe, is published in *Graham's Magazine* in Philadelphia.

SEASON'S GREETINGS Christmas cards are introduced.

Punch, London's satirical magazine, goes on sale.

1842 The polka, an exuberant dance of Czechoslovak origin, comes into fashion.

1843 The first Christmas card, designed by John Calcott Horsley, shows a Victorian family raising their glasses in a toast to an absent friend.

1845 Thomas Cook of Leicester, England, organises tours to temperance meetings and to Liverpool and North Wales, heralding the era of the package holiday.

1848 Chewing gum, called 'The State of Maine Pure Spruce Gum', is produced commercially by John Curtis on a Franklin stove in his kitchen.

MR FEZZIWIG'S BALL An original illustration from Charles Dickens's *A Christmas Carol.*

The Pre-Raphaelite Brotherhood is formed by Dante Gabriel Rossetti, William Holman Hunt and John Millais.

BOOKS Mikhail Lermontov's *A Hero of Our Times* (1840); Charles Dickens's *A Christmas Carol* (1843); Charlotte Brontë's *Jane Eyre* (1847); Emily Brontë's *Wuthering Heights* (1847).

Lifestyle Changes

1840 Britain's GPO issues the first adhesive postage stamps: the Penny Black and the Twopenny Blue.

Construction of the Houses of Parliament begins, under the direction of Sir Charles Barry (completed in 1860).

1842 Samuel Morse lays the first submarine telegraph cable in New York Harbour, heralding an age of inter-continental communication.

PENNY BLACK The world's first stamp is issued.

1843 The first telegram is dispatched along a cable between Paddington and Slough, England, by William Cooke's double-needle, electromagnetic telegraph.

1845 Prince Albert launches the SS *Great Britain*, the first iron-hulled, screw-propelled ocean liner, designed by Isambard Brunel and built in Bristol, England.

Baking will never be the same again after self-raising flour is put on the market by Henry Jones of Bristol, England.

1846 Dr John Collins Warren, at Massachusetts General Hospital, Boston, removes a tumour from the jaw of a printer anaesthetised by ether.

GOLD RUSH Fortune-hunters dig for riches in California.

1848 The California Gold Rush begins.

1849 Safety pins are patented by Walter Hunt in New York and by Charles Rowley in Britain.

1850s

News of the World

1850 Zachary Taylor dies and Millard Fillmore becomes 13th US President.

1852 The Republic of South Africa is established.

Franklyn Pierce is elected US President.

Louis Napoleon declares himself Emperor of the French.

1853 The Crimean War between Turkey and Russia begins.

1854 Britain and France ally themselves with Turkey and declare war on Russia; the allies lay siege to Sebastopol (which Russia will surrender next year) and gain victories at Inkerman and Balaclava.

US Commodore Matthew Perry negotiates a treaty with Japan, opening up the country to Western influence.

The Republican Party is formed in the USA.

1855 Tsar Nicholas I of Russia dies after a reign of 30 years and is succeeded by his son Alexander II.

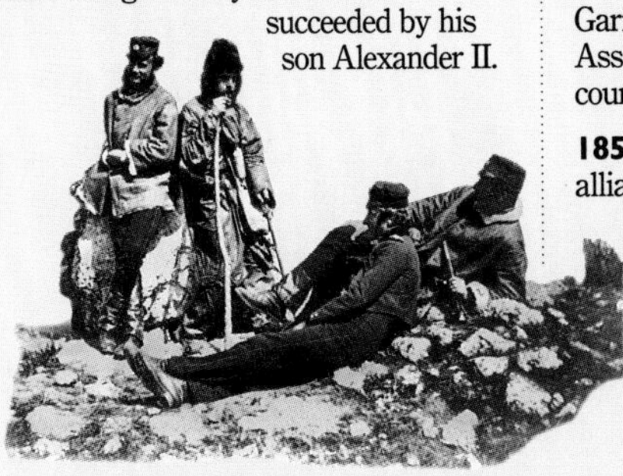

1856 The Crimean War ends with Russia's capitulation.

1857 The East India Company loses control of India following the mutiny by natives in the army (in 1858 the British Crown takes control of the country).

Garibaldi forms the Italian National Association in his attempt to unify his country.

1859 France and Sardinia form an alliance against Austria, which is defeated at the battles of Magenta and Solferino.

Crimean Campaign British soldiers are sent to fight against the Russians.

Leisure and Learning

1850 The first magazine competitions are published in *The Family Friend*, London, with prizes worth 50 guineas.

1853 The first aquarium opens at Regent's Park Zoo, London.

1855 The first Hyde Park orator is a carpenter talking about food prices.

The *Daily Telegraph* goes on sale in London.

1859 Horizontal bars and swings are erected in Queen's Park and Philips Park in Manchester, England – the first time a municipal authority has sited a children's playground in a park.

BOOKS Charles Dickens's *David Copperfield* (1850); Herman Melville's *Moby Dick* (1851); Harriet Beecher Stowe's *Uncle Tom's Cabin* (1851); Dickens's *Bleak House* (1852); Henry Thoreau's *Walden* (1854); Gustave Flaubert's *Madame Bovary* (1856-57).

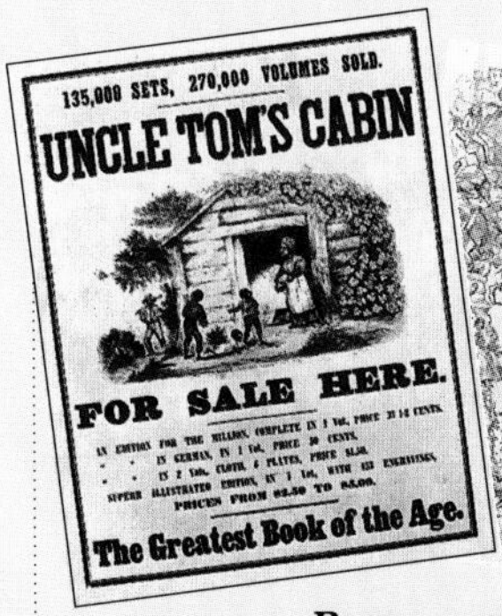

Bestsellers Growing literacy creates more readers and bestselling novelists.

Extra Colour The discovery of synthetic dyes provides new colours for clothes and fabrics.

Lifestyle Changes

Queen of Inventions The sewing machine transforms a whole area of housework. Singer's model has the advantage of a foot pedal, rather than relying on hand power.

1850 Levi Strauss, a Bavarian who had emigrated to San Francisco during the gold rush, makes the first jeans.

1851 The International Exhibition begins in London.

Sewing machines for the home are produced by Isaac Singer of Boston.

1852 The world's first hospital for children opens at Great Ormond Street, London.

The first free public lending library in Britain opens in Manchester, lending more than 77,000 books in its first year.

1853 Queen Victoria permits the use of chloroform during the birth of her seventh child, thereby popularising anaesthesia in Britain.

1853 Vaccinations against smallpox are made compulsory in Britain.

1856 A synthetic dye, mauveine, is discovered by 18-year-old William Perkin in London, thereby precipitating the search for other man-made dyes.

1857 The rue Impériale in Lyons, France, is the first street to be permanently lit by electric lighting.

1859 British scientist Charles Darwin publishes *On the Origin of Species by Natural Selection*, laying the foundations for a new understanding of evolution.

The first oil rig is erected by Edwin Drake of Titusville, Pennsylvania, after he struck oil.

1860s

News of the World

1860 The first Italian Parliament gathers in Turin, while Garibaldi's redshirts take Naples and Palermo, and Garibaldi declares Victor Emmanuel (who is King of Sardinia) King of Italy.

Abraham Lincoln is elected 16th US President, causing South Carolina to break away from the Union.

1861 Frederick William IV of Prussia dies and is succeeded by William I.

The American Civil War begins after the Confederate States of America are formed at the Congress of Montgomery.

Queen Victoria's husband, Prince Albert, dies (his memorial is built in Hyde Park in 1862).

1864 Abraham Lincoln is re-elected as US President.

1865 The American Civil War ends with the surrender of the Confederates at Appomattox Courthouse in Virginia.

Actor John Wilkes Booth assassinates Lincoln during a performance at Ford's Theatre in Washington DC.

OUTGUNNED Unionist fire-power helps win the war.

1865 Andrew Johnson becomes US President, and Congress passes the 13th Amendment to the constitution, abolishing slavery.

1866 Upheaval in Europe, as Prussia and Italy go to war with Austria.

1867 The British North America Act establishes the Dominion of Canada.

1868 Benjamin Disraeli becomes British Prime Minister but soon resigns; William Gladstone becomes the next Prime Minister.

Revolution in Spain forces Queen Isabella to flee to the safety of France.

1869 Ulysses S. Grant, victorious leader of the Union, is elected US President.

Leisure and Learning

1860 The Dry Martini is invented by bartender Jerry Thomas at the Occidental Hotel, San Francisco.

1861 A Whitsuntide Working Men's Excursion to Paris, with travel arrangements by Thomas Cook, may be the first overseas package holiday.

The Meteorological Office in Britain publishes a daily 'weather forecast' (a term coined by the Met Office's Superintendent) in *The Times* newspaper.

Mrs Beeton publishes *The Book of Household Management.*

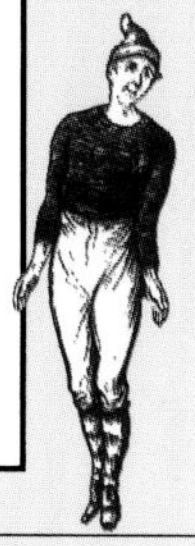

ON THE BALL The first professional football teams are formed.

1863 Association Football rules are drawn up and published in England.

The prototype of the modern four-wheeled roller skates is patented by James Plimpton of New York.

1865 The Erie, produced by the Repeating Light Co. of Springfield, Massachussets is the first pocket lighter.

1866 Cadbury's introduce boxes of assorted chocolates, with delicacies such as raspberry soft centres and spice-flavoured bonbons.

BOOKS Wilkie Collins's *The Woman in White* (1860); George Eliot's *The Mill on the Floss* (1860); Dickens's *Great Expectations* (1861); Victor Hugo's *Les Misérables* (1862); Lewis Carroll's *Alice's Adventures in Wonderland* (1865); Leo Tolstoy's *War and Peace* (1863-69); Fyodor Dostoyevsky's *Crime and Punishment* (1866); Wilkie Collins's *The Moonstone* (1868).

STRANGE WORLD Alice ventures through the looking glass.

Lifestyle Changes

1861 A tartan ribbon on a black velvet background is the image on the first colour photograph – a transparency prepared by Thomas Sutton in collaboration with Scottish scientist James Clerk Maxwell.

1862 Belgian engineer Etienne Lenoir, working in Paris, builds the first motor car with an internal combustion engine; in 1863, he takes it for a six-mile drive that takes him three hours.

1863 The Metropolitan Railway, a four-mile stretch of underground railway between Paddington and Farringdon Street, opens to the fare-paying public.

1864 The International Red Cross is founded in Geneva, in response to the Swiss philanthropist Henri Dunant's appeal in 1862 for volunteer societies to attend the wounded on the battlefield.

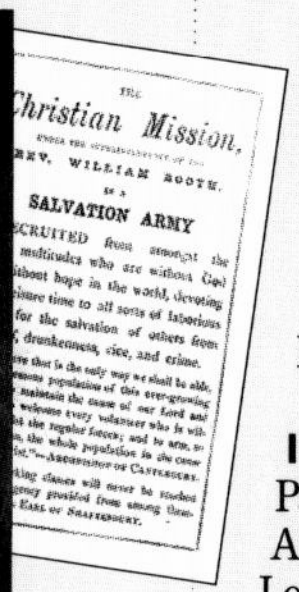

EVANGELIST William Booth founds the Salvation Army to save the bodies and souls of the poor.

1865 The Salvation Army has its origins at a meeting conducted by William Booth at Whitechapel Burial Ground, London.

1866 The first plastic, named Parkesine after its inventor Alexander Parkes, is manufactured in London.

1868 The Trades Union Congress (TUC) is founded at Manchester, England.

Tungsten steel, which is much harder than ordinary steel, is invented by Englishman Robert Mushet.

1870s

News of the World

1870 France and Prussia go to war and Napoleon III is defeated; rebels in Paris declare a Third Republic while the Prussians besiege the city.

The Italians declare Rome their capital.

1871 William I, King of Prussia, becomes German Emperor at Versailles.

The Paris Commune reigns for two months but is defeated in a bloodbath in which up to 30,000 Parisians are killed.

Grandeur and Decadence A cartoonist voices the popular judgment on Napoleon III.

'Dr Livingstone, I presume?' asks Henry Stanley, on meeting the British explorer, who had not been seen for five years, at Ujiji on Lake Tanganyika.

1872 During the civil war in Spain, Don Carlos, the Bourbon pretender to the throne, and his Carlist supporters are defeated at the Battle of Oroquista by the new king, Amadeos I. (In 1873, Spain is declared a republic.)

Zulu Chief Cetshwayo is held by the British in Cape Town, South Africa.

Ulysses S. Grant is re-elected US President.

1874 Benjamin Disraeli becomes British Prime Minister for the second time.

1876 Turkish troops massacre Bulgarians, and Serbia and Montenegro declare war on Turkey. As a result, Sultan Abdul Aziz and his successor are deposed and a new Ottoman constitution is drawn up.

1879 In South Africa, Zulus massacre British troops at Isandhlwana but are eventually defeated and their chief, Cetshwayo, captured.

Leisure and Learning

Tom Thumb The diminutive American showman, real name Charles Stratton, was just 40 inches tall.

1871 Bank Holidays are instituted in England and Wales.

P.T. Barnum opens *The Greatest Show On Earth* in Brooklyn, New York.

1872 The first mail-order catalogue is issued by the recently incorporated Army & Navy Stores in London.

The Football Association (FA) Cup is inaugurated.

The first lawn tennis club is established at Leamington Spa, England.

1873 The traveller's first pocket dictionary is the *Bona Fide French and English Dictionary* by John Bellows.

Cable cars run along the Clay Street Hill Railroad in San Francisco.

1874 The first Impressionist exhibition is held in Paris.

1875 Gilbert and Sullivan's first comic operetta, *Trial By Jury*, is performed.

Milk chocolate is made for the first time by Daniel Peter, son-in-law of François-Louis Cailler who produced the first eating chocolate at Vevey, Switzerland, in 1819.

1879 The Echo Farms Dairy in Brooklyn, New York, delivers milk to its customers in glass milk bottles instead of pouring it into pitchers from barrels on milk wagons.

BOOKS Jules Verne's *20,000 Leagues Under the Sea* (1870); Jules Verne's *Around the World In Eighty Days* (1873); Leo Tolstoy's *Anna Karenina* (1873-77); Thomas Hardy's *Far From the Madding Crowd* (1874); Mark Twain's *Adventures of Tom Sawyer* (1875); Emile Zola's *Nana* (1879).

Lifestyle Changes

Listening In A user winds the handle of Alexander Graham Bell's telephone to operate it.

1870 The writing ball typewriter is invented by Pastor Malling Hansen in Denmark. (In 1872, Christopher Sholes and James Denmore of Milwaukee in the US produce a typewriter with the letters arranged in the now familiar QWERTY formation.)

The first lightweight, all-metal bicycle, the Ariel, is patented by James Starley and William Hillman of Coventry – their machine is also the first to possess wire-spoked tension wheels.

1871 Swedish engraver Carl Carleman discovers a way of reproducing photographs in printer's ink, enabling halftone illustrations to grace the pages of papers and magazines.

1875 Third-party accident insurance is introduced by London & Provincial Carriage Insurance Co.

1876 'Come here, Watson, I want you' – Alexander Graham Bell's words to his assistant in Boston, Massachusetts, are the first coherent message conducted along the inventor's newly patented telephone.

1877 The Phonograph, invented by Thomas Alva Edison in New Jersey, is the first equipment to record and play back sound.

1879 The first telephone exchange in London begins operation.

1879 Chemists Constantin Fahlberg and Ira Remsen discover saccharin – 300 times sweeter than sugar – at Johns Hopkins University, Baltimore.

The prospect of electric lighting for all becomes a reality as Thomas Edison of New Jersey demonstrates the first practical incandescent filament light bulb. At around the same time in Britain, Joseph Swan demonstrates his own independently developed light bulb.

Lighting up Thomas Edison's light bulb uses an innovative platinum filament.

1880s

News of the World

1880 Benjamin Disraeli, now Lord Beaconsfield, resigns as British Prime Minister and is succeeded by William Gladstone.

1881 US President James Garfield is assassinated by Charles Guiteau at a Washington DC, railway station and is succeeded by Vice-President Chester Arthur.

Tsar Alexander II of Russia is assassinated by nihilist terrorists at St Petersburg and is succeeded by his son, Alexander III.

Germany, Italy and Austria form a Triple Alliance.

NEVER CAUGHT Jack the Ripper terrorises London's East End, but his identity remains a mystery.

1886 William Gladstone introduces a Home Rule Bill for Ireland.

1887 Queen Victoria celebrates her Golden Jubilee as the first Colonial Conference opens in London.

1888 German Emperor William I is succeeded by his son Frederick III, who dies after three months and is succeeded in turn by his son William II, known as the Kaiser.

Benjamin Harrison is elected 23rd US President.

Jack the Ripper murders at least five women in London's East End.

1889 Austrian Crown Prince (Archduke Rudolf) kills himself at a hunting lodge at Mayerling.

Brazil becomes a republic.

Leisure and Learning

1880 Bingo can now be played after it is developed from the Italian game of *tumbula*.

1886 The Statue of Liberty is dedicated in New York.

1887 Sir Arthur Conan Doyle introduces his supersleuth, Sherlock Holmes, in *A Study in Scarlet*.

1888 The first beauty contest is held at Spa, Belgium.

The gramophone, playing sound recordings on discs rather than cylinders, is invented by Emile Berliner in Washington, DC; in 1894, the gramophone will be electrically operated and commercially produced.

MUSIC ON DISC Berliner's gramophone plays flat, grooved discs.

STEREOSCOPE Super-imposed images create a 3D effect.

1889 The first jukebox, a nickel-in-the-slot machine equipped with four listening tubes, is installed at the Palais Royal Saloon, San Francisco.

The world's first fruit machine, the Liberty Bell, is designed by Charles Frey in San Francisco: it pays out one coin for a pair of horshoes and ten coins for three bells.

BOOKS Robert Louis Stevenson's *Treasure Island* (1882); Mark Twain's *Huckleberry Finn* (1884); Rider Haggard's *King Solomon's Mines* (1885); Robert Louis Stevenson's *Doctor Jekyll and Mister Hyde* (1886); Jerome K. Jerome's *Three Men in a Boat* (1889).

PEN NAME Samuel Langhorne Clemens, better known as Mark Twain.

Lifestyle Changes

1880 The Connecticut Telephone Co. installs the first public telephone call-box in its office at New Haven.

1881 The first electric power station, the Central Power Station in Godalming, England, taps hydroelectric power from a local river and starts generating current for public and domestic consumption.

1882 Dr Werner von Siemens demonstrates his prototype for the trolley bus in Berlin.

Henry Seely patents his electric iron in New York.

1883 The first artificial fibre – a kind of silk made from nitro-cellulose – is produced by Joseph Swan at Newcastle-upon-Tyne, England, in his attempts to improve the filaments of his electric light bulb.

1885 Karl Benz's three-wheeled, single-cylinder, petrol-driven vehicle is constructed in Mannheim, Germany.

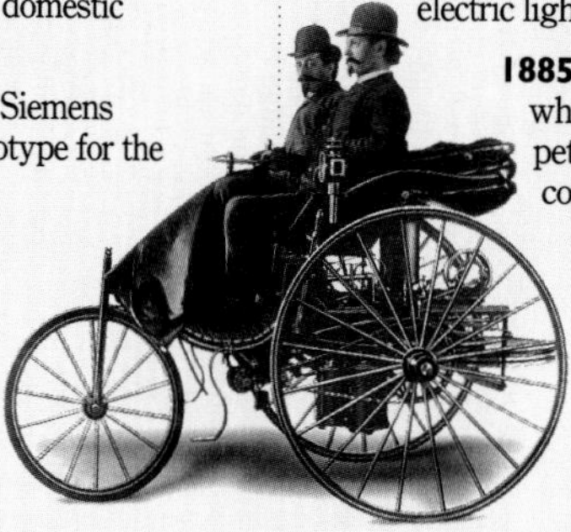

PETROL POWER Benz's three-wheeler heralds the age of the car

1886 Coca-Cola makes its debut at Jacob's Pharmacy in Atlanta, Georgia, after pharmacist John Pemberton formulates a headache and hangover cure from coca leaves, kola nuts and fruit syrup.

ELECTRIC IRON Electricity took some of the tedium out of ironing.

1887 Contact lenses are created by Dr Eugen Frick in Zurich, Switzerland, and then manufactured by Zeiss of Jena, Germany.

1889 Vehicle Excise Tax – two guineas per year for all four-wheeled steam and motor road vehicles – is introduced in Britain.

1890s

News of the World

1890 Japan holds its first general elections.

Luxembourg separates from the Netherlands and becomes a nation.

1892 William Gladstone becomes British Prime Minister for the fourth time.

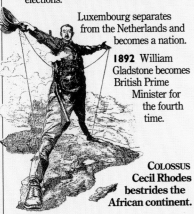

Colossus Cecil Rhodes bestrides the African continent.

1892 Scottish miner Keir Hardie is elected to the British Parliament as a Labour MP (in 1893 he helps to found the Independent Labour Party).

1893 Grover Cleveland is elected 24th US President.

1894 Korea and Japan declare war on China and defeat the Chinese at Port Arthur (the war ends in 1895, China recognising the independence of Korea).

Captain Alfred Dreyfus is arrested and convicted of treason in France (he is pardoned by presidential decree in 1899).

1895 Rhodesia is formed from British South Africa Company territory south of the Zambezi and named after the Prime Minister of the Cape Colony, Cecil Rhodes.

Russian revolutionary Vladimir Ilich Ulyanov (later known by his pseudonym, Nikolai Lenin) forms The League of Struggle for the Emancipation of the Working Class at St Petersburg.

1898 The US declares war on Spain, causing Spain to hand over Cuba, Puerto Rico, Guam and the Philippines for $20 million.

The Boxers are formed in China as an anti-Western organisation.

1899 British attempts to take over the Transvaal and its rich deposits of gold cause the Boer War in South Africa.

Leisure and Learning

1890 *Comic Cuts*, an eight-page weekly produced by Alfred Harmsworth, is the first comic; it achieves a circulation of about 300,000 after a month.

1891 Travellers' cheques requiring countersignatures are invented by Marcellus Berry of American Express – the first cheque was cashed for $50 in Leipzig.

1894 The Kinetoscope Parlor on Broadway opens for business giving the first commercial presentation of a motion picture.

J. Lyons' white-fronted teashop opens in Piccadilly, London, offering a novel menu of Welsh rarebit, canned spaghetti on toast, cakes and buns.

Comedy King The first weekly comic is an instant hit.

1896 The first screen kiss is shared between May Irwin and John Rice in *The Widow Jones*, filmed by Raff and Gammon in New York.

Chop Suey is devised by Li Hung-Chang's chef in New York in an attempt to appeal to both American and Chinese tastes.

1896 The first modern Olympic Games are held in Athens.

1897 The Sunday colour supplement of the *New York Journal* hosts the first newspaper comic strip – *Yellow Kid.*

BOOKS Oscar Wilde's *The Picture of Dorian Gray* (1890); Thomas Hardy's *Tess of the D'Urbervilles* (1891); H.G. Wells's *The Time Machine* (1895); Edmond Rostand's play *Cyrano de Bergerac* (1897).

Moving Pictures The cinematograph projected a series of images from a strip of film.

Lifestyle Changes

Role of Gas Gas becomes more widely used in the home for heat and light.

1890 The first surgical rubber gloves are worn by Nurse Caroline Hampton at Johns Hopkins University Hospital, Baltimore.

1891 Germany introduces the first scheme for old age pensions.

Free state education is introduced in Britain.

1892 A dentist from New London, Connecticut, devises the first toothpaste tube.

1893 French police demand that their country's motorists take a driving test and subsequently carry a driving licence.

A passenger elevator with push-button control is built by Otis for a private residence in New York.

1895 King Gillette invents the safety razor.

X-rays are discovered by William Roentgen in Würzburg, Germany, and soon after are used clinically to examine a gunshot wound.

1896 Radio makes its debut at Toynbee Hall, London, when its inventor, Guglielmo Marconi, demonstrates his wireless to the public.

Close Shave Gillette's safety razor has a replaceable blade and a guard to prevent the user from cuts.

Radioactivity is discovered by French scientist, A.H. Becquerel.

1899 Aspirin powder is produced commercially by Bayer in Germany.

Index

NOTE: Page numbers in *italics* denote illustrations; there may also be textual references on these pages.

ACKNOWLEDGMENTS

Abbreviations
T = Top; M = Middle; B = Bottom
R = Right; L = Left.

1 Culver Pictures Inc. 2–3 The Bettman Archive. 4 Private Collection,TL; The Museum of English Rural Life, TR; The Granger Collection, M; Giraudon, BL; The Frank Sutcliffe Gallery, Whitby, BR. 5 The Bettmann Archive, TR; The Granger Collection, ML; Ullstein Bilderdienst, MR; Bilderarchiv Weber-Kellermann, BL; Private Collection, BR. 6 The Bridgeman Art Library. 7 The Bridgeman Art Library, TR, ML; The Granger Collection, TL; Ullstein Bilderdienst, B. 8 Wallington Hall, Northumberland: *Industry of the Tyne: Iron and Coal* painting by William Bell Scott/The Bridgeman Art Library. 9 The Granger Collection, T; Laurie Winfrey, B. 10 Private Collection. 11 Punsch of Munich, T; Musée Carnavelet, Paris: *Boulevard des Italiens* lithograph by Eugen von Guerard/The Bridgeman Art Library. 12 Musée des Beaux-Arts, Mulhouse: *The Siege of Paris* by Gustave Doré/The Bridgeman Art Library, T; The Bettmann Archive, ML. 13 The Mansell Collection. 14 Culver Pictures Inc, MR; The Mary Evans Picture Library, BR. 15 The Granger Collection, T; The Mary Evans Picture Library, BR. 16 The Victoria and Albert Museum, London, TL; The Bettmann Archive, TR; Culver Pictures Inc, MR, B. 17 Culver Pictures Inc, T; The Mansell Collection, B. 18 E.T. Archive, T; The Bettmann Archive, BL; The Mary Evans Picture Library, BR. 19 Bradford City Art Gallery: *Signing The Register* painting by James Charles/E. T. Archive; The Mansell Collection, BL, BR. 20 From: *Dear Lord Rothschild* by Miriam Rothschild published by Balaban and Hutchinson Limited, TR, MR; Historisches Museum, Frankfurt, ML; The Mary Evans Picture Library, M; Hulton-Deutsch, B. 21 The Mansell Collection, TL, TR; From *Rothschild: A Story of Wealth and Power* by Derek Wilson published by Andre Deutsch, BL; Hulton-Deutsch Collection, BR. 22 The Granger Collection, T; The Bettmann Archive. 23 The Mary Evans Picture Library, MR; The Bettmann Archive, B. 24 The Granger Collection, T; The Mary Evans Picture Library, B; Musée Toulouse-Lautrec, Albi: *The Salon in the rue des Moulins* painting by Henri Toulouse-Lautrec/The Bridgeman Library, TL; The Granger collection, TR. 26 The Tate Gallery, London: *The Awakening Conscience* painting by William Holman Hunt/ The Bridgeman Art Library. 27 S.P.A.D.E.M., BL; The Mansell Collection, BM; Photograph by Nadar, Private Collection, BR. 28 Culver Pictures Inc, BL; The Granger Collection, BR. 29 The Victoria and Albert Museum, London. 30 Culver Pictures Inc, TR; Private Collection, M. 31 Arthur Lockwood, TL; The Mary Evans Picture Library, TR; Culver Pictures Inc, B. 32 The Mary Evans Picture Library, TR; The Granger collection, M; Hulton-Deutsch Collection, B. 33 The Granger Collection, TL, TR; Hulton-Deutsch Collection, TM; Ullstein Bilderdienst, B. 34 The Mary Evans Picture Library, BL, BM; Culver Pictures Inc, BR. 35 Roger-Viollet, T; The Granger Collection, TR; Culver Pictures Inc, B. 36 Jean-Loup Charmet. 37 The Granger Collection. 38 The Mary Evans Picture Library. 39 Museum of the City of New York, T; Jean-Loup Charmet, MR. 40 The Mary Evans Picture Library, T; From, *The Gastronomic Regenerator*, 1846 and *The Modern Housewife*, 1851 by Alexis Soyer, B. 41 Goteborgs Koustmuseum, Sweden/The Bridgeman Art Library, London, T; Jean-Loup Charmet, M. 42 The Bettmann Archive. 43 The Mary Evans Picture Library, TL; The Granger Collection,TR; Culver Pictures Inc, MR. 44–45 The Mansell Collection. 45 The Mary Evans Picture Library, ML, MR. 46 Private Collection, T; The Mansell Collection, BL; Arthur Lockwood, BR. 47 The Granger Collection. 48 Roger-Viollet, TL; Jean-Loup Charmet, M; The Mary Evans Picture Library, B. 49 Private collection, TL; Culver Pictures, TR; Drawing by Sidney Paget/The Granger Collection, BR. 50 The Bettmann Archive, T; Robert Opie Collection, BR. 51 Robert Opie Collection, BL; Culver Pictures Inc, BM, The Granger Collection, MR. 52 Culver Pictures Inc, T; E.T. Archive, MR. 53 Arthur Lockwood, T; Private Collection, MR, B. 54 Robert Opie Collection, TL; The Granger Collection, TR; The Mary Evans Picture Library, BL; Robert Opie Collection, BR. 55 The Bettmann Archive, T, MR; The National Gallery of Washington, DC: *A Friendly Visit,* painting by William Merrit Chase/The Bridgeman Art Library, ML. 56 The Bettmann Archive, TL; Robert Opie Collection, TR; Culver Pictures Inc, BL; The Mary Evans Picture Library, BR. 57 The Bridgeman Art Library, T; Roger-Viollet, TR. 58 Private Collection T, B. 59 Culver Pictures Inc, T; Robert Opie Collection, ML; The Mary Evans Picture Library, MR. 60 Culver Pictures Library Inc, TL; Robert Opie Collection, TR, B. 61 Jean-Loup Charmet, The Mansell Collection, BR. 62 The Mary Evans Picture Library, TL, TM; Robert Opie Collection, TR. 63 Musée Carnavalet, Paris: *The Boulevards* painting by Jean Beraud/The Bridgeman Art Library. 64 Private Collection, The Tate Gallery, London: *St. Martins-in-the-Fields* painting by Logsdale/E.T. Archive, BL; Private Collection, BR. 65 The Granger Collection, T; The Bettmann Archive, TR, Musée D'Orsay Paris: *Dark Landscape* painting by L.E. Meurier/ Giraudon. The Bridgeman Art Library, BR. 66–67 Drawing by Peter Morter. 66 The Mary Evans Art Picture Library, T. 67 Culver Pictures Inc, T. 68 The Granger Collection, T, M, BR. 69 International Museum of Photograph, T; Staten Island Historical Museum, B. 70 Private Collection, TL; The Bettmann Archive, TR, BL. 71 The Bettmann Archive, Private Collection, MR. 72 Sheffield City Museum, T; The Granger Collection, B. 73 Culver Pictures Inc, ML, MR; Arthur Lockwood, B. 74–75 The Science Museum, London. 74 The Granger Collection, TL; Private Collection, BR. 75 The Tate Gallery, London: *Omnibus Life in London* painting by W. M. Egley/The Bridgeman Art Library, TL; From: *Victorian Delights* by Robert Wood published by Evans Brothers Ltd, 1967, TM; Private Collection, TR; City of Bristol Museum and Art Gallery *Launch of the Great Britain at Bristol*/ The Bridgeman Art Library, BL; Daimler/Private Collection, BR. 76 Hulton-Deutsch, TR; The Mary Evans Picture Library, ML; Marconi, M; The Royal Photographic Society, BL; Museum of Photography, Bradford/ Kodak Museum, BR. 77 The Granger Collection, TL; The Bettmann Archive, M, BR. 78 *Florence Nightingale At Scutari,* painting by Jerry Barrett, (detail), National Portrait Gallery, London, T; Mary Evans Picture Library, M, B. 79 The Bettmann Archive, T; Ullstein Bilderdienst, M; Hulton-Deutsch Collection, B. 80 The Granger Collection, TL; Culver Pictures Inc, B. 81 The Granger Collection, TR, BL. 82 The Bettmann Archive, TR; Arthur Lockwood, BL; The Bettmann Archive, BR. 83 The Mansell Collection, TR; Culver Pictures Inc, B. 84 Culver Pictures Inc, T; E.T. Archive, B. 85 Manchester City Art Gallery: *Dinner Hour at Wigan* painting by Eyre Crowe/The Bridgeman Art Library, T; Hulton-Deutsch, MR. 86 The Granger Collection, TL; House of Worth, London: *Cinq Heures Chez Paquin* painting by Henri Gervex. 87 Historisches Museum Der Stadt, Vienna: *The Court Ball* painting by W. Gause/The Bridgeman Art Library, T; Musée Carnavalet, Paris: *La Soiree* painting by Jean Beraud/The Bridgeman Art Library, B. 88 Gallerie d'Arte Moderna, Venice: *The Guidini Family* painting by G. Favretto/Scala, TR; Musée d'Orsay, Paris: *New Orleans Cotton Exchange* painting by Edgar Degas, MR; The Frank Sutcliffe Gallery/Private Collection, BL. 89 Culver Pictures Inc. 90–91 The Bettmann Archive. 90 The Frank Sutcliffe Gallery/Private Collection. 91 Private Collection. 92 Musée de Roubaix: *The Potato Harvest* painting by E. Masson/Giraudon, The Bridgeman Art Library, T; Dansk Folkemuseum, Nationalmuseet, Lyngby/Royal Library Copenhagen, B; The Frank Sutcliffe Gallery/Private Collection, BR. 93 The Mary Evans Picture Library, T; The Bridgeman Art Library, BL; Birmingham City Museums and Art Gallery: *The Last of England* painting by Ford Madox Brown/The Bridgeman Art Library, BR. 94 Culver Pictures Inc; State Library, South Australia/Private Collection, B. 95 Royal Agricultural Society of England: *Country Meeting of the Royal Agricultural Society of England, 1842* painting by Richard Ansdell (detail). 96 Christopher Hussey, From: *A Country Camera 1844–1914* by Gordon Winter published by Penguin Books, 1973, BL; King Street Galleries, London: *An English Homestead* painting by J.F. Herring Snr/The Bridgeman Art Library. 97 Private Collection TL, TM,TR. 98–99 Drawing by Gill Tomblin. 100 Professor J.H. Hutton, From: *A Country Camera 1844–1914* by Gordon Winter published by Penguin Books, 1973, BR; The Granger Collection,TL. 101 Culver Pictures Inc, TR, M. 102–103 The Mitchell Library, New South Wales, Australia. 104 Culver Pictures Inc. 104–105 The Granger Collection. 106 The Bridgeman Art Library, TL; Galleria d'Arte Moderna, Florence: *Un Incontro* painting by Gioli Francesco/Scala. 107 The Granger Collection. 108 The Bettmann Archive, B. 109 Manchester City Art Gallery: *Work* by Ford Madox Brown (detail). 110 The Granger Collection, TL; Private Collection, TR. 111 Private Collection, TL; Jean-Loup Charmet, TR, B. 112 The Granger Collection, TR; Staten Island Historical Museum, BL; Cambridgeshire Constabulary, BM; The Mary Evans Picture Library, BR. 113 The Police College Library, Bramshill House Hampshire, T; Avon and Somerset Police, M; Lincolnshire Police, BR. 114 The Mary Evans Picture Library, TL; Private Collection, TR; Ullstein Bilderdienst, B. 115 Private Collection, T; The Mansell Collection, B. 116 The Mary Evans Picture Library, T; The Victoria and Albert Museum, London: *The Governess* painting by R. Redgrave/The Bridgeman Art Library, B. 117 The Bettmann Archive, TR; The Granger Collection, M; Private Collection/ Photography Norman Brand, B. 116–117 Culver Pictures Inc. 118 The Mary Evans Picture Library, TL; Private Collection, M. 119 Arthur Lockwood, TR; Archives Photographiques, From: *Nadar* by Nigel Gosling published by Secker and Warburg, 1976, M, B. 120 The Walker Art Gallery, National Museums and Galleries on Merseyside: *Eventide* painting by Sir Hubert von Herkomer, TL; The Mary Evans Picture Library, M; Barnado's Photographic Archive, BL. 121 The Mary Evans Picture Library, TL,TR; Robert Opie Collection, BL; Cadbury Brothers Ltd, Bournville, BR. 122 The Bridgeman Art Library, TL, TR. 123 The Granger Collection, TM; The Mary Evans Picture Library, TR; Private Collection, B. 124 The Granger Collection, TL; Fotomas Index, MR. 125 Private Collection, TL; Photograph by John Thompson: Courtesy John Hillelson, BM; Private Collection, BR. 126 The Massachusetts Hospital, Boston. 127 Private Collection, TL; The Bridgeman Art Library, BM. 126–127 The Bettmann Archive. 128 The Granger Collection, TL; The Bridgeman Art Library, B; Private Collection, BR. 129 Private Collection, TL, TR; The Granger Collection, BL; The Mary Evans Picture Library, BR. 130 The Bridgeman Art Library, TL, TM; Culver Pictures Inc, TR, ML, M; The Bettmann Archive, MR. 131 Private Collection. 132 The Bridgeman Art Library, M; The Mansell Collection, BL. 133 Hulton-Deutsch Collection. 134 The Bettmann Archive. 135 Private Collection, TL; The Bridgeman Art Library, TR. 134–135 The Fine Art Society, London: *View over London from Hampstead Heath* painting by John Ritchie/The Bridgeman Art Library. 136 The Mary Evans Picture Library, TL, B; The Granger Collection, TR. 137 *La Plage de Trouville,* painting by Paul Rossert, Private Collection/The Bridgeman Art Library, London, T; The Mary Evans Picture Library, ML, BR; E.T. Archive, BL. 138 Culver Pictures Inc, TL; Ullstein Bilderdienst, TR, B. 139 Graphic 1880, T; E.T. Archive, B. 140 Robert Opie Collection, TR; Museum of London, ML; E.T. Archive, MR; Robert Opie Collection, BL, BM; Culver Pictures Inc, BR. 141 Robert Opie Collection, TL, BL, BR; E.T. Archive, TR; Culver Pictures Inc, ML, MR. 142 Private Collection, ML; Culver Pictures Inc, B. 143 Culver Pictures Inc, TL, TM, TR; The Bridgeman Art Library, B. 144 Hulton-Deutsch Collection, ML; Jean-Loup Charmet, MM; The Royal Photographic Society, Bath, MR, B. 145 The Royal Photographic Society, Bath, TL, TM, TR, MR; Hulton-Deutsch Collection, ML, BL; Jean-Loup Charmet, MM; Victoria & Albert Museum, London/Bridgeman Art Library, London, BM. 146 Culver Pictures Inc, TL. 147 Culver Pictures Inc, TL; Private Collection, TR. 148 Culver Pictures Inc, TL; The Bridgeman Art Library, ML; Reece Winstone, B. 149 Culver Pictures Inc, TR, BR; Private Collection, BL. 150 Toucan Archives, T; E.T. Archive, ML, MR, BR; National Postal Museum, BL. 151 Hulton-Deutsch Collection, T; Toucan Archives, ML, BL; Fotomas, MM; Michael Holford, MR; Hulton-Deutsch Collection, BR. 152 Hulton-Deutsch Collection, T; The Mary Evans Picture Library, ML, MM; E.T. Archive, MR, BL, BR. 153 Toucan Archives, TL, TM; E.T. Archive, ML; Science Museum, London, BL; Michael Holford, BR. 154 From: *Illustrated Police News*, British Library, London, ML, BR; Robert Opie Collection, MM; The Granger collection, MR; E.T. Archive, BL. 155 Toucan Archives, T; E.T. Archive, ML, MR; Giraudon, BL; The Mary Evans Picture Library, BR.

Front cover: Culver Pictures, B; The Science Museum, London/Photography Eileen Tweedy, ML; E.T. Archive, M; Robert Opie Collection, BL, M; Private Collection, BR.
Back cover: The Granger Collection, TL; Private Collections, TR, BR; Culver Pictures, M; Robert Opie Collection, MR.

The editors and publishers are grateful to Routledge and Kegan Paul for their kind permission to quote from *The Victorian City: Images and Realities* edited by H.J. Dyos and Michael Wolff 1973